William Hodges, 1744–1797: the Art of Exploration

edited by GEOFF QUILLEY and JOHN BONEHILL

with contributions from David Bindman, Natasha Eaton, Charles Greig, Harriet Guest, Nicholas Thomas, Giles Tillotson, Beth Fowkes Tobin, Pieter van der Merwe.

Foreword by Sir David Attenborough

March 10th 1793   Geo. Dance

William Hodges 1744–1797: the Art of Exploration

Catalogue to the exhibition at the

National Maritime Museum, Greenwich,
5 July–21 November 2004

and the

Yale Center for British Art, New Haven,
27 January–24 April 2005

Published for
THE NATIONAL MARITIME MUSEUM, GREENWICH
THE YALE CENTER FOR BRITISH ART, NEW HAVEN
by
YALE UNIVERSITY PRESS, NEW HAVEN AND LONDON

Most of Hodges's oil paintings held by the National Maritime Museum, and many others in the collection, can be viewed on-line on the Maritime Art Greenwich website at www.nmm.ac.uk/mag.

Pictures and prints of NMM copyright images may be ordered from the Picture Library, National Maritime Museum, Greenwich, London SE10 9NF; tel. 020 8312 6600.

© National Maritime Museum, London, 2004
www.nmm.ac.uk

For information about this and other Yale University Press publications, please contact:

U.S. Office: sales.press@yale.edu   www.yalebooks.com
Europe Office: sales@yaleup.co.uk   www.yaleup.co.uk

Set in Bembo by Bestset Typesetters, Hong Kong, Ltd.
Printed in Italy by Conti Tipocolor

ISBN   0-300-10376-X cloth
          0-948-06558-3 paper

A catalogue record for this book is available from the Library of Congress and the British Library

10 9 8 7 6 5 4 3 2 1

Frontispiece: Fig. 1 George Dance R. A., *Portrait of William Hodges, R. A.*, pencil and colour on paper, Royal Academy of Arts, London.

Contents

Foreword by Sir David Attenborough

Why should this exhibition of William Hodges's paintings, assembled more than two hundred years after his death, be the first to be devoted to his life's work? He has, after all, in addition to his great gifts as a landscape painter, a very remarkable claim to fame. He was both the first and the last professional European artist to have encountered a civilization as yet entirely unaffected by European ways. Neither the Spanish conquistadors in Mexico nor the Jesuit missionaries in medieval Japan, who both had that extraordinary experience, included a trained artist among their number. But Captain Cook had Hodges. The pictures this young man produced during his encounter with Polynesia not only capture the outward appearance of those societies, but reveal in a fascinating way how he and his companions evaluated what they saw. They are also extremely beautiful. Yet neither of Britain's great national art galleries has a single one of them. The reason may well be that Hodges, when he painted them, was a Government employee.

He was not, however, the Government's first choice. Captain Cook, in 1772, was preparing to leave in the *Resolution* on his second great voyage of discovery. The Admiralty gave particular instructions that the expedition should collect and make detailed records of the people and places, the animals and the plants that it encountered. This work was to be done by a wealthy young naturalist, Joseph Banks. He had been with Cook in the Pacific three years earlier and as a consequence was now something of a celebrity. For this new voyage he decided he would need a team of thirteen servants, musicians and cooks. He also engaged the fashionable society painter, Johann Zoffany. But the *Resolution* could not give his entourage the accommodation Banks thought it deserved, so he demanded the building of an additional deck. This was done, but on the ship's first outing, Cook decided she was now unseaworthy and the Navy Board had the additions removed. Banks was outraged and withdrew

from the expedition in a huff taking Zoffany with him. The Admiralty now had the job of finding replacements. As naturalists they appointed the German-born father and son, Johann and George Forster; and then, to replace Zoffany, the young and little known landscape painter, William Hodges.

So it was that when Hodges returned from this epic voyage in the Pacific, the Admiralty very properly claimed not only the pictures he had painted on the voyage, but also the larger, more finished canvases based on them that he produced in his London studio. Some of these until only about twenty years ago hung on the oak-panelled walls of the Morning Room of Admiralty House to delight those who had the good fortune to be invited to dine there by their Lordships. It was a vision not to be forgotten but not one that could be shared by the general public. Gradually, over the years all of these Government possessions were transferred to the care of the National Maritime Museum in Greenwich. Some, however, did escape official clutches. Hodges's drawings from the voyage consist of exquisite crayon portraits of Pacific Islanders, detailed sketches of coastlines and watercolours of flowers, icebergs and coral islands – some of which were kept by Cook himself in a portfolio that was eventually acquired by the Mitchell Library in Sydney. Hodges retained in his studio one or two of the quick oil sketches made in Tahiti. His major pictures, however, seem to have been regarded by the artistic establishment as of merely topographical significance and of interest only to those concerned with the history of maritime exploration.

Hodges was still a young man when he returned from the Pacific – a mere thirty-one years old. He now had a taste for the exotic and soon afterwards found favour with another great institution in the burgeoning British Empire, one that to some seemed almost an independent state in itself – the East India Company. Under the protection of its Governor General, Warren Hastings,

Hodges travelled widely in India and painted a great number of pictures that were acquired by officers of the Company. He viewed the Indian landscape in a rather different way from that in which he had seen the Pacific. This was not an unknown, untainted Eden. This was the site of an ancient civilization that had long since passed its zenith, and Hodges recorded it in pictures that sometimes bustle with commercial activity but at other times have an elegiac quality, a portrayal of glories long gone.

When Warren Hastings was finally impeached for corruption, Hodges's Indian pictures lost their appeal to the general public. Back home he struggled to establish himself as a painter of British landscapes. In 1794 he mounted a paying exhibition, the centre-piece of which was a pair of huge moralizing landscapes, *The Effects of Peace* and *The Consequences of War*. Members of the royal family, headed by the Duke of York, visited it and roundly condemned the pictures for their radical, anti-war message. The general public, it seems, did not care for them either. We cannot properly judge them today for, together with many of those he painted of British scenes, they are now lost. Within weeks of the exhibition closing, Hodges put all his pictures into a hurriedly arranged sale, abandoned painting altogether and left London for Devon to take up banking. His business failed and he died in relative obscurity.

Since that time, art historians have largely ignored him. Now – at last and for the first time – the full range of his work can be seen and assessed. It demonstrates, surely, that William Hodges has – until now – been the most unjustly neglected British painter of the eighteenth century.

Preface by Roy Clare, Director, National Maritime Museum

This catalogue and our exhibition are the first-ever international celebration of the full span of William Hodges's remarkable career. He has deserved to be better known since he stepped ashore from Captain Cook's *Resolution*: now, after more than 200 years, the National Maritime Museum is proud to be rectifying this matter, and especially to be doing so in association with the Yale Center for British Art and assisted by the Paul Mellon Centre for Studies in British Art, London.

Sir David Attenborough has greatly encouraged our preparations for this premiere. We are most grateful to have had his knowledgeable support and very much look forward to his address at the conference that follows the opening of the exhibition. His vividly evocative foreword to this catalogue affirms his personal enthusiasm for the subject and explains how the Museum has come to hold so many excellent works from Hodges's artistic legacy to Britain. The best are included in this show, with others of great interest and quality, generously lent by institutional and private owners from around the world. We are very grateful to them all.

This happy conjunction of public and private loans, adding to the inherent strength and quality of the Museum's holdings, also highlights the exceptional nature of Inigo Jones's Queen's House as a venue for their display. Since 2001, when it was re-opened by His Royal Highness the Prince of Wales, this seventeenth-century 'House of Delight' has lived up to that early description in another context, growing in confidence as the primary gallery for the Museum's rich and diverse art collections.

Now there are plans to draw on these world-class assets for further shows, building on the reputation that has been initiated, while capitalizing on the expertise of Dr. Geoff Quilley (our Curator of Maritime Art and also the curator of this exhibition) and other talented colleagues here in Greenwich. Together, in the past few years, we have begun a stimulating programme that will reveal further surprises and encourage new audiences, amid a steady revaluation of the Museum's capacity in this area.

It is perhaps fitting that one of our heralds should be a hitherto relatively obscure artist, whose significant and beautiful works are a consequence of Britain's historic and enduring taste for ambitious maritime endeavour. In this light, I hope that you will share my enjoyment of William Hodges this year and find cause to return to the Queen's House again and again.

Roy Clare
Director
National Maritime Museum

Preface by Amy Meyers, Director, Yale Center for British Art and
Brian Allen, Director, Paul Mellon Centre for Studies in British Art

The Yale Center for British Art is proud to collaborate with the National Maritime Museum in presenting *William Hodges 1744-1797: the Art of Exploration*, an exhibition examining the career of an artist whose beautiful but long-neglected representations of Polynesia and India allow us to glimpse the ways in which British naval explorers and mercantile adventurers viewed the topographies, peoples, and natural productions of vast regions of the globe that were rapidly falling subject to an expanding British empire. Although the vicissitudes of politics, taste, and personal fortune caused the majority of Hodges's works to descend into obscurity within his lifetime, our own imperatives, as members of a post-colonial society of increasing complexity, have caused us to seek out his work and to appreciate it for all that it reveals of the original imperatives that lie at the heart of our own global culture.

The Yale Center maintains a special interest in Hodges since its founder, Paul Mellon, was among the first connoisseurs of British art, in the mid-twentieth century, to rediscover the aesthetic and intellectual power of the artist's work. Mr. Mellon added significant paintings, drawings, and prints, as well as associated illustrated publications on India and Captain James Cook's expeditions, to his vast holdings on the history of British exploration and empire, forming a body of material that now serves as one of the major study collections on this important subject. It is consequently fitting that we are working with the National Maritime Museum—the very richest repository of Hodges's work—to resurrect the artist's corpus and to turn it in the light of current scholarship.

To this end, the Yale Center's sister institution, the Paul Mellon Centre for Studies in British Art in London, has lent enthusiastic support for research toward the exhibition and has partnered with the National Maritime Museum to organize a broad-ranging symposium, entitled *The Art of Exploration*, that will place Hodges' work in context. The Yale Centre also has been privileged to host the curator of the exhibition and co-organizer of the symposium, Dr. Geoff Quilley, Curator of Maritime Art at the National Maritime Museum, as a guest scholar in New Haven. We are certain that this cross-institutional collaboration will augment the study of the visual culture of empire through a model study of one of the most important artists to have travelled the globe in the service of his nation at the end of the eighteenth century, and we hope that this productive project will lead to many more collective explorations of like kind.

Amy Meyers
Director
Yale Center for British Art

Brian Allen
Director
Paul Mellon Centre for Studies
in British Art

List of Lenders

The Alkazi Collection, London; Anglesey Abbey, The Fairhaven Collection (The National Trust); The British Library; The British Museum, London; Lord Egremont; Government Art Collection; Charles Greig; Hunterian Museum, The Royal College of Surgeons of England; Inchcape Family Estates Ltd.; The Richard Kelton Foundation; James Mackinnon; Manchester Art Gallery; The Mitchell Library, State Library of New South Wales, Sydney; National Library of Australia; National Museums and Galleries, Wales; His Grace the Duke of Norfolk; Pym's Gallery, London; Royal Academy of Arts, London; Standard Chartered Bank, London; Tate; Wolverhampton Art Gallery; Yale Center for British Art, New Haven, and other private lenders who wish to remain anonymous.

List of Contributors

David Bindman is Durning-Lawrence Professor of the History of Art, University College London.

John Bonehill is Curatorial Research Fellow, National Maritime Museum, Greenwich.

Natasha Eaton is Simon Research Fellow, School of Art History and Archaeology, University of Manchester.

Charles Greig is an independent art historian.

Harriet Guest is Professor of English Literature, University of York.

Geoff Quilley is Curator of Maritime Art, National Maritime Museum, Greenwich.

Nicholas Thomas is Professor of Anthropology, Goldsmith's College, University of London.

Giles Tillotson is Reader in the History of Art, Chair of Art and Archaeology, School of Oriental and African Studies, University of London.

Beth Fowkes Tobin is Professor of English, Arizona State University.

Pieter van der Merwe is General Editor, National Maritime Museum, Greenwich.

Acknowledgements

We are indebted and extremely grateful to all our lenders, and to the following institutions and individuals, without whose support this exhibition and catalogue would not have been possible: The Paul Mellon Centre for Studies in British Art, for generously providing a Curatorial Research Grant for the employment of John Bonehill, and to the Centre's Director, Brian Allen, for unstinting support from the outset; Sir David Attenborough for his inspiration and for communicating his enthusiasm for Hodges's work; the Yale Center for British Art, and its Director, Amy Meyers, for their support and co-operation in preparing the exhibition on its transfer to the YCBA, including the generous provision of a Guest Fellowship for Geoff Quilley, and for their participation in co-organizing the parallel conference, *The Art of Exploration*, which the Paul Mellon Centre also generously supported; Richard Kelton, President of the Kelton Foundation, and John Mitchell and Son (Fine Paintings), for their support towards the costs of preparing the catalogue; James Mitchell of John Mitchell and Son (Fine Paintings), whose enthusiastic support for the project from its inception, resulting in the 'preview' exhibition at John Mitchell and Son, has been most helpful; Charles Greig, for unfailing support, encouragement and invaluable advice at all times; the staff of the British Library, the Royal Academy Library and National Art Library; John Nicoll and Beatrix McIntyre of Yale University Press, for their patience, encouragement and professionalism; finally, all the staff at the National Maritime Museum, Greenwich, not least among the Curatorial Team, for their continued support and faith in this project. Certain individuals at the National Maritime Museum have been in various ways highly instrumental in seeing the project to its conclusion; they know who they are, but essentially this has been a hugely significant team effort, led by Geoff Quilley.

R.C.

William Hodges, artist of empire

GEOFF QUILLEY

The artistic career of William Hodges RA (1744–97) coincided precisely with the decline and foundation, respectively, of what have been termed 'the first and second British empires'.[1] At the close of the Seven Years' War in 1763, when Britain established itself as the foremost imperial nation of Europe, Hodges was coming to the final year of his apprenticeship under Richard Wilson, the leading British landscape painter of the day, and emerging as an important member of the younger generation of British painters. Hodges's subsequent career revolved around two major – indeed, by eighteenth-century standards, epic – voyages, both intimately connected with the rise of empire. The first, Captain James Cook's second voyage to the Pacific (1772–75), to which Hodges was appointed official draughtsman, has justly been noted as one of the most important single contributions to the understanding of world geography and the natural sciences. It was also a key moment in the foundation of the methodologies of ethnography and anthropology, as they would develop in the nineteenth century, and Hodges's works from the voyage have frequently been cited in this connection.[2] However, coming at a time when the British were seeking to consolidate their maritime empire, against the backdrop of Wilkite riots in London and growing colonial rebellion in America, the military and strategic importance of Cook's voyage should not be overlooked.

Hodges's second major journey, to India (1780–83), was made under the patronage of the first Governor General, Warren Hastings, and with the full support of the East India Company, which is given due acknowledgement in Hodges's subsequent publications of Indian subjects. It coincided with a period of concentrated British military action against local rulers, in particular the conflict with Chait Singh that would figure prominently in Hastings's later impeachment. Not only was Hodges reliant on East India Company forces in paving the way for him to travel through the contested territories west of Bengal, but his painterly subjects also frequently represent overtly the recent and ongoing history of British conquest in India (cat. nos 55-59).

It is not just that the rise of empire facilitated Hodges's art, providing him with subjects and making him surely the most widely travelled artist of his day, it also provided commercial opportunities for the artist-entrepreneur, which operated within a specifically metropolitan context: 'empire' was itself given visual and conceptual definition by Hodges's (and, of course, others') representations of the non-European world. At the very least, they provided or consolidated the cognitive assimilation of the territories depicted, by making an explicit connection, through the visual artefact, between those territories and the British metropolis.

Hodges's importance lies, therefore, in four principal areas, the first and most striking of which is that he was the first professional landscape artist (British or otherwise) to represent such extensive global territories so profusely and on such a scale; and that this artistic production was the result of a complex symbiosis between the development of British art and the rise of British global dominion. Secondly, he figures crucially, within the larger context of the history of eighteenth-century colonialism, in being pivoted between colonial and metropolitan spheres: his work and career provide an important case study of the exchanges, relations, alignments and misalignments, congruences and fractures between the metropolitan and non-metropolitan spaces of empire. This relates to a series of issues, from the large question of Hodges's role in representing the non-European world through the filter of a 'European vision',[3] to how he tempers and adapts his visions of the Pacific and India to suit the cultural and economic demands of the metropolitan audience for art. In this connection, thirdly, it is significant that his career flourished at a moment not just of imperial expansion, but also of the explosive expansion of the British art world, with the formulation of a distinctive, influential and increasingly professionalized art establishment, headed by the newly formed Royal Academy. Parallel with the redefinition of the nation's cultural and political self-image provoked by its changing imperial horizons (of which Hodges was himself a catalyst), the theoretical and practical values of art and aesthetics were also subject to constant revision through this period. Perhaps the most marked changes occurred with respect to landscape painting, which from the 1790s was increasingly associated with discourses on national identity and the question of what might properly constitute the character of a national style of painting.[4] Discussion of landscape, as both physical topography and visual representation, was particularly mediated through reference to the cult of the 'picturesque', and in this regard the aesthetics of landscape have been critically linked to the imperial context.[5] But wider connections between imperialism and the discourse of landscape at this period surely cannot be overlooked.[6] Here Hodges is a key figure, in proposing landscape painting, in theory and practice, both as the obvious means of recording the topographies of empire, and (most revolutionary) also as a suitably philosophical medium for evaluating them and commenting on their significance.[7]

Given such apparent importance, therefore, Hodges's significance lies, finally, in the consequent anomaly that after his death he was largely forgotten and was later effectively excised from the orthodox history of British art as it was academically articulated during the twentieth century. He was known, if at all, only as Cook's artist or as one of the early British artists in India. Until now there has been no fully representative monographic exhibition devoted to him.

If, in the picture of Hodges's career, empire provided the ground on which his art was composed, its frame was war. He both was born and died during periods of war, and for nearly half of his life Britain was involved in major – and increasingly global – conflicts. Born in London, in 1744, the son of a smith, when the country was in the middle of the War of the Austrian Succession, Hodges's artistic training, first at William Shipley's drawing school, followed by his apprenticeship to Richard Wilson, overlapped with the Seven Years' War, as a result of which Britain acquired unprecedented colonial possessions, principally in India, North America and Canada, and the Caribbean.[8] On his return from Cook's voyage in 1775, Britain was launching itself into the internecine colonial conflict of the American Revolutionary War; and his time in India coincided with the final phase of the First Maratha War and the bulk of the Second Mysore War. Hodges, indeed, witnessed British engagements in India at first hand, celebrating the 'opportunity which falls to the lot of but few professional men in my line; I mean that of observing the military operations of a siege'.[9] War, openly or discreetly addressed, is a recurrent subject for his art, whether in the context of Tahiti, or India, or his final one-man exhibition in 1794–95 of *War* and *Peace*. As a consequence, war, both as subject for that exhibition and also as the wider cultural background against

which it was produced and received, was critically influential upon the turn of events that led to his death.[10] For not only was the exhibition closed down at the prompting of the Duke of York, on the grounds that the treatment of such subjects was dangerously radical, in Britain's first year of war with Revolutionary France, but this disgrace also led Hodges to abandon painting, auction his remaining pictures – including *War* and *Peace* – and to invest his funds in a banking partnership in Devon, for which he abandoned London and moved to Brixham in 1795. The unstable financial climate caused by the ongoing war with France in 1797 led to the failure of the bank and Hodges died immediately upon his return from the journey to Dartmouth to close it. There was mention of financial corruption and also rumour that Hodges had committed suicide, but these issues remain unresolved.[11] What is significant is the centrality of war to Hodges's career and to its demise. However, this is not to say that he was an advocate of war. On the contrary, his writings frequently lament the ruinous impact of war upon the practice of art, as well as other aspects of civilized culture. However disingenuous this may see, given his reliance, particularly in India, upon the military both for his security and his painterly subject matter, it betokens a sentimental idealization of peace, as the opposite of 'the great scourge of human nature, the great enemy of the arts, war',[12] that is, in the first place, typical of the gestures of late eighteenth-century discourse of sensibility, and, secondly, allied to a form of nostalgia for the past that suffuses Hodges's sense of history with respect to the monuments, ruins and landscapes comprising the majority of his art.

There is, therefore, a complex dialectic at the heart of Hodges's work, that is also a dialectic of empire: between imperialism as enlightened, Enlightenment practice *vis-à-vis* the discovery, documentation and classification of the world; and imperialism as the function of militarized conquest and the imposition of colonial order. It is also a dialectic between the imperial present and the imperial past, which is further informed by the widespread comparison made throughout the eighteenth century between Britain as a modern commercial empire and the classical precedent of imperial Rome, famously documented in Gibbon's monumental history. At its centre, therefore, is the representation of history, which Hodges can be seen to engage at several levels. He draws on comparisons between Pacific or Indian culture and classical civilization, for example in the overt classicization of Pacific Islanders in the post-voyage 'landing' paintings (cat. nos 34–36); in the links attempted between the architecture of Benares [Varanasi] and classical Greece; or in the classical Roman light in which Akbar's tomb and other Mughal ruins are shown.[13]

History itself, as a discursive field of study, was undergoing profound changes at this period, in the face of the material evidence about the composition, extent and history of the world that was being produced by travel, particularly that undertaken by Cook. This entailed radical revisions to the accepted, theologically dominated accounts of the world and human development.[14] On the one hand, therefore, Hodges's body of work, in its sheer range and extent, could be taken as a visual counterpart to Edmund Burke's celebrated comment to William Robertson in response to the latter's *History of America* of 1777:

> We possess at this time very great advantages towards the knowledge of human Nature. We need no longer go to History to trace it in all its stages and periods. History from its comparative youth, is but a poor instructour . . . But now the Great map of mankind is unrolld at once; and there is no state or Gradation of barbarism, and no mode of refinement which we have not at the same instant under our View. The very different Civility of Europe and China; The barbarism of Tartary, and of Arabia. The Savage State of North America, and of New Zealand.[15]

The importance of painting to this change in the perception of history should not be underestimated, and it is relatively easy to see how Hodges's drawings of Pacific Islanders (cat. nos 16, 17, 21, 22) or views of Pacific landscapes accord with such an image of the world as consisting of a living history that was being progressively brought to light by geographical exploration.

On the other hand, Hodges's observations, particularly in *Travels in India*, on the dreadful effects of war were closely aligned with a moral discourse on despotism. This in turn pertained to a larger debate in Europe on the morality, benefits and dangers of empire, that was especially acute for Britain in the wake of the loss of the American colonies. It becomes most pronounced in his description of Agra and Emperor Akbar's tomb nearby at Sikandra (1606–12, fig. 23). Agra he terms 'the once splendid and imperial city' built by Akbar in the mid-sixteenth century, but now the 'whole of this spot, as far as the eye can reach, is one general scene of ruined buildings'.[16] The panoramic view from the balcony of one of the minarets of Akbar's tomb confirms this impression and enables a correspondingly expanded historical overview, in which the clear view of the landscape is metonymic with a broad view of history:

> From the summit of the minarets . . . a spectator's eye may range over a prodigious circuit of country, not less than thirty miles in a direct line, the whole of which is flat, and filled with ruins of ancient grandeur: the river Jumna is seen at some distance, and the glittering towers of Agra. This fine country exhibits, in its present state, a melancholy proof of the consequences of a bad government, of wild ambition, and the horrors attending civil dissentions; for when the governors of this country were in plenitude of power, and exercised their rights with wisdom, from the excellence of its climate, with some degree of industry, it must have been a perfect garden; but now all is desolation and silence.[17]

The ravages of war are linked to imperial decline, parallel to the manner in which the extent of Hodges's vision of landscape is linked to his facility for historical judgment.[18] It is not insignificant, therefore, that the site from which this sight is made available is the tomb of Akbar, for Hodges the great founder of the Mughal empire, 'whose great actions have resounded through the world, and whose liberality and humanity were his highest praise'.[19] Mughal decline is associated more widely with the corrupting effects of luxury:

> The private luxury and vices of the Musselman princes too frequently reduce them to a state of real poverty, even with large revenues; and too often they delegate to artful, designing, and avaricious characters, the management and concerns of the state, and become virtually the plunderers instead of the parents of their subjects . . . Thus it is that the people at large retain no real regard for their governors, and the natural consequence is, that the princes are frequently left, in the hour of distress, quite destitute of support, and an easy prey to any invader.[20]

This is a local, colonial adaptation of a longstanding metropolitan argument, deriving ultimately from classical sources, about the deplorable effects of luxury upon the political state.[21] Broadly put, this held that the manly virtue required to protect the individual, family and public society, through the right and ability to bear and use arms, was subject to corruption from external sources. These were mostly to do with climate or commerce and consumption. In the individual, climate or the indulgence of luxury commodities (such as sugar or coffee) might enervate the body and lead to indolence and dissipation, with consequent impact upon the individual's morality and public spiritedness. At a larger public level, the body politic could be corrupted through the cultural development of a 'false' sense of taste caused by the over-importation of foreign or luxury goods, or through the increasing influence of trade and commerce – with a consequent political empowerment of the merchant class – causing the promotion of private financial interests over those of the state. The result would be a decline in public virtue and the social ties entailed in it, a greater propensity to internecine conflict, and the exposure of the state to invasion from its enemies. For a nation such as Britain, self-styled as a commercial maritime empire, such notions could sound particularly ominous. Moreover, they were increasingly associated by British theorists with the acquisition of empire. As early as 1767, Adam Ferguson explicitly linked imperialism to despotism:

> What may not the fleets and armies of Europe, with the access they have by commerce to every part of the world, and the facility of their conveyance, effect, if that ruinous maxim should prevail, That the grandeur of a nation is to be estimated from the extent of its territory; or, That the interest of any particular people consists in reducing their neighbours to servitude?[22]

Hodges's account of Indian luxury, therefore, should be understood in the much larger context of prevailing attitudes to empire among the British public. He displaces any overt concern with British imperial activity onto an account of the imperial history of India, and surrogates the British military presence via a lament

on the effects of 'civil dissentions' and a complaint over the reduced opportunities for the painter 'in a country . . . over-run by an active enemy' (no matter if the country more properly belonged to the 'active enemy', and despite his later welcome of the rare opportunity to witness 'the military operations of a siege').[23] However, in his account of the past Mughal empire there is clearly an Ozymandian admonition for eighteenth-century imperial Britain, which is pitched dialectically against his frequent accounts of the present benefits brought to India by the British presence. This dialectic emerges for Hodges as the split between war and peace, and is aesthetically expressed through the representation of landscape as the repository of history.

The idea that all regions of the world were, in Burke's words, 'at the same instant under our View' had a metropolitan as well as a colonial aspect, and could be taken to refer to the increasing amount of visual culture available in London representing the non-European world, whether in exhibitions or in private collections. This is not to mention the growth of prints and book illustration. There is a real sense in which the world was becoming increasingly visible 'at the same instant' though visual representation. What is perhaps most arresting about Burke's vivid image of the 'map of mankind', however, is not just the interesting elision it proposes of history and mapping, to suggest that one is the exact correlate of the other, but also the necessarily visual register it ascribes to the making of history: history is present in the world, and is available to be seen and visually recorded, in the manner of a map or a painting.

This has important implications for the art of Hodges, who saw himself increasingly as an artist-historian. In promoting his views of India, he makes direct comparison between his work and the exacting methods demanded of the writing of history:

Judging that these representations would give a true idea of the general features of that favoured country and climate, and in some respects of the former and present state of India, I have chosen to consider myself as their portrait painter, who, though his taste has a right to select the most characteristic features of his originals, to chuse the properest point of view, and place them in the best light, must still submit his genius and fancy to the strictest rules of veracity. Like the historian, he may adorn his work with every beauty of stile and composition; but like him he is bound to the rigid canon of truth: like him he must delineate things as they are, not like the poet, as imagination may suggest, they ought to be, or might be. It would be needless to expatiate here on the respective rank, merit, and difficulty of portrait or history painting, or of plain historical subjects, contrasted with fanciful and poetical compositions. I must beg leave to say, that fanciful compositions are more easy and pleasing to the composer than useful and instructive to the beholder, who finds his account generally better in exact, lively, and graceful representations of truth and reality.[24]

This is a complex passage, which needs to be considered in the light of Hodges's own artistic self-promotion as well as prevailing debates over the relative capacities for the various genres of painting to treat philosophical or historical subjects.[25] The principal point for my argument here is the centrality of the representation of history to Hodges's art. What emerges very strongly when his work is viewed as a whole is the dominance and consistency from an early date of the themes of war and peace, and of the relation of painting to history; also the way these two aesthetic concerns closely interleave, to culminate in the 1794–95 exhibition of the historical landscapes of *War* and *Peace*.[26]

The concern with representing history can be seen also in Hodges's depiction of architectural monuments. On his return from Cook's voyage, he toured Wales and central England, producing several paintings concerned with the iconography of medieval monuments and ruins (cat. no. 73, fig 62). While these paintings broadly correspond to the contemporary antiquarian interest in the ancient monuments of Britain, other works celebrate new architecture, though frequently this is associated with the historical longevity of the aristocracy. For example, Hodges's *View of Sandbeck in Yorkshire, the seat of the Earl of Scarborough* (fig. 2), exhibited in 1770 and 1771, was later engraved for W. Watts's *The Seats of the Nobility and Gentry*. The description states that the building was designed by James Paine, with the pediment of the portico containing 'a fine Alto Relievo, by the ingenious Mr. *William Collins*'.[27] While many such views were of buildings by Paine, who appears to have been an important source of support and patronage to Hodges in his early career, the concept of history presented here is, in direct contrast to the later views of Mughal monuments in India, that of a longstanding, medieval-derived, dynastic class, which far from declining into oblivion under the effects of luxury, was continuing and flourishing, and indeed adding to the cultural capital of the nation by patronizing new architecture. A similar treatment is accorded to Warren Hastings' commissioning of new building in India:

> Calcutta . . . was soon raised to a great and opulent city, when the government of the kingdom of Bengal fell into the hands of the English. For its magnificence, however, it is indebted solely to the liberal spirit and excellent taste of the late Governor General; and it must be confessed, that the first house was raised by Mr. Hastings which deserves the name of a piece of architecture.[28]

The prosperity denoted by such building is also associated for Hodges with peace. His views and descriptions of Calcutta correspond with his description of the painting of *Peace* exhibited in 1794–95. Where Calcutta, under British control, boasts 'a range of beautiful and regular buildings; and a considerable reach of the river, with vessels of various classes and sizes, from the largest Indiaman to the smallest boat of the country', the scene of *Peace* comprises

> A sea-port thronged with shipping, expressive of Commerce; the great public buildings denote its riches; a large bay opening to the ocean, merchant ships going out, others returning,

shew the extension of its trade to the most distant quarters of the globe.[29]

Hodges's association of architecture, historical lineage and dynastic continuity with peace and prosperity, therefore, appears to apply overwhelmingly to metropolitan history. Metropolitan historical progress, even when relocated to the colonial sphere, is contrasted with non-European historical retardation or inertia. It is significant that his 'historical landscape' of *Peace* was openly intended to be a national allegory, 'Exemplifying the happy state of England in the year 1795'. This was contrasted with 'War, shewing the misery of internal commotion', showing the same landscape overrun by Turkish invaders.[30] 'Internal commotion', however, was something Hodges associated strongly, as already suggested, with the decline of the Mughal empire. Indeed, it appears to be civil discord as a form of conflict that poses the greatest problems for him. In other contexts, particularly in the Pacific, the capacity for war could be represented as a mark of social and civilizational progress. The majestic *War Boats of Tahiti* (cat. no. 30), by far the largest of the paintings executed for the Admiralty, registers the awesome impact that the sight of the Tahitian naval forces preparing for war had upon Cook's expedition, and might be seen as a positive representation of military prowess as a sign of civilization, analogous to the theories of contemporary thinkers such as Lord Kames, who argued that war, when conducted in a civilized rather than a barbaric way, must be a cause of improvement in the commercial state, since it inculcated public virtue and was an antidote to luxury.[31]

Hodges's history, therefore, is an imperial one, which, while it operates as an assimilative discourse, connecting different parts of the empire within an overall order, also registers difference between the metropolitan and the colonial spheres. On the one hand, Hodges presents 'truth' as the universal premise on which his art is based, and states his intention 'to give the manners of mankind in the varied shades from the Savage in the wilds to the highly civilized in the palace'. He thus seeks to embrace the 'manners of mankind' in a paternalistic, broadly Anglican imperial vision, which parallels the attempts to establish linguistic connections across different regions of the Pacific or Asia by J. R. Forster, or the later comparisons made by Sir William Jones between Sanskrit and ancient Greek or Latin (which echo closely Hodges's own remarks on the relation of classical to Hindu architecture).[32] On the other hand, such assimilation does not entail the erasure of difference. Again, this comes across most strongly in Hodges's representations of architecture. Where, for example, Agra and Akbar's tomb are fixed in an irretrievable past and steeped in discourses of imperial decline and loss, by contrast, equivalent British sites are presented as part of a living tradition, denoting an antiquity that is not a signifier of the alienated cultural difference of the past from the present, but is instead the marker of the present being informed by and legitimized by the past. It is rare for Hodges to give textual accounts of British buildings in that way that he did with Indian ones, but he did so in the case of Windsor (cat. no. 74). The painting, *View of Windsor Castle from the Great Park*, was exhibited at the Royal Academy in 1787 to favourable reviews, and was engraved with a textual description added. After claiming that Windsor 'is universally allowed to be the most magnificent and pleasantly situated Castle in the Island of Great-Britain', this goes on to outline the continuous history of the building from its foundation by William the Conqueror, through the institution of the Order of the Garter, to the development of the town in the seventeenth century. It concludes by giving a summary of the composition of the present-day Corporation and the number of Members of Parliament returned. This wider, ongoing social and cultural context for Windsor is matched by the breadth of the view in the print, which

> includes a wide range of Country. The Chapel at Eaton is situated in the Valley a little to the left of the rising Ground on which the Castle stands. On the right, in the Distance Harrow is seen; and some Peeps of the River Thames. The white Building in the Front of the Castle is the Queen's-Lodge, which the present Royal Family make their principal Country Residence.

This list of sites visible in the scene amounts effectively to a taxonomy of monarchical presence, implicitly as an unbroken line of dynastic descent from William I to the present day, which is integrated with the local political composition of Windsor. The transition in the description from past to present tense is gradual and logical: there is certainly no comparison with Akbar here. The Castle and other sites around Windsor are naturalized as part of the landscape, in a way that renders landscape as the natural repository of history. This is parallel but inverse to the representation of Agra, where the landscape is produced as evidence of the history of 'bad government', in its mismanagement, lack of cultivation and being littered with ruins: in this imperial context, the traces of history in the landscape are out of harmony with its naturalness. What is of greater import, of course, is the ideological function of representing landscape-as-history through images that are proclaimed to be transparent renditions of the 'manners of mankind' in 'exact, lively, and graceful representations of truth and reality'.

However, Hodges's representations of the non-European world were of course mediated by the formal structures of exhibition, reproduction and critical discourse by which his works were received and judged among his largely London audience. Nor was Hodges working in isolation or in a cultural vacuum: as a member of the Royal Academy from 1787, he was the associate of Joseph Farington and other high-ranking Academicians, including Sir Joshua Reynolds. He appears to have had contact with Joseph Wright of Derby, and his views of the non-European world were supplemented by other artists, notably John Webber, Johann Zoffany, Tilly Kettle and the Daniells. He was also for a time in the early 1790s scene painter at the Pantheon in London.[33] The claim, therefore, made by Hodges himself, that his works were clothed only in 'the simple garb of truth', or that they may be taken as somehow transparent

records of visual reality, must therefore be treated with great scepticism.[34] This may seem obvious when dealing historically with his art in an eighteenth-century context but it applies equally to the way his work has been discussed in recent art history. The teleological fallacy, for example, which sees Hodges as a step towards the more naturalistic art of Turner and Constable, to be crowned by the 'pure' vision of the Impressionists, represents the history of landscape painting as a progressive movement away from artificial convention and towards realism and an increasing closure of the separation between the physical landscape and its painted representation.[35] This historiography has its own imperial dimension. As W. J. T. Mitchell has written, the 'semiotic features' of such accounts of the development of landscape in western culture

> and the historical narratives they generate, are tailor-made for the discourse of imperialism, which conceives itself precisely (and simultaneously) as an expansion of landscape understood as an inevitable, progressive development in history, an expansion of 'culture' and 'civilization' into a 'natural' space in a progress that is itself narrated as 'natural'.[36]

Although Mitchell's account of the history of landscape painting is over-generalized, it offers a suggestive route into understanding the relationship between the representation of landscape and imperial history. He criticizes, perhaps unfairly, Bernard Smith's *European Vision and the South Pacific*, the great pioneering account of the importance of Pacific exploration to the development of European art and culture. A central figure in Smith's book is Hodges, for his daring use of *plein-air* techniques in a move towards a more naturalistic or empirical vision. Mitchell instead criticizes Smith for treating the Pacific as

> a spatial region that was there to be 'opened', 'discovered', and constructed as an object of scientific and artistic representation . . . The real subject is not the South Pacific but European imperial 'vision', understood as a dialectical movement towards landscape understood as the naturalistic representation of nature.[37]

This is in no way to belittle Smith's magnificent achievement in opening up this whole area of scholarly enquiry. It is simply to identify the historiographical lineage of that achievement. In this regard, there is a further question of Smith's account of Hodges as the precursor of Turner and Ruskin in his 'fearless attempts to break with neo-classical formulas and to paint with a natural vision':[38] if he has such important status in the development of a modernist vision of landscape, why has he been left in effective obscurity for the past two centuries? In attempting to answer this, it has to be further questioned what is the relationship between imperialism and modernism, and whether it is possible to identify an 'imperial' history of collections and collecting, parallel to the imperialist history of landscape that Mitchell detects, even down to the late twentieth century. Hodges, again, is peculiarly interesting in this respect.

Despite Hodges's importance in eighteenth-century British

art, and the visual quality of his art, this is the first exhibition devoted solely to the artist, covering the entire range of his work. His invisibility to art-historical scrutiny has to do with the widely varied collecting of his work, which in turn results from the imperial context within which it was produced. The paintings relating to Cook's voyage were mostly made for the Admiralty, and via this route the majority have ended up at the National Maritime Museum. Even being in a public collection has not necessarily led to their being publicly displayed. The remarkable *View in the Island of New Caledonia* (cat. no. 29), since its first Royal Academy exhibition in 1778, has rarely – and certainly not in the last ten years – been on exhibition.

By contrast, his other works, particularly the Indian subjects, were generally produced for private East India Company patrons, most notably Warren Hastings and Augustus Cleveland, often in the colonial context. These have been dispersed through private sales, frequently unrecorded, and have remained overwhelmingly in private collections. A large number of Hodges's paintings in Augustus Cleveland's collection appeared in the sale of Cleveland's effects in Calcutta on 4 February 1794. Many of these disappeared without record, while others have resurfaced, but without provenance for the intervening period (cat. no. 66). On the other hand, his European, British, historical and literary subjects are now substantially untraced: many were sold by Hodges in the hasty and dismal sale of his works following the closure of the 1794–95 exhibition (Christie's, 29 June 1795), and remain unlocated. Others appeared for sale after Hodges's death, particularly at the European Museum sales at Christie's, but generally went for very low prices.[39] By an interesting irony, subsequent interest in collecting Hodges's work has rested with his overtly imperial production rather than his domestic landscape imagery. He is known as an artist of empire, but this very categorization has marginalized him in the history of British art. What might be termed the 'imperial history of collections', therefore, has also had a determining effect upon the priorities of art-historical discourse and research.

As a result, the critical assessment of Hodges has separated him into distinct parts, to classify him either as Cook's artist or the artist in India, while his contribution to British landscape imagery has tended to go almost unnoticed. It is surely critical, however, to take account of his total output within the larger context of eighteenth-century Britain as an imperial nation: such a reconsideration would also reciprocally comprise a critique of the history of collections, by referring this history itself to a wider imperial frame of reference. Hodges in this sense stands as an instructive case study for the wider relation of art to empire.

Hodges's art makes us question our own understanding of history, whether that is the history of global exploration, the history of eighteenth-century British art, or the history of collecting and display that has enabled or disabled the viewing of such work and the understanding of its wider significance. More specifically, it makes us question our relation to our own, shared imperial past. At a moment when there is considerable debate in Britain[40] about the relevance of the history of empire, especially to education, serious critical engagement with Hodges's work is perhaps more important than ever.

1   Harlow (1952–64).
2   See particularly Joppien and Smith (1985b).
3   Smith (1985).
4   Kriz (1997).
5   Tillotson (2000).
6   Mitchell (2002).
7   See Hodges (1793), 17, 154–6, and the essays by Natasha Eaton and Beth Fowkes Tobin in this volume.
8   The details of Hodges's life are given in Stuebe (1979).
9   Hodges (1793), 85.
10 See Harriet Guest's essay in this volume.
11 Farington (1978–98), vol. 8, 2860–3.
12 Hodges (1793), 5.
13 See the essays by Nicholas Thomas, Natasha Eaton and Giles Tillotson in this volume.
14 Pocock (1999b).
15 Burke, letter to William Robertson, 9 June 1777.
16 Hodges (1793), 113.
17 Ibid., 123.
18 Barrell (1992).
19 Hodges (1793), 122.
20 Ibid., 103–4.
21 Sekora (1977).
22 Ferguson (1767), 154.
23 Hodges (1793), 8.
24 Hodges (1787), np.
25 See Beth Fowkes Tobin's essay in this volume.
26 On this exhibition, see Harriet Guest's essay in this volume.
27 Watts (1779), no. 10.
28 Hodges (1793), 15–16.
29 See Appendix below, and Stuebe (1979), 351.
30 Ibid., 350–4; see also Harriet Guest's essay in this volume.
31 Kames (1773); see my ' "Tahiti revisited": the historicizing visual order of the Pacific in the art of Cook's voyages', forthcoming.
32 Forster (1982); Hodges (1787); see also Giles Tillotson's essay in this volume.
33 See Price (1987).
34 Hodges (1793), iv.
35 Stuebe (1979), 91; Smith (1985), 56–80 and Smith (1992), 111–34; see also Tillotson (2000), 53–4, for a critique.
36 Mitchell (2002), 17.
37 Ibid., 19.
38 Smith (1985), 80.
39 See Stuebe (1979), nos. 619–21, 627–8, 630–3, 636–8, 640–3.
40 This is not to say, of course, that such debate has not been conducted for many years in other parts of the globe.

Overleaf: detail of cat. no. 11 [*A view of Point Venus and Matavai Bay, looking east*], August 1773.

'This hapless adventurer': Hodges and the London art world

John Bonehill

William Hayley's *Life of George Romney, Esq.*, first published in 1809, offers a particularly vivid recollection of the London art world in the closing decades of the eighteenth century. His biography of one of that scene's leading portrait painters, aside from its narrative of Romney's life and career, comprises various anecdotes of the professional and social milieu of the time, reflections on the competitiveness and fierce rivalries that often existed between artists, as well as a number of pen-portraits of figures the poet had come to know personally. These include several verses dedicated to contemporary artists, such as the following epitaph to the frustrated career and sad demise of his friend, William Hodges:

> Ye men of genius, join'd to moral worth,
>   Whose merits meet no just rewards on earth,
> Ye fair, who in your lot, tho' lovely, find
>   To grace and virtue fortune still is blind,
> Sigh o'er the names recorded on this stone!
>   And feel for characters so like your own!
> To active Hodges, who with zeal sublime,
>   Pursued the art, he lov'd, in every clime;
> Who early traversing the globe with Cook,
>   Painted new life from nature's latent book;
> Who with a spirit that no bars controul'd,
>   Labour'd in Indian heat, and Russian cold,
> Yet clos'd (with virtues by the world allow'd)
> A life of labour in affliction's cloud[1]

Hayley's lines are part tribute to the artist's wanderlust, part lament for Hodges's failure to achieve the measure of praise the writer clearly thought he deserved. The disparity between the energies Hodges devoted to his artistic career and the singular lack of reward that blighted his final years led Hayley to reflect:

Ill fortune seemed continually to attend all the exertions, and all the wishes of the kind-hearted and high-spirited Hodges. With uncommon industry, and considerable talents, he could not gain a comfortable subsistence by his art, and when, in honest indignation, he renounced the pencil for the more lucrative business of a provincial banker, the public storm, that shook even the bank of the nation, utterly overwhelmed this hapless adventurer, and all his hopes.[2]

Making a living in the overcrowded metropolitan art world of the period was a precarious business: Hayley's summation of Hodges's career makes the point that there was no correlation between hard work and fame, and that for all an artist's industriousness, resourcefulness and idealism, rewards were hard won.

This essay explores Hodges's attempts to secure the public acknowledgement Hayley thought denied to him, through an examination of the artist's relationship to the major developments in the London art scene of the late eighteenth century: its expanding exhibition culture; the emergence of an art press; and an ever more sophisticated print market. For Hodges's early training and first steps as a professional artist coincided with the formative moments of these novel transformations in the British art world, and his subsequent career might be taken as a paradigmatic case study in their effects. Within two years of Hodges being articled to Richard Wilson's studio in 1758, the first exhibition of the Society of Artists – founded by his old teacher, William Shipley – opened its doors to a public that had formerly little access to contemporary painting. With the founding of the Royal Academy in 1768, and its promotion of a disinterested, civic-minded art, as part of its liberal-humanist agenda, competition between artists for the recognition of that public (or more properly 'publics') became increasingly fractious and intense. Such was the rivalry and such the uncertainty of the artist's position, that those concerned to make a living from art were forced to adopt any number of expedients, with Hodges accepting commissions for paintings from a diverse range of institutional bodies and individual patrons from across the social spectrum, as well as working as a print maker and publisher, theatrical scene painter, essayist and author, before turning to banking. While some of these activities saw Hodges cultivate the image of artist-historian and a learned, scholarly profile befitting a gentleman, and so tallying with the view of the artist being promoted so influentially by the Royal Academy, others might be more readily identified with the lowly status of businessman, jobbing craftsman or mechanic.[3] Indeed, the uneven, at times *ad hoc*, pattern of Hodges's career is indicative of the uncertain place of artists in Georgian culture more generally, caught as they were between the commercial pressures of the market and – as embodiments of genteel politeness – the need to disguise the entrepreneurial skills needed to succeed.[4] Nowhere were these tensions more in evidence than in the annual exhibitions of the arts that had so rapidly established themselves in the wake of the Society of Artists' initial show, and which had become the most important advertisement for an artist's work.

Exhibition and display

It should be remembered that Hodges was often geographically remote from the very market place on which he was most dependent. What made his work so notable for contemporaries like Hayley was that he 'Pursued the art, he lov'd, in every clime', yet the lengthy absences this visual exploration of exotic cultures required placed him on the fringes of domestic developments. That Hodges was all too aware of the need to maintain a presence of sorts on the metropolitan scene when physically absent is apparent from early in his career. He began exhibiting at the Society of Artists in 1768, and continued to enter works to this body or the Free Society of Artists for several years. In the summer of 1774 he showed at the latter several scenes of exotic subjects, at a point when he was, of course, on the other side of the globe accompanying Cook. Those paintings on display in London had been shipped back home from the Cape of Good Hope in late 1772, and included views of Madeira, St. Jago and Table Mountain (see cat. nos 1, 2). This career-mindedness is striking, but it is also interesting that Hodges chose to remain faithful to the Free Society of Artists – at least for the time being – in an increasingly Academy-dominated art world. And it might be wondered whether Hodges's choice was informed by the professed aims of the Society of Artists, from which that body had earlier split but with which it maintained links.[5] For Shipley saw the Society as:

> an effectual means to embolden enterprise, to enlarge science, to refine Art, to improve Manufactures, and extend our

Commerce; in a word, to render Great Britain the school of instruction, as it is already the centre of traffic to the greatest part of the world.[6]

Hodges's *A View of the Cape of Good Hope*, which in the Free Society of Artists exhibition catalogue is identified as having been 'taken on the spot, from on board the *Resolution*, Capt. Cooke', might be interpreted as epitomizing this mixture of patriotic and mercantilist sentiment. Not only did it result from one of the country's most prominent and prestigious enterprises in enlarging the sphere of knowledge, but had arrived on the walls of the exhibition as part of that global 'traffic' in goods of which London was celebrated as the centre. Shipley's Society was already a major agency in the nation's colonial projects and schemes, spreading ideals of agricultural improvement and trade. To judge from the kinds of imagery consistently on show at the Society's exhibitions they may have actively encouraged the production of scenes with a colonial theme.[7]

Hodges's views of distant, foreign curiosities, whether seen in the print shop window or on the crowded walls of the London exhibition rooms, might then jostle for attention alongside a host of images that took as their theme the nation's expanding global network of colonial outposts and trade routes, and all similarly imbricated in those circuits of colonial commerce celebrated by Shipley. This consistent engagement with an imagery drawn from the country's ventures abroad is testament both to the seemingly insatiable appetite of metropolitan culture for knowledge of its colonial interests, and to the capacity of artists to respond to the commercial possibilities which that fascination opened up. Subjects drawn from the nation's imperial activities were thus central to the emergence of an exhibition culture in the latter half of the eighteenth century. This meant, of course, that exotic subjects in themselves would not guarantee professional acknowledgement.

Competition for recognition on the heavily laden walls of Somerset House, as depicted in Johann Ramberg's view of the 1787 Royal Academy exhibition, where several of Hodges's exhibits for that year are visible, necessitated a tactical approach to display (fig. 16). Hodges had begun displaying his work at the Academy on returning from Cook's second voyage. By this time, it was well established as the primary arena for playing out professional rivalries, publicizing an artist's work and cultivation of a public profile. There was a need, therefore, to exhibit to effect, and analysis of the works Hodges showed suggest that he consistently sent work that capitalized on the extent of his travels but also advertised his erudition, range and versatility, through works that self-consciously recalled such acknowledged masters as Claude, Rosa, Canaletto or Vernet. They also drew not only on his travels but also on antiquarian, architectural, biblical and literary subjects, illustrating Shakespearean drama or (one of his last Academy exhibits) the contemporary Gothic fiction of Ann Radcliffe.[8] Hodges's choice of submissions was also designed to display his connections, allegiance and sympathies with the patrons his work attracted, whether the Admiralty, Hastings and the East India Company, or leading architects such as James Paine.

Outside of this most competitive of arenas, the 1780s saw a marked increase in the opening of alternative exhibiting spaces, ones that might even reconcile the Academy's public agenda with the private concerns of the market place. These were ventures that might link the morally edifying with the commercial by offering artists the opportunity to produce works that might aspire to the condition of history painting, but allow them to defray their expenses by selling engravings after the paintings. Hodges forged links with two such enterprises in John Boydell's Shakespeare Gallery and the European Museum, only to find them suffering from the contraction of the market in the 1790s. It was in this harsh climate, and in emulation of the tactics adopted by these more overtly commercial galleries, that Hodges conceived his disastrous one-man show of 1794–95.

These were difficult times for London's artistic community, with a glut of artists competing for fewer clients and the international trade in prints effectively halted. War with Revolutionary France was cited as the reason for the unusually low number of works on display at the 1794 Academy exhibition. It is in this context that Hodges's grand exhibition of *War* and *Peace* originated. This was not an unusual tactic: the format of the individual exhibition with an admission fee had been successful for several artists, and there were handsome profits to be made.[9] Indeed, by the mid-1790s it was a well-established route for an artist to make money, in addition to forging their credentials as a painter of serious intent.

Although history painting occupied a privileged position in academic doctrine, it was not financially remunerative.[10] But the format of the one-man exhibition provided a source of income from display rather than from sales. Thus, such shows were presented as an ingenious mode of responding to artists' material needs, while also keeping their art in the service of the public. This novel form of display enabled the public to participate in art both physically and symbolically, granting them access to painting by sharing in it through the payment for the entry ticket, or subscription to an engraved version of the painting on display. This was in line with those who argued that the founding of a native school of history painting – an increasingly pressing concern in the wake of the founding of the Royal Academy – would contribute to the country's commercial prosperity. Boydell, for example, in making a gift to the City of London in 1793, explicitly linked commercial prosperity to the growth of a British school of painting and printmaking.[11]

This argument was also forwarded as justification for several instances of one-man exhibitions, surely familiar to Hodges through the involvement of those we know him to have been close to. It was central to Joseph Wright of Derby's one-man exhibition at Robin's Rooms, Covent Garden of 1785, where the centrepiece had been an enormous canvas depicting *A View of Gibraltar during the Destruction of the Spanish Floating Batteries*, a subject that undoubtedly enabled the artist to exploit his trademark handling of spectacular light effects. In the show's catalogue,

William Hayley made the correlation between a notable recent British military victory over the French and artistic progress. This was a glory in which the country's military and artistic communities could share, and again ascend to their deserved, rightful prominence:

> Rival of Greece, in arms in arts,
>   Tho' deem'd in her declining days,
> Britain yet boasts unnumber'd hearts,
>   Who keenly paint for public praise;
> Her battles yet are firmly fought
>   By chiefs with Spartan courage fraught:
> Her painters with Athenian zeal unite
>   To trace the glories of the prosp'rous fight,
> And gild th' embattl'd scene with Art's immortal light.[12]

Hayley's characterization of Britain as the natural, virtuous heir of classical culture had been a common assertion throughout the eighteenth century. Britain's unique constitutional freedoms, akin to the democratic ideal represented by Athens, were seen as the animating principles, in this case, of its military strength and its artistic progress.[13] For Hayley, British arms' vanquishing of the despotic Bourbon powers at Gibraltar would now inspire a reciprocal connection between British military prowess, the progress of a native school of painting and the commercial exhibition, for which his words originally appeared. It was in this spirit that Hodges surely conceived of his own speculative venture into the one-man show, centering on his two epic paintings of *War* and *Peace*, suitably noble in theme and execution. However, as Harriet Guest demonstrates, the political situation had rendered any potentially 'patriotic' intent on Hodges's part clearly problematic, and the view of the nation's doubtful military prowess that those works implied made his situation quite different from that in which Wright and Hayley were working a decade previously. Staging such shows was always a gamble, and much was obviously riding on the success of *War* and *Peace*, from both a financial and critical standpoint. For Hodges, it must have appeared a viable commercial venture, but also one enabling him to assert his credentials as a painter of an elevated form of landscape and so secure his position in the London art world.

Hodges and the press

If maintaining a presence on the walls of the city's increasing number of exhibition venues was crucial to professional acknowledgement, then that competition for attention was also played out in the contemporary press, which devoted increasing column-inches to the machinations of the art world as the century progressed.[14] Hodges's work did not always fare well with critics, who faulted him for the spatial anomalies occasionally found in his work, his lack of finish, or simply compared him unfavourably with various contemporaries. Few artists were entirely immune from criticism but Hodges's exhibiting career was peppered with unfavourable or equivocal reviews.

A flavour of the kind of critical commentary Hodges's work was to attract, off and on, throughout his career is first apparent in the much-cited response of the *Morning Chronicle* to the Pacific scenes he exhibited at the 1777 Academy exhibition. While his paintings were to be welcomed for their 'curiosity', and the information they afforded on exotic cultures, they were perceived as being marred by certain technical failings:

> Mr HODGES, who in last year's Exhibition had several views of bays, & c. about the Island of Otaheite, had this year a large piece exhibiting the war boats of that Island, and a view of part of the harbour of Ohamane-o, & c. The public are indebted to this artist for giving some idea of scenes which before they know little of. It is surprising however, that a man of Mr Hodges's genius should adopt such a ragged mode of colouring; his pictures all appear as if they were unfinished, and as if the colours were laid on the canvas with a skewer.[15]

For this reviewer, the artist's liquid paint effects and 'ragged mode of colouring' robbed them of the kinds of topographical accuracy such novel subjects warranted. This apparent inability to negotiate between the need to describe the particular and the striving for general effects was a recurrent complaint levelled at Hodges's painting. Criticism of this kind was, of course, inextricable from what were considered sto be the artist's inappropriate attempts to offer a more elevated form of landscape painting. In 1792, the *St. James's Chronicle*, long hostile to the artist's work, observed of his sole Academy exhibit that year, *A Cottage Scene in the New Forest*:

> Mr. Hodges, in landscape can produce pleasing effects of light and shadow, and his colouring is often good; but from his figures, and particularly from his attempts to combine History with Landscape, we hope prudence and good taste will deliver us.[16]

Critics also suggested that the painter's work was too 'mannered',[17] or that his experiments with somewhat monochromatic palettes in the late 1780s and early '90s were simply dull. It was said of the *View of Part of the City of Benares* that 'This Picture is void of Force. One flat tame Colour is spread from one Corner to the other; which is rendered more fatiguing to the Eye, as the light Parts of the Clouds are tinged with it'.[18] Such criticisms had their origin for many commentators in the failings of his master, Wilson. Edward Edwards suggested that, like Wilson, his painting had 'too much the appearance of neglect, which has been considered as the effects of slovenliness, united with the affectation of mastery'.[19]

This was answered in an account of Wilson that appeared in the *European Magazine and London Review* for June 1790:

> There are persons who object to Mr. Wilson's pictures not being sufficiently finished in the foregrounds; and it must be admitted, that to look very near them, they are not so highly finished as many Dutch works we see; but they at all times agree with the whole: That was his great wish and constant aim; when That was accomplished, he left his picture. He did not possess the phlegmatic industry to labour upon the down of a thistle.[20]

It seems likely that the author of this essay was Hodges himself, and that it was as much a defence of his own work as his master's. Hodges's sensitivity to criticism of his technique has been pointed out by Bernard Smith, who sees the relatively smoother finish of pictures like *A View in the Island of New Caledonia* as, in part, a response to the harsh criticisms meted out to earlier exhibited works (cat. no. 29).[21] Certainly, other works, such as Hodges's 1787 Royal Academy diploma piece, *The Ghats at Benares*, might also be seen as tempering that 'ragged mode' he had become known for (cat. no. 61). However, rather than being a response to negative criticism, it is possible that Hodges adopted a less vigorous, less impasto-heavy approach depending on the context in which such works were to be received, the artist on this occasion adopting an appropriately academic finish. This seems more likely given that Hodges did not always moderate or adjust his handling, and continued to exhibit works characterized by the fluid materiality of the paint, or which were to all intents and purposes studies, such as *The Landing at Erramanga* (cat. no. 35). It might be that the artist persisted with what to many critics appeared a cavalier approach to finish, at least in part, as a means of asserting his difference from any competitors. It was not only the novelty of the subject matter that marked these works as 'Hodges', but the *bravura* handling of paint.

Hodges's defence of Wilson's 'grand manner' is significant, not only in terms of the way it can be seen to offer a defence of his own working practices but in that it amounts to the artist's first attempt in print to argue for a form of landscape painting to be realized in generalized or abstracted terms. This was later made explicit in his catalogue for his one-man show, where he again identified himself with his tutor.[22] Hodges's stentorian statement of intent on that occasion was a still more explicit validation of the painter's attempts to 'give dignity to landscape painting'. While certain critics were clearly hostile to such claims, others were more favourably disposed to Hodges's way of working; the *Morning Post* writing of one of his last exhibited works, *The Abbey, from the Romance of the Forest* (R.A. 1794): 'This Artist's forte seems to be the conception of grand and poetic scenery; where the minor excellencies of execution and detail are unattended to in the broad expansion of the *idea*'.[23]

Hodges's validation of Wilson then was an important part of his attempts to cultivate the kind of profile so necessary for public recognition. Such biographical vignettes of contemporary artists littered the periodical press at this time, the *European Magazine* especially. Such was the social prominence of many Academicians and so public their quarrels, that artists' lives had become subject to increasing scrutiny. These often brief, but usually flattering, portraits did much, as John Brewer has shown, to create a more general public awareness of artists as individuals and found a 'link between life and work'.[24] They were important vehicles for generating publicity and establishing an artist's public image. In this context, it is notable that in his encomium on Wilson, Hodges not only alluded to and defended a manner of painting he himself had been much criticized for adopting, but also closed the article with a somewhat laudatory self-portrait. According to the essay's conclusion, chief among the school Wilson had left behind was

> Mr. Hodges, whose works in the Admiralty, his representations of Asiatic manners and scenery, and pictures in the Shakespeare Gallery, are entitled to that high degree of praise which genius has a right to demand, but which merit like theirs frequently declines accepting.[25]

Hodges's claims to 'genius' here are obviously meant to reinforce the arguments of the foregoing article, in its promotion of a generalized approach to landscape. It is entirely in keeping with contemporary attempts to define such a designation, such as Alexander Gerard's 1774 *Essay on Genius*, which characterized it as 'properly the faculty of *invention*'.[26]

Evidently, Hodges had established some links with the *European Magazine* by this time, as they also reproduced several engravings after his Indian subjects. Such ties were important to the artist. Few of Hodges's pictures from the 1790s survive, yet, by all accounts, those years that immediately precede his abrupt withdrawal from the art world in early 1795 were especially busy, and saw the painter engaged in a range of attempts to maintain a certain public profile, in part, through an association with the periodical press. In May 1792, the *Literary and Biographical Magazine* carried a short, anecdotal life of Hodges himself, accompanied by a portrait of the artist after Richard Westall (fig. 34).[27] This amounted to little more than a brief synopsis of the artist's chief claims to public interest; his work for Cook in the Pacific and for Hastings in India. However, Hodges himself was probably the author of this puff, since he had evident links with the periodical. It had already reproduced an engraving after his view of the Cape of Good Hope, alongside a description of the port by Anders Sparrman, whom J. R. Forster had recruited there as an assistant botanist on the *Resolution* voyage. It later also featured plates after his Indian pictures, such as the *View of Pagodas at Deogur*, as well as an extended, extremely positive review of the *Travels*. Hodges's energies had been variously directed in the year or two leading up to the appearance of this article. There was his disastrous, if still lucrative, stint as 'Inventor and Painter of the Decorations' for Robert Bray O'Reilly's recently established opera at the Pantheon concert and assembly rooms.[28] He was also busy preparing the *Travels* for publication, and finalizing a journey to St. Peterburg. According to press reports Hodges made the voyage to Russia, the month the *Literary and Biographical Magazine* article appeared, 'with some large pictures he has lately painted by command of the Empress of Russia'.[29] It is hardly surprising then that given this feverish activity the painter had only one picture

on show at the lately opened Academy exhibition.[30] And he may have conceived the periodical biography as a means of maintaining a presence on the metropolitan scene when geographically removed and all but absent from its premier showcase. If so, then the placement of the article was astute. For by association with the *Literary and Biographical Magazine*, Hodges recommended himself towards a particular kind of learned clientele. In its pages, his work might be evaluated alongside accounts not only of other artists, whether illustrious ancients or contemporaries, but also the scientific papers and Orientalist scholarship that comprised the majority of its contents.

Below the engraving after Westall's 'very strong resemblance'[31] that accompanied Hodges's biographical anecdotes, the legend describes the artist as 'Landscape Painter to the Prince of Wales'. What right Hodges had to this title is unclear, but it is certainly consistent with the kinds of circles the artist moved in at that moment.[32] And it is likely the Prince had recommended Hodges for the post of scene painter at the Pantheon Opera House, for which the monarch's son had acted as a consultant. It is also consonant with the artist's evident professional ambitions, as evidenced by the close identification with notable patrons on other occasions. Despite these connections it seems likely that Hodges's situation was at this time less than secure. Indeed, the frenetic activity of this period might have been partly an attempt to recover from or disguise the results of his financially ruinous foray into the print market.

Hodges and the print market

If Hodges's risky move to India was occasioned, according to Farington, by 'the little encouragement for Landscape painting', then the gamble appeared to pay off.[33] On returning with what the diarist described as 'a very decent fortune', Hodges immediately began acquiring the trappings of success, leasing a townhouse in Queen Street, Mayfair.[34] According to Edwards, this was 'where he built a handsome painting room'.[35] A well-appointed studio conveyed a sense of wealth and taste, and an image of the artist as a man of refinement and learning. It also had an important commercial function in providing further exhibition space for the display of works to prospective clients. His election to the Academy at this time conferred an additional degree of professional and social acceptance. However, according to Edwards's no doubt partial account of the artist, Hodges was to soon find himself in a situation that 'injured his fortune'.[36] This was a reference to the losses incurred from his 1785–8 publication of the forty-eight aquatints comprising *Select Views in India* (cat. no. 68).

Thanks in part to the emergence of an exhibition culture, the British print trade was in a buoyant state. With improvements in technology and the conditions for expansion in place, an increasingly dynamic, sophisticated market saw printmakers and sellers catering for a diverse, international range of consumers.[37] Hodges's

Indian views sold on the Continent and were aimed squarely at the upper end of the market: his *View of the Gate of the Tomb of the Emperor Akbar, at Secundrii*, and *A View of the Tomb of the Emperor Shere Shah, at Sassaram in Bahar*, were published as a pair retailing at 2 guineas, whilst his *Views in India* were sold in fours at £1 10s.[38] Obviously, this restricted potential clientele. While Hodges surely sought a degree of exclusivity in this, he cannot have anticipated the lack of demand for such luxurious items.

This was clearly an error of judgement, and, at least for Edwards, one to be aligned with the artist's misguided ambition:

> It is not pleasant to reflect, that although this gentleman had, in the early part of his life, many of those difficulties which are consequent to the pursuits of professional profit and fame, yet he was not in mature age prudent to retain that decent competency which he had acquired in India. This mistaken conduct was probably owing to his desire of appearing as an artist of high rank, and to the hope of thereby procuring employment.[39]

While Hayley's verse tribute praised the artist's lofty purpose and lamented the lack of opportunities the marketplace afforded such noble ambitions, here those same qualities are judged 'mistaken'. Both accounts are certainly partial. However, while their relative assessments of Hodges's career differ markedly regarding his high-minded attempts to appear 'as an artist of high rank', they both agree he was undone by his ambitions. As his former tutor Wilson had found before him, market conditions simply would not sustain the didactic, moralizing form of landscape painting the artist advocated.[40] And the Duke of York's censorship of his attempts at such painting made Hodges's place in the art world of the mid-1790s even more untenable.

On 12 February 1795, Hodges was elected to the Society of Antiquaries, where he was welcomed as 'a gentleman well known to the Public by his extensive travels and the valuable views he has published of many remains of Antiquity in India equally new and curious'.[41] The learned, scholarly profile Hodges so carefully cultivated for much of his career is clearly acknowledged by such a recommendation. And contacts established through the Society would doubtless have provided potential avenues of support. Yet by the end of the following month he had determined on leaving London for Devon, and investing in a bank with the attorney Thomas Gretton. A sale of his paintings at Christie's on 29 June 1795 was to be his last significant involvement in the art world.

1   Hayley (1809), 260–1.

2   Ibid., 259.

3   On Hodges's cultivation of this image, see below and the essays by Geoff Quilley and Beth Tobin in this catalogue.

4   For an astute analysis of the contradictions this entailed, see Brewer (1995).

5   On the complex history of these two groups, see Allen (1992).

6   [Mortimer] (1763), vol. 1, 12.

7   Graves (1907).

8   For a list of those pictures Hodges exhibited during his lifetime, see Stuebe (1979), 363–5.

9   In the Great Room at Spring Gardens in the summer of 1781, John Singleton Copley's epic contemporary history painting *The Death of the Earl of Chatham* had been displayed to great critical and commercial effect, with exhibition and print generating a profit in excess of £5000. See Prown (1966), vol. 2, 275–91.

10 On the risks attached to the production of history painting in this period, see Lippincott (1995).

11 See Bruntjen (1985), 75–88.

12 *A Catalogue of Pictures* (1785), unpaginated. This was only one of several such exhibitions devoted to this particular theme. For a discussion of this phenomenon, see my 'Exhibiting war: John Singleton Copley's *The Siege of Gibraltar* and the staging of history', in John Bonehill & Geoff Quilley (eds.), *Conflicting Visions: War and Culture in Britain and France, c.1700–1830* (Aldershot, forthcoming).

13 For the translation of these arguments into the context of contemporary British debates over the function of art in civil society, see Barrell (1986), 33–9 and *passim*.

14 On the forms, functions and language of art criticism in this period, see Hallett (2001).

15 The *Morning Chronicle*, 28 April 1777, 2.

16 The *St. James's Chronicle; or, British Evening-Post*, 10–12 May 1792, 4. Cf. also the *St. James's Chronicle*, 23–25 March 1790, 2

17 *Evening Mail*, 2–4 May 1791, 3.

18 Ibid., 6–8 May 1788, 4.

19 Edwards (1808), 244. Cf. also Pilkington (1824), vol. 1, 443.

20 [Hodges] (1790), 402–5, 404.

21 Smith (1992), 131.

22 See Appendix. It might be noted here that this identification with Wilson also took the form of compositional borrowings (see cat. no. 27).

23 The *Morning Post*, 24 May 1794, 2.

24 Brewer (1997), 319.

25 [Hodges] (1790), 405.

26 Gerard (1774), 8.

27 'Biographical Anecdotes of William Hodges, Esq.', *The Literary and Biographical Magazine, and British Review*, vol. 8 (May 1792), 321–2.

28 For further details on this period, see Price (1987).

29 The *Morning Chronicle*, 24 May 1792, 4.

30 This was *A Cottage scene in the New Forest, Hampshire*.

31 The portrait had been exhibited at the R.A. the previous year, and described thus by the *Morning Chronicle*, 6 May 1791, 3.

32 For further discussion of this milieu, see the essays by Harriet Guest and Natasha Eaton in this volume.

33 Stuebe (1979), 43.

34 Ibid., 51.

35 Edwards (1808), 242–3.

36 Ibid., 245.

37 For a comprehensive account of these developments, see Clayton (1997).

38 The *Morning Herald*, 18 January 1787, 1.

39 Edwards (1808), 243–4.

40 Solkin, (1982), 19–20.

41 I am grateful to Adrian James, archivist at the Society of Antiquaries, for this information.

Hodges and attribution

CHARLES GREIG

William Hodges's marginalization from the canon of British art history, and his absence from monographic exhibitions devoted to British artists have had important consequences for the attribution of his works. Paintings have been – and no doubt continue to be – unrecognized as being by Hodges, misattributed to other artists, or works by other artists have been wrongly attributed to Hodges. The issue is particularly complicated in this instance, since so many works by the artist remain untraced. It is further compounded by the facts that Hodges is known to have collaborated on several works with other artists, notably the animal painter Sawrey Gilpin, and that he rarely signed his works, the signature varying from the use of the initials 'H' and 'WH' to the full surname and a date. Added to these difficulties of authentication has been the confusion from an early date, noted frequently by Farington, between Hodges's works and those of his mentor, Richard Wilson. This has caused Hodges, at one extreme, to be dismissed as a mere copyist or, at the other, denounced as a faker of Wilsons, even though there is no evidence to support such a claim.[1]

Serious scholarship into Hodges has only really begun over the last thirty years, and has been confined principally to just two, albeit excellent, works: Isabel Stuebe's *The Life and Works of William Hodges* (1979), a published Ph.D. dissertation comprising a catalogue of Hodges's works, and Rüdiger Joppien and Bernard Smith's *The Art of Captain Cook's Voyages. Volume Two: The Voyage of the Resolution and Adventure 1772–1775* (1985), which deals only with Hodges's works relating to Cook's voyage.[2] Inevitably, many issues remain unaddressed or unsolved in these studies, and many more have arisen since their publication. This essay is concerned with the issues of attribution surrounding Hodges, particularly since the publication of these books.

Works reattributed to Hodges

In 1758, at the age of fourteen, Hodges was articled to Richard Wilson, the leading British landscape painter of the day, for a period of seven years. Just one painting by Hodges deserves mention here that was probably painted, at least in part, while he was still apprenticed to Wilson; *David Garrick and his Villa at Hampton* (fig. 3). It is generally agreed that the figures are by Zoffany and the background by Hodges, though this was rejected by Stuebe

Fig. 3 William Hodges and Johann Zoffany, *David Garrick and his Villa at Hampton*, c.1765, oil on canvas, 61.0 x 73.7cm. John Wyndham Collection, Petworth House.

Fig. 4 William Hodges, *A View of Part of the South Side of the Fort at Gwalior*, 1783, oil on canvas, 34.3 x 48.3 cm. Henry E. Huntington Museum, San Marino, California.

and also by Constable in his biography of Wilson.[3] Recent research, however, has uncovered much greater collaboration between Zoffany and Wilson than was previously accepted.[4] It seems not unlikely, therefore, that Zoffany may have employed Wilson's most talented pupils, Hodges and Carr, to paint the backgrounds to some pictures. Certainly, the style of the landscape in this picture is sufficiently close to Hodges's early work to render such an attribution plausible.

Ironically, from the late eighteenth century, the problem seems to have been reversed: a number of works, clearly by Hodges, were attributed to Wilson. Farington mentions several, including a view of London Bridge in the hands of a dealer in 1799, 'who calling it by Wilson asks 40 guineas for it'.[5] An early *View on the Rhine* of 1772 was recently sold in London with an attribution to Wilson.[6] The fine small oil sketch of Gwalior (Huntington Library, fig. 4), probably done on the spot in India, was long thought to be a view near Rome by Wilson, until correctly identified by Robert Wark.[7] Similarly, the *View of Funchal* (cat. no. 1) was thought to be by Wilson as late as the 1950s.

Two drawings from Hodges's journeys in India have recently been identified. A sepia drawing with white highlights of *The Gate of a Caravanserai at Rajmahal* (cat. no. 51) turned up unrecognized at a minor London auction twenty years ago and is now in the India Office Library. The second drawing, *Ruins at Rajimahl* (cat. no. 50), had long been attributed to Thomas Daniell and was offered as such by Christie's in 1996.[8] It shows part of the ruins of Prince Shuja's palace at Rajmahal and is drawn in grey wash over pencil with touches of the same green and yellow that Hodges used in some of his drawings of Tahiti. It is inscribed in Hodges's hand on the reverse, though unusually for him it is done on blue paper.

Another Rajmahal subject has recently come to light. Attributed to Thomas Daniell as a 'View of Gyah', it emerged after cleaning as the long lost painting by Hodges, *A View of the City of Raujemahal*,

sold at the Warren Hastings sale in 1797 (cat. no. 48).

Four large oil paintings from Augustus Cleveland's collection came up for sale in 1991, including *A Camp of a Thousand Men formed by Augustus Cleveland* (cat. no. 62).[9] Despite their stylistic consistency with Hodges's other work, and the fact that this one was inscribed in his hand on a label on the reverse, their attribution was questioned and they remained unsold at the time. However, there can be no doubt that these are autograph works.

Works known through exhibition or publication

On leaving Wilson's studio in 1765, Hodges joined the Society of Artists and exhibited a number of paintings and watercolours there during the following seven years. Very few of these can now be traced. In March 1956 Christie's sold Hodges's earliest recorded painting, *A View of London Bridge from Botolph Wharf*, signed and dated 1766, the year it was exhibited.[10] It is surprising perhaps how different it is from Wilson; only in the loose handling of the paint and the subtleties of the palette is the latter's influence recognizable. Already, Hodges had begun to develop an individual style that characterized his art throughout the rest of his life, centred on an interest in atmospherics and the play of light on a landscape, evident here in the great cloud formations with their reflections in the river, and in the architectural details of the warehouses on the bank, picked out in bright flashes of impasto. The dramatically foreshortened perspective was to become a device that Hodges used to great effect in many later paintings.

Several English views prior to 1772 were commissioned by the architect James Paine, an early patron and also a director of the Society of Artists up to that year. He bought the *View of the Welch*

Fig. 5 William Hodges and William Pars, *The Pantheon, Oxford Street, London*, 1772, oil on canvas, 228.6 x 304.8cm. Temple Newsam House, Leeds City Art Galleries.

Fig. 6 William Hodges, *A View of the Pagodas at Deoghur*, c.1786, oil on canvas. Private collection.

Bridge at Shrewsbury at the 1770 exhibition. Two paintings of this subject have been sold in recent years.[11] The first, painted on panel and signed and inscribed on the reverse, was probably Paine's picture. While the composition of each is similar, there are variations in the arrangement of the foreground figures, and the boat is omitted in the second painting. The latter's looser composition suggests that it may be the original version made on the spot. If so, it is the only known *plein-air* sketch by Hodges that predates the Cook voyage. Stylistically, both works resemble the *View of London Bridge from Botolph Wharf*, and there is a striking similarity in the figures, one of which – the standing figure in the boat of the Sotheby's version – was subsequently adapted for the Maori warrior holding a club, in *Cascade Cove, Dusky Bay* (cat. no. 26).[12] The subject of Shrewsbury Bridge would have had particular appeal for Paine, himself a designer of several bridges. He later commissioned Hodges to paint his most celebrated, Richmond Bridge, while still under construction. The painting, exhibited at the Royal Academy in 1778, is lost.[13]

Several other exhibited paintings were views of buildings designed by Paine. Only two are known: the *View of Worksop Manor* (cat. no. 72) and *A View of a Greenhouse at Weston in Staffordshire, the Seat of Sir Henry Bridgman, Bart*, exhibited at the Society of Artists in 1772, but now unlocated. At the same exhibition was *The Pantheon, Oxford Street* (Temple Newsam, fig. 5), for which Hodges apparently collaborated with William Pars to paint the figures,[14] and also four views of Germany and Switzerland. Two of these

small oval landscapes appeared at Sotheby's in 1994.[15] A third painting, *A View on the Rhine*, recently came to light, inscribed 'From Lord Palmerston's Collection', establishing a firm connection at this date between Hodges and Palmerston, who recommended him as the official draughtsman for Cook's second voyage upon Zoffany's withdrawal.[16]

After returning from India, between 1785 and 1788 Hodges exhibited many works at the Royal Academy, done in England and based upon his drawings of Indian subjects. About half of these remain untraced. Those that are known tend to differ from works done in India itself, being more carefully and classically composed than the relatively unstructured works done in the subcontinent. *A View in the Jungle Ferry* [Jungleterry] *in Bengal* (cat. no. 64), exhibited in 1786, was rediscovered in 1988, as was *The Pagodas at Deoghur* (England, private collection), engraved in 1787 as no. 22 in *Select Views in India* (fig. 6). A further Jungleterry view (cat. no. 65) has been in the collection of the Earl of Egremont since the 1830s, but was overlooked by Stuebe and other scholars. Listed as 'Camels in a Wood' in the catalogue for Petworth House, it has only recently been identified as a lost Jungleterry scene, probably the *View in the Jungle Ferry in Bengal, the animals painted by Mr. Gilpin*, exhibited at the Royal Academy in 1785. Another painting engraved for *Select Views* and painted around the same time, *A View of a Mosque at Mounheer* (cat. no. 53), is probably Hodges's most accomplished scene of an Indian architectural subject, the details of which are reminiscent of his early views done in England. In preparing the plates for *Select Views* Hodges also appears to have worked up some of the drawings done on the spot into more accurate watercolours prior to engraving, a small number of which have come to light in recent years.[17]

The rare late English landscape, *A Cottage, a Study from Nature* (cat. no. 75), was exhibited in 1787. The anonymity of its subject, however, suggests that similar works may have been attributed to other artists. By contrast, one of the most remarkably distinctive works to appear recently is the *Landscape, Ruins and Figures* (cat. no. 76), exhibited at the Royal Academy in 1790, which casts an entirely new light on Hodges's work at this time and the diversity of material that he was experimenting with. This is a true *capriccio*, unlike any other work known by the artist, though it may be suggestive of his approach to the range of other subjects he was working on at this time, particularly the paintings on literary and historical subjects and the later allegories on war and peace, almost all of which are now untraced.

Works wrongly attributed to Hodges

Hodges's works from his period in India have presented great problems of attribution, due to the lack, until very recently, of scholarly interest in, and specific information about, British artists working in India in the eighteenth century. Numerous paintings of Indian subjects by other hands have been given to Hodges on scant evidence, and his work has conversely been attributed to Thomas Daniell. However, through reference to Hodges's own publications of his Indian works, particularly the *Travels in India* (1793), the ninety drawings at the Yale Center for British Art, formerly in the Warren Hastings Collection, and the records of the sales of Hodges's works from the collections of his two principal patrons in India, Warren Hastings and Augustus Cleveland, more accurate attributions may be achieved.

A painting of *The Esplanade in Calcutta*, taken from a viewpoint close to Fort William, is one of three paintings in the Victoria Memorial Hall, Calcutta, attributed to Hodges by Dr and Mrs Archer (the other two are views of Murshidabad and Allahabad).[18] They, together with another version of this Calcutta view (private collection, Scotland), were all painted by an artist thoroughly acquainted with Hodges's work. It has been suggested that they are inferior works by Hodges, but it is more likely that they are by another hand, possibly George Farington, brother of Joseph, who arrived in Calcutta shortly before Hodges departed and painted in a style that shows the influence of Wilson.[19]

Similarly, two paintings of the ruined palace at Rajmahal, one in the Victoria Memorial Hall, Calcutta, the other – its pair – in an English private collection, have been consistently attributed to Hodges, even though they are stylistically dissimilar: the composition of each is at variance with Hodges's known work, they lack his vigorous brushwork, the skies show none of his concern with atmospheric conditions, and they have a uniform smoothness of

finish. Most telling is the use of tone and colour: Hodges's tonal contrasts are absent. Rather, the techniques employed in these two paintings, and in another by the same hand of the Rajmahal Hills that has also been attributed to Hodges, suggest that they were produced at the end of the eighteenth century by a Dutch or Flemish painter. Apart from François Balthazar Solvyns, whose work is well known and rather different in style, the Dutch landscape painter, Flories Croese, was in Calcutta at that time and is recorded in Lucknow in 1801. He was employed by Lord Wellesley to decorate the ceilings of Government House, Calcutta.[20] The Victoria Memorial Hall picture was engraved by James Moffat in 1800, suggesting a similar date for the original, so Croese may be the artist of these views.

The attribution to Hodges of two portraits of Cherokees in the collection of the Royal College of Surgeons goes back to the early years of the nineteenth century, but is difficult to understand, other than by their being mistakenly grouped with Hodges's portrait of Omai in the same collection (cat. no. 40). The handling of the paint in these portraits bears little resemblance to Hodges's work, the outlines are softer and the finish smoother. They almost certainly relate to an embassy that arrived in England in October 1790, accompanied by William Augustus Bowles who acted as their guide and interpretor. According to press reports they were painted by Opie in early 1791.[21] However, there is an engraving after a painting by T. Hardy of Bowles, again of 1791, which recalls the two paintings of Cherokees in the Royal College of Surgeons. It seems possible then that Hardy was the artist.[22]

Other works come to light since 1985

Opinion is divided on which of Hodges's oil paintings from Cook's voyage were done on the spot or during the voyage, and which were worked up in England after his return. Of the New

Fig. 7 William Hodges, *A View in the Island of Madeira*, 1777, oil on canvas. Captain Cook Memorial Museum, Whitby.

Fig. 8 William Hodges, *Italianate Landscape,* c.1790?, oil on canvas. Christie's Images.

Zealand views, only one, the *View in Pickersgill Harbour* (cat. no. 5), done *en plein air* in April 1773, was reasonably identifiable as having been made on the voyage. However, the recent discovery of a small oil painting on panel (perhaps ship's timber) casts new light on the artist's work at this period (cat. no. 6). It is a coastal profile of Dusky Bay, closely resembling the wash drawings of the same location (cat. no. 4) and clearly painted *en plein air* from an elevated position, the deck or great cabin of the *Resolution.* The appearance of this work begs the question of how many similar small studies were done and remain lost.

Of the Tahiti views, in addition to those small studies done on the spot that are now in the National Maritime Museum, a previously unrecorded painting of Vaitepiha Bay came up for sale in 1992 (cat. no. 10). The provenance of this painting is of particular interest: it was purchased from Hodges towards the end of his life by George Woodward (founder of the British Society of Artists), and is clear evidence that Hodges retained for himself some of his voyage work. Another fine and previously unrecorded painting, this time of Matavai Bay (cat. no. 12), may also have been made on the voyage, or else very shortly after Hodges's return. A further view of Matavai Bay, presented to the National Maritime Museum by Mrs H. J. Braunholtz in 1987, was thought by Stuebe to be a copy and was ignored by Joppien and Smith entirely. However, it is possible that it is a later version by Hodges himself, despite the somewhat pedestrian execution, painted possibly as late as the 1790s.

A View in the Island of Madeira appeared at Sotheby's in 2001, uncleaned in its original condition, as 'A View of an Italianate Coastline' (fig. 7). That is indeed what it appeared to be but for the inclusion of a dragon tree and the typical small boats of Madeira. Cleaning revealed Hodges's signature and the date '77'. Its vibrant palette is far removed from the 1772 view of Funchal, and is so topographically inaccurate that it is closer to a *capriccio.*

From a second visit to the Continent in the late 1780s, Hodges exhibited a number of European views at the Royal Academy in 1789 and 1790, all now missing. However, a small painting probably dating from that period recently appeared at Sotheby's, and shows an unidentified bridge and figures in a boat in the foreground (fig. 8).[23]

The disastrous exhibition in Bond Street in 1794–95 put an end to Hodges's painting career and prompted him to quit London for Brixham, where he died virtually bankrupt two years later. For the next 170 years this extraordinary and most widely travelled artist was almost entirely neglected. It would be a fitting memorial to Hodges, were this long overdue exhibition and reappraisal of his work to result in many more of his lost works emerging and being correctly attributed.

[1] See Waterhouse (1953), 168. This eminent scholar described Hodges as 'probably the most accomplished painter of fake Wilsons' and claimed that 'his style in 1772 was so close to his master's that rather more than the evidence of the eye is needed to distinguish between the two'. No copies of Wilson's work can now be attributed to Hodges and the evidence of the few surviving paintings done by him prior to 1772 suggest that he had already evolved a style subtly different from Wilson's.

[2] Since the publication of these works a significant number of previously lost paintings and drawings by Hodges have been identified (27 oil paintings and 6 drawings). These span Hodges's entire career and enable a better insight into the development of the artist's style and technique, particularly regarding which of his Indian works were completed in India and which were worked up back in London after his return. Stuebe attempted no such distinction.

[3] There has been much confusion surrounding this picture. The attribution to Hodges first surfaced in C. H. Collins Baker, *Catalogue of the Petworth Collection* (1920), no. 107. Any connection to Zoffany was excluded in Manners and Williamson, *Life and Works of Johann Zoffany,* published in the same year. Constable makes no mention of the painting whatsoever while Stuebe (1979) included it in her list of 'Pictures misattributed to Hodges' (359) with a note that the figures had been attributed to Zoffany. In 1976 Mary Webster included the painting with a full attribution to Zoffany alone in her National Portrait Gallery catalogue *Johan Zoffany* (no. 13). The two figures are clearly by Zoffany but the landscape, though cleverly executed, is more tentative than the backgrounds in other paintings by Zoffany of the same period. The architectural details of the house, the brushwork and atmospheric details certainly resemble those in Hodges's *View of London Bridge from Botolph Wharf* of 1766 and other early views.

[4] I am grateful to Mrs Penny Treadwell for generously providing this information, which will be included in her forthcoming *catalogue raisonné* of Zoffany's work.

[5] Farington (1978–98), vol. 4, 1151; see also vol. 8, 3053; vol. 9, 3377; vol. 13, 4497; vol. 16, 5724.

[6] Christie's, *British and Victorian Paintings,* 13 March 1998 (58).

[7] Robert R. Wark (comp.), *The Huntington Art Collection* (San Marino CA, The Huntington Library, 1970), p. 22.

[8] Christie's, *The P&O Collection of Watercolours by Thomas and William Daniell,* 24

September 1996. This collection had originally been put together by the Bromley-Davenport family of Capesthorne Hall in Cheshire after the death of Thomas Daniell in 1839. The family sold the collection in 1951 to Stevens and Brown of Godalming, who then sold it to Messrs Gooden and Fox in the same year. The following year it was sold to the Peninsular and Oriental Steam Navigation Company. There appears to be no record of how the Bromley-Davenport acquired the view of *Ruins at Rajimahl* nor indeed how it was attributed at that time.

9 Christie's, *British Paintings*, 16 November 1991 (37–40: the property of Sir George Christie). These four paintings were painted for Augustus Cleveland and descended by marriage through the Cleveland family to the vendor. The titles of the other three paintings are *Paharia Tribesmen with Bows and Arrows, and a Bengali Girl in a Wooded Landscape, a Cascade beyond*; *A Paharia Village surrounded by Trees*; *A Group of Indian Musicians playing Saranghi, a Tambura and Tablas, with a Girl dancing on a Terrace.*

10 This painting, which measured 63.5 × 76 cm, was acquired by the dealer Montague Bernard in the late 1940s and was advertised for sale (illustrated) in the *Burlington Magazine* 91 (February 1949). It was again illustrated in W. G. Constable, *Richard Wilson* (1953), plate 152a. The painting remained unsold until offered by Christie's, 23 March 1956 (89), when it was sold to Cevat for £105. It is now untraced.

11 The first at Sotheby's, *British Paintings*, 21 November 1979 (61). It is signed and inscribed verso in Hodges's hand 'The Old Bridge at Shrewsbury'. It was resold at Christie's, *British Paintings*, 16 July 1982 (46). The second was sold at Sotheby's, *British Paintings*, 18 November 1981 (3).

12 This large painting, done for the Admiralty, is based on a small oil sketch, *A Maori standing before a Waterfall in Dusky Bay*, recently acquired from an English private collection by the Southland Museum and Art Gallery, New Zealand. A further painting, *A Maori standing on a Rock, Dusky Bay* (Auckland City Art Gallery) shows the same figure in an identical pose. Painted on a circular mahogany panel, it was clearly done well after the voyage, and the cascade has been replaced with a romanticized mountainous background.

13 Stuebe (1979), no. 516. The painting was engraved by Valentine Green and Francis Jukes, published 1 January 1780.

14 Mortimer and Jones (1772) list under paintings by Hodges '133 A view in the Pantheon in Oxford Road (the figures by Mr Parrs, *unfinished*)'. Pars and Hodges studied together at William Shipley's drawing school in the 1750s.

15 Sotheby's, *British Paintings*, 9 November 1994 (85), with titles: *View on the Rhine in Germany* and *View of the Mountains of Switzerland*, each oil on canvas, oval, 37 × 47 cm. As with the other larger *View on the Rhine* these small paintings had belonged to Henry Temple, 2nd Viscount Palmerston, and descended at Broadlands until sold by Edwina, Countess Mountbatten.

16 See Connell (1958), 100–9.

17 Three of these (England, private collection), formerly in the Oppé Collection, have the following titles: *The Fort of Gwalior from the North West; South Side of the Fort of Gwalior; The Fort of Bidjegur*. A fourth watercolour (now in the same English private collection but with unknown provenance) is entitled *The Ruins of a Palace at Gazipoor on the River Ganges*.

18 The *View of the Esplanade in Calcutta* (VMH ref. R.2848) and *View of the Fort of Allahabad at the Confluence of the Rivers Ganges and Jumna* (VMH ref. R.2849) were purchased for the Victoria Memorial Hall by Sir Evan Cotton in 1937. The *View of Part of the City of Murshidabad, with the Bhagirathi River in the Foreground* (VMH ref. R.3080) was formerly in the Tagore Collection and sold to the VMH in 1956. These, together with the other version of *The Esplanade in Calcutta*, are characterized by their unusual compositions: each is painted in a series of horizontal planes with an open sky taking up two thirds of the canvas. There is nothing comparable in Hodges's landscapes.

19 A signed portrait by George Farington of his brother, Richard Atherton Farington, with a landscape background, was sold at Sotheby's, 18 November 1987 (45). The handling of the landscape closely resembles that in these four Indian views.

20 'Some foreign European artists working in India', *Bengal Past and Present* 40, part 11 (October–December 1930), 83. The original ceiling decorations in Government House, Calcutta, have long since disappeared.

21 *The Diary; or, Woodfall's Register*, 8 Jan. 1791, 3.

22 For further details on the visit and reproduction of the engraving, see Pearson (1976). I am grateful to John Bonehill for this information.

23 Christie's, *British Pictures*, 26 November 2002 (59). This painting had previously been attributed to J. C. Ibbetson and, in the 1980s, to William Marlow. The crisp handling of the paint and sharply accented highlights are entirely consistent with Hodges's work of the 1790s. The barge filled with rustic figures recalls his drawing *A Party of Maoris in a Canoe* (La Trobe Library, State Library of Victoria, Melbourne).

'Philanthropy seems natural to mankind': Hodges and Captain Cook's second voyage to the South Seas

DAVID BINDMAN

The three voyages undertaken by Captain James Cook to the South Seas in the years 1769–80, especially the second voyage of 1772–75 in the ships *Resolution* and *Adventure*, as is well known, decisively transformed the way Europeans looked at the world beyond Europe. It was not that Cook *discovered* the South Sea islands for Europe – he was after all only one in a long line of British, Dutch and French explorers to travel there – but he opened the South Seas to the European imagination when the Franco-British Enlightenment was at its height. He established the geographical disposition of the islands of the South Seas, but perhaps more important the three voyages enabled natural scientists of the highest distinction like Joseph Banks, the father and son Johann Reinhold and George Forster, and Daniel Solander, and artists like Hodges and Webber, to visit, study, document and depict the islands and their inhabitants, and make them a key to understanding the nature and development of the human species.[1]

In his three years on the *Resolution* on Cook's second voyage, Hodges was to observe, draw and paint peoples and sights whose existence had been perceived in Europe almost entirely through fantasy and fable. His paintings have left a richly compelling picture of the light, the vegetation and the peoples encountered, but, it goes without saying, mediated through his own sensibility, experience as an artist, ideas of the period, and the paintings' function as record. The paintings of the South Seas, though all but a few were delivered to the Admiralty a few years after his return, do not contain a clear narrative, nor are they consistent in format or in the relationship between figures and setting. Some may have been painted on the voyage, but the more obvious set pieces were certainly done in London in the two or three years after his return in 1775.[2]

Despite Hodges's presence in the accounts of the voyage by Cook, both Forsters, and William Wales the astronomer,[3] his own voice is entirely to be found in the paintings and drawings. Not a single word of conversation on the voyage is attributed to him though he was involved in or overheard the most animated and learned conversations on board ship and on shore visits. On the basis of Hodges's thoughtful account of India, first published in 1793,[4] and the pamphlet that accompanied his later lost paintings of *Peace* and *War*, it is clear that he was a 'philosophical' artist, concerned to make his paintings objects of moral reflection. As he notes in connection with *Peace* and *War*

> My pictures will constantly be lessons, sometimes of what results from the impolicy of nations, or sometimes from the vices and follies of particular classes of men. These illustrations will be wide and various – from Europe and Asia, wherever the moralist can draw the substance of his animadversion, I shall select as the subject of my pictures. The task is arduous and new, but I resolve to pursue it with vigour and fidelity.[5]

If Hodges's second voyage paintings were by no means programmatic and respond sensitively to the beauty and strangeness of the South Seas, we can expect them to bear the imprint of the urgent debates among his learned companions prompted by what they encountered on the voyage.

Reading meanings in paintings, and especially in landscape paintings, is never straightforward, but it is a reasonable assumption that Hodges's awareness of current theories of human typology and development would have been stimulated by the argumentative Forsters and their adversary William Wales, who were nonetheless united in admiration for his work and his ability to depict light and atmosphere, subjects of particular interest to them as scientists. As Bernard Smith has pointed out, Hodges brought with him the classical tradition of landscape learned from his master Richard Wilson, and also a knowledge of art theory and a strong sense of the moral purpose of landscape painting, expressed in continuities between past with the present, the potency of memory, the value of the past as virtuous example, and the possibility of the virtuous life in nature.[6] But the voyage to the South Seas raised an urgent need to place the 'new' peoples within existing frameworks of human development, and to test common assumptions about humanity.

Though other artists and draughtsmen accompanied Cook on all three voyages, Hodges was beyond question the most gifted and the one most imaginatively attuned to the task. Yet he was not the first choice as artist to the voyage and his appointment was the consequence of fortunate contacts and an unforeseen event; the decision of Sir Joseph Banks, who had been on the first voyage, not to join the expedition.[7] Hodges was not the botanical draftsman on board (that was George Forster's job), and though he made detailed drawings of notable people he encountered in the South Seas and some coastal views for navigation purposes, his main work was to gather material for landscape paintings. He was thus able to bring to new sights an individual response, claiming implicitly the same privilege as George Forster, author of the most elegant account of the voyage, who noted that scientists were not mere recorders, but 'We go by analogy & judge from what we have seen before'. In describing his own task as chronicler Forster claimed that 'it was necessary for every reader to know the colour of the glass through which I looked', and that colour was formed by experience and conviction.[8]

Cook and the Forsters clearly saw Hodges as an artist with a particular sensibility and insight that went beyond literal observation. Hodges appears in their accounts often with an admiring comment on his artistic qualities as well as his ability to record accurately. In Dusky Sound in New Zealand, Johann Reinhold Forster, in his published account of the voyage, noted that

> Some of these cascades with their neighbouring scenery, require the pencil and genius of a Salvator Rosa to do them justice: however, the ingenious artist, who went with us on this expedition has great merit, in having executed some of these romantic landscapes in a masterly manner.[9]

In his journal he made even more extravagant claims for Hodges: 'The canvas was gradually animated with the most romantic scenery of this country, & nature seemed amazed to see her productions imitated by the Son of Apellos [sic]'.[10] Behind such comments there is an appreciation of Hodges's ability to depict the totality of their experience of the South Seas, the interconnections between light, atmosphere, climate, means of sustenance and the way of life of the peoples encountered, and the impact of their own presence.

Classical landscape painting, of the kind inherited by Hodges from his master Richard Wilson, with its images of 'the Garden of Eden', 'the Golden Age', 'Arcadia', 'l'Île de Cythère', or scenes of ancient Greece and Rome, contained within itself a simple but powerful anthropological theory. It proclaimed, often with great pathos, that mankind had fallen away from its original state of happy perfection (and happy ignorance) into the complexity and even decadence of modern times. From this it was a simple step to identify the seemingly paradisical life of Tahiti as corresponding to the infancy of mankind, before life in Europe had become dominated by competition and self-seeking, but above all by the knowledge that came with maturity. Bougainville, the French explorer who had visited Tahiti in 1770, described it by evoking a series of idyllic paintings of the kind painted by Boucher and other artists.[11] Cook and the Forsters were wary of such sentimentalism, though they were susceptible to its effects especially when faced with the beauty of Tahiti and the hospitality of its inhabitants. As George Forster noted of some plantations in Tahiti: 'we found them indeed to answer the expectations we had formed of a country described as an elysium by M de Bougainville'.[12] Despite a fondness for applying Arcadian imagery to beautiful and fertile landscape, the Forsters as natural philosophers saw Tahiti and the other South Sea islands as a kind of laboratory, representing the different stages of humanity on its long road to improvement; one could experience the unfolding history of mankind by travelling from one island to another, with virtually every stage from complete barbarism to relative civility (though not, of course, the commercial stage) represented by an island or a people.[13] George Forster in comparing Tahitians and ancient Greeks as naval warriors, concludes 'that men in a similar state of civilization resemble each other more than we are aware of, even in the most opposite extremes of the world'.[14] His father divided 'the Human Species in the South-Sea Isles' into two 'varieties' or 'races', with the inhabitants of Tahiti and the Friendly and Society Isles and some others at the more civilized end, while at the other end were the more 'savage' peoples of New Caledonia and the New Hebrides, with New Zealanders somewhere in the middle.[15]

For the Forsters and other observers on the voyage, then, the inhabitants of the South Seas raised a number of fundamental anthropological questions: What level of savagery/civilization did each of the peoples represent, in relation to each other and to Europeans? Did the peoples of the South Seas belong to 'races' that were different from each other and from other 'races' in the world? What was the relationship between their level of savagery/civilization, the climate in which they lived, and their methods of subsistence? How were their ways of life affected by political systems? What prospects of improvement did each people have, and what was the danger of regression? Did the encounter with the Cook voyages and those who might come after bring improvement or threat to their way of life? What was the role of the arts in gauging levels of civilization? Was, as George Forster suggested, 'philanthropy . . . natural to mankind'?

Such questions were debated at great length and often inconclusively in all the accounts of the voyage, but how far can Hodges's paintings be said to comment on them, given not only the difficulty of reading the multiplicity of signs presented by a landscape painting, but the understanding that a landscape painter had also to represent persuasively the sights he saw? To begin to answer this question I want to focus on just two paintings of Tahiti that each exist in two versions, of *Otaheite Peha [Vaitepiha] Bay* and *Matavai Bay*. The first versions of each are in Anglesey Abbey and the Yale Center for British Art respectively (cat. nos 31, 32) and were probably exhibited as a pair at the Royal Academy in 1776, while the second versions painted for and belonging to the Admiralty are in the National Maritime Museum (cat. nos 28, 33), and were probably painted at a slightly later date.[16]

Tahiti was only one of the many islands in the South Pacific visited by Cook but it already had the largest place in the European imagination. Though earlier explorers had been there it had been 'discovered' by Captain Wallis in 1766 and named King George the Third's Island.[17] Wallis was there for five weeks to observe the transit of Venus, and some of his men thought they saw the much sought-after southern continent in the distance. Cook stopped there on the first voyage in 1769, and such was Tahiti's aura in the second half of the eighteenth century that it became the object of sentimental ideas that had previously been applied to the Caribbean. As Peter Hulme put it, 'Sentimental sympathy began to flow out along the arteries of European commerce in search of its victims',[18] but Hodges's companions, especially the Forsters, were to become aware of the complex realities of the South Seas.

Vaitepiha and Matavai Bay were the main harbours used by Cook's two ships on their fourteen-day stay in Tahiti in August–September 1773, and they were the subject not only of paintings by Hodges but of poetic descriptions by George Forster in his *A Voyage round the World*, published in 1777, the same year as Cook's official account of the voyage which had engravings after Hodges's designs. It is impossible to know whether Hodges's paintings or George Forster's descriptions came first, or whether the author of one was aware of the other. For that reason it is best to see the paintings and the verbal descriptions as parallel responses to two of the most stirring and dramatic views experienced on the whole voyage. However it is worth remembering that Johann Reinhold Forster firmly believed, on the voyage and when he returned to England, that he and his son and not Cook were to be official chroniclers of the voyage. So it is not far-fetched to suggest that the Forsters might have discussed with Hodges the choice and nature of the illustrations to the volume, and that these views could have been considered for them.

Forster's first sight of Tahiti is of the harbour of Vaitepiha, described in the rapturous set-piece forming the opening of his account of the island:

> It was one of those beautiful mornings which the poets of all nations have attempted to describe, when we saw the isle of O-Taheite, within two miles before us . . . The mountains, clothed with forests, rose majestic in various spiry forms, on which we already perceived the light of the rising sun: nearer to the eye a lower range of hills, easier of ascent, appeared, wooded like the former, and coloured with several pleasing hues of green, soberly mixed with autumnal browns. At their

foot lay the plain, crowned with its fertile bread-fruit trees, over which rose innumerable palms, the princes of the grove. Here every thing seemed as yet asleep, the morning scarce dawned, and a peaceful shade still rested on the landscape. We discerned however, a number of houses among the trees, and many canoes hauled up the sandy beaches. About half a mile from the shore a ledge of rocks level with the water, extended parallel to the land, on which the surf broke, leaving a smooth and secure harbour within.[19]

Forster wonders not only at the natural beauty of the island, but at its fecundity. The passage is as saturated with classical echoes as are Hodges's two paintings of Vaitepiha. The description of the Claudean beauty of the scene wrapped in the morning light, then moves on to evoke its strangeness by alluding to the palm and bread fruit trees in the foreground. Similarly Hodges's paintings of the subject create an initial burst of glorious light and distance, but only by examining the paintings closely can we pick out signs of an exotic world previously unknown to us.

In an equally rapturous description of the bay of Vaitepiha itself Forster emphasizes the connection between the beauty of the scene and its fecundity and productivity:

> We contemplated the scenery before us early the next morning, when its beauties were most engaging. The harbour in which we lay was very small, and would not have admitted many more vessels besides our own. The water in it was as smooth as the finest mirrour, and the sea broke with a snowy foam around us upon the outer reef, the plain at the foot of the hills was very narrow in this place, but always conveyed the pleasing idea of fertility, plenty, and happiness. Just over against us it ran up between the hills into a long narrow valley, rich in plantations, interspersed with the houses of the natives. The slopes of the hills, covered with woods, crossed each other on both sides, variously tinted according to their distances; and beyond them, over the cleft of the valley, we saw the interior mountains shattered into various peaks and spires, among which was one remarkable pinnacle, whose summit was frightfully bent to one side, and seemed to threaten its downfall every moment. The serenity of the sky, the genial warmth of the air, and the beauty of the landscape, united to exhilarate our spirits.[20]

While the description does not correspond in every respect to Hodges's paintings, their similarity in feeling is obvious.

The presence of the Tahitian women in Hodges's paintings is partly explained by Forster's enthusiastic account of their sexual appeal, to which the sailors (and clearly Forster himself) were susceptible:

> the simplicity of a dress which exposed to view a well proportioned bosom and delicate hands, might also contribute to fan their amorous fire; and the view of several of these nymphs swimming nimbly all round the sloop, such as nature

had formed them, was perhaps more than sufficient entirely to subvert the little reason which a mariner might have left to govern his passions.

Furthermore 'their easy position in the water, and the pliancy of their limbs, gave us reason to look on them almost as amphibious creatures'.[21]

We might conclude that Hodges's *Otaheite Peha* paintings represent an idyllic-sentimental view of Tahiti as an earthly paradise or locus of erotic nostalgia, encapsulated in the later and familiar title of 'Tahiti Revisited'. Joppien and Smith saw the painting as representing Tahiti 'in its pristine independence, untouched by European contact'.[22] They noted that the presence of an idol or fetish supposedly worshipped by the Tahitians, and a shrouded corpse lying on a bier in the right hand corner, suggested the classical theme, often attempted by Richard Wilson, of *Et in Arcadia Ego*. Yet the lack of males in the picture makes it hard to see it as a total view of Tahiti; a truly idyllic scene surely would show amorous contact between the sexes. The male presence in the painting is displaced to the learned gentlemen and sailors coming upon Tahiti for the first time, and the fortunate spectators at the Academy or in the Admiralty, who relive that moment of first encounter, privileged to watch the women disport themselves uninhibitedly as if unaware of being watched. While the beauty of the landscape and the erotic air of the picture contributed to its London success, the unashamed nakedness of the girls could also signify their lack of 'civilized' modesty.

The *Resolution* and *Adventure* moved to Matavai Bay on August 1773 where they were greeted enthusiastically by the inhabitants, many of whom had fond memories of Cook's previous visit. Forster's description of the Bay is as rapturous as that of Vaitepiha:

> We now discerned that long projecting point, which from the observation made upon it, had been named Point Venus, and easily agreed, that this was by far the most beautiful part of the island. The district of Matavai, which now opened to our view, exhibited a plain of such an extent as we had not expected, and the valley which we traced running up between the mountains, was itself a very spacious grove, compared to the little narrow glens in Tarraboo.[23]

Forster's response to the beauty of the scenery is accompanied in his text by an appreciation of the moral character of the Tahitians, who seemed to have forgotten the difficulties of Cook's previous stay there:

> we now saw the character of the natives in a more favourable light than ever, and were convinced that the remembrance of injuries, and the spirit of revenge, did not enter into the composition of the good and simple Tahitians . . . philanthropy seems natural to mankind.

In the first version of *Matavai Bay* (cat. no. 31) the figures, far from being indolent as in *Otaheite Peha*, are evidently all male and engaged in vigorous activity, rowing boats of different kinds in the harbour. Three spectacular war canoes are conspicuous in the middle and far distance, one of which has the high priest in full regalia, as if on the way to battle. These war canoes are a reminder of the recent war in Tahiti,[24] but they are also examples of Tahitian ingenuity and 'artfulness', indicative of a people who could think beyond the necessities of life. The boat on the left has a lovingly depicted 'natural' sail, as do others in the foreground and background, and this suggests an ingenuity underlined by the activity on the ship on the left.

There are important changes in the Admiralty version of *Matavai Bay*. It no longer has the Tahitian warships, the figures on the left are substantially changed, the *Resolution* and *Adventure* are anchored in the middle ground, and, further behind to the left, the Cook expedition's large tent can be seen on the promontory.[25] On the left there is a noble gesturing figure apparently directing operations, and the figure with hands behind his back (a prisoner?) in the first version is now placed beneath the mast, his former position taken by an almost naked mother and suckling child. These changes point to two important issues not highlighted in the first version: the consequences, good or bad, of the intervention of Europeans upon a 'primitive' society, while the presence of a mother and child and fishing boats hints at the forms and methods of its subsistence.

In brief, the main and not necessarily mutually exclusive theories of human development current in the 1770s were the relatively new one based on the differentiation of 'race', and the other that assumed the decisive effect on human character of climate and means of subsistence.[26] Johann Reinhold Forster, when he wrote up his considered reflections on the voyage for publication in 1777, categorized the Tahitians as the most physically beautiful and therefore the most civilized of the peoples of the South Seas. His son George, on the other hand, also with hindsight, was less absolute in attributing exceptional beauty to the Tahitians, and reflected more on the effects of climate and the potential for change among the South Sea islanders.

In Hodges's paintings the issue of race only surfaces intermittently in his paintings for two possible reasons: his figures are normally too sketchy to allow for the identification of facial and other features, and secondly, in the 1770s, climatic and subsistence theory had a longer history and had been more thoroughly absorbed by laymen than ideas of race.[27] There is ample evidence in Hodges's *Travels in India* that he was thoroughly conversant with the effects of climate on the character of the peoples of India, and was attentive to their means of sustenance.[28] In its post-1750s form as developed in the Scotland and France of the Enlightenment, subsistence theory posited four stages of human development; hunting and gathering; the pastoral; the agricultural, and the commercial, the highest, dominant in the most advanced states of Europe. In the second *Matavai Bay* painting the presence of the Cook expedition's ships could represent the mobility and technological advance reached by a commercial society like Britain, but what does the painting say of the stage reached by the Tahitians? For both Forsters the Tahitians clearly belonged to the third or agricultural stage, and both versions of *Matavai Bay* – especially the second – show activities compatible with that stage. While fishing in its basic form is carried out in the first or hunter-gatherer stage, the way it is undertaken in the painting, collaboratively, harmoniously and with ingenuity, is characteristic of a society in a prosperous agricultural phase. In the words of Lord Kames:

> the true spirit of society, which consists in mutual benefits, and in making the industry of individuals profitable to others as well as to themselves, was not known till agriculture was invented. Agriculture requires the aid of many other arts.[29]

Those arts are visible in the ships the Tahitians have built, and in the wholly co-operative nature of their activity. Joseph Banks, who had visited Tahiti on Cook's first voyage, and George Forster doubted nonetheless that Tahiti could ever aspire to become a commercial society; the latter predicted decline rather than further improvement.[30] Even so Tahiti would have appeared to them and to Hodges very far from the state of nature in which North American Indians and Africans were then presumed to live.

On the evidence of the second version of *Matavai Bay* it is arguable that Hodges had to a degree absorbed the progressive social thought of his sophisticated travelling companions, but this does not adequately account for the meaning of the views of *Otaheite Peha*. If they had been primarily market-driven and designed to appeal to fashionable taste then it is hard to explain why he would have repeated the composition for the Admiralty. If on the other hand we assume it to have some 'philosophical' content, it could be seen to represent the threat to Tahitian peace and industry, noted by George Forster, in the temptations of indolence, sensuality and superstition. If that is one of the 'arguments' of the painting then it is only hinted at, and is overwhelmed by the beauty of the scene which demonstrates the way in which climate contributes to the growth and fecundity of the landscape.

The paintings of *Otaheite Peha* and *Matavai Bay* belong to the genre of landscape painting, and as such their 'truth-effect' rests not on specific moments but on the depiction of the continuum of daily life. They can be contrasted typologically with the group of three small paintings in the National Maritime Museum that show landings in the New Hebrides, at Tanna, Erramanga and Mallicolo,[31] which were engraved for the official publication of Cook's account of the second voyage (cat. nos 34-36). These are, as Smith has noted, history paintings within the recently established sub-genre of contemporary history painting, pioneered by Benjamin West. They describe a specific *event*, the primal encounter, when European sailors confront, on one occasion violently, unknown peoples for the first time, to be greeted either by yielding friendliness or vigorous hostility. The inhabitants of New Caledonia were agreed by Cook and both Forsters to be less beautiful and more savage than the Tahitians, and

Johann Reinhold Forster placed them in a lower racial category than the inhabitants of the Society and Friendly Isles. The men of Mallicolo [Malakula] were regarded by Cook as 'the most ugly, ill-proportioned people I ever saw'.[32] There are signs that in his painting of *Mallicolo* Hodges has attempted to depict the simian cast noted by Cook and Johann Reinhold Forster in the faces in the foreground, and he has carefully depicted the characteristic penis sheath of the facing figure in the central group, a detail censored by the clergyman-editor from the published version of Cook's journal of the voyage. The smallness of relative stature noted by the observers is perhaps signalled in the figures of the officers on the first boat (Cook standing on the stern), who appear elongated by contrast. Though the Malakulans in the foreground are to a degree individualized, those behind form part of a mass of bodies, which contrast with the graceful individuality of the standing officers but also the more regularly organized seated sailors, the ones in the background bearing parallel rifles with bayonets attached. There are, then, not two but three orders of humanity in these paintings: the officers, the sailors who obey their orders, and the natives on the shore. The sailors on board the two ships are frequently remarked upon by Cook and the Forsters as an unstable and untrustworthy presence, threatening to pass venereal disease to the women of the islands and thereby round themselves, drink too much, steal from or be stolen from by the natives, or attempt to desert.[33]

If the Malakulans were at least friendly, in *The Landing at Erramanga*, the natives on the shore evidently appeared not to have peaceful intentions, and Cook opened fire upon the chief of the party. We know that Hodges was not present but pieced together the scene from Cook's journal shortly after it was written,[34] so it is likely to correspond to Cook's sense of the event. Cook is seen as a commanding and decisive figure but the natives are here even more of an undifferentiated mass than the Malakulans, though they are more individualized and heroic in the published engraving by J. K. Sherwin.[35]

Hodges's paintings of *Otaheite Peha* and *Matavai Bay* are by comparison less direct in their representation of the confrontation of old and new, and offer perhaps a more reflective view of the South Seas. They are steeped, as are George Forster's accounts, in a vision formed by poetic and visual responses to the Roman campagna, but this is not the same as saying that they represent a reconciliation of the classical and the naturalistic.[36] I have argued implicitly that the classical tradition, far from inhibiting realism or merely framing it, could provide ways for landscape painters to express profound ideas beyond simple observation. Hodges's 'artistic' qualities, so admired by his fellow voyagers, enabled him to give visual form to the continuum between climatic conditions, the organic forms of nature, and the different ways that people lived and responded to European visitors. In other words his classical background as an artist was not a hindrance to his task on the voyage, but on the contrary it formed the mental equipment that enabled him to carry out so successfully the brief given him by the Admiralty. As Cook himself

wrote: Hodges's brief from the Admiralty was to 'give a more per‑
fect idea' of the scenes they observed 'than could be formed from
written description only',[37] and it is this 'perfect idea' that links
him to the implicit idealism of the classical tradition.

[1] The literature on the Cook voyages is, of course, enormous, but the most
comprehensive account of the visual images made on them and afterwards is
treated exhaustively in Joppien and Smith (1985a‑b and 1988).

[2] For a full catalogue, see Joppien and Smith (1985b), nos. 2.1–2, 150.

[3] Forster (1977; 2000); Forster (1778; 1996); Wales (1778).

[4] Hodges (1793).

[5] See Appendix below.

[6] Smith (1985b), 62f.

[7] On the circumstances surrounding Hodges's appointment, see Joppien and
Smith (1985b) and pp. 74‑5 below.

[8] Bindman (2002), 128.

[9] Joppien and Smith (1985b), 24.

[10] Forster (1982), vol. 2, 265.

[11] Bindman (2002), 123–6.

[12] Forster (1777; 2000), 269.

[13] For Burke's remark in 1777, 'the Great Map of mankind is unrolld at once;
and there is no state or Gradation of barbarism, and no mode of refinement
which we have not at the same instant under our View' see Geoff Quilley, '
"Tahiti Revisited": the historicizing visual order of the Pacific in the art of
Cook's Voyages', forthcoming.

[14] Forster (1777; 2000),

[15] Bindman (2002), 126–7.

[16] Joppien and Smith (1985b), nos. 2.42–3, 2.48–9; and Quilley, *op. cit.*

[17] Beaglehole (1974), 131–3.

[18] Hulme (1986), 229.

[19] Forster (1777; 2000), 253.

[20] Ibid., 266.

[21] Ibid., 265.

[22] Joppien and Smith (1985b), 62.

[23] Forster (1777; 2000), 318.

[24] See Quilley, *op. cit.*

[25] Joppien and Smith (1985b), 62–3.

[26] The standard work on the subject is Meek (1976).

[27] Bindman (2002), 58f.

[28] Hodges (1793), passim.

[29] Quoted in Meek (1976).

[30] Quilley, *op. cit.*

[31] Joppien and Smith (1985), nos. 2.126, 2.128, 2.134.

[32] Cook (1955–67), vol. 2, 466.

[33] See, for instance, Forster (1777; 2000).

[34] Wales (1778), 74.

[35] For a specific comparison see Bindman (2002), figs. 39, 40.

[36] As is argued by Smith (1985b), 62–4.

[37] Cook (1777), vol. 1, xxxiii.

Hodges as anthropologist and historian

NICHOLAS THOMAS

James Cook's *Voyage Toward the South Pole*, published in 1777, the official account of the famous navigator's second voyage, was arguably unprecedented among travel books. This was not because of the work's literary accomplishment. For his writing, Cook offered the somewhat disingenuous apology of a 'plain man' at sea since youth.[1] What was new was rather the remarkable standard of the book's illustration. Previous voyage narratives, even those such as Anson's that had been opulently produced, had included few prints. Such images as did appear were generally concocted by metropolitan artists on the basis of the text, and derived nothing from field sketches or any other putatively primary visual sources. Now, the purchaser of Cook's *Voyage* got as part of the bargain sixty-four finely engraved plates, of which more than half were based on portraits and views drawn in the course of the expedition by William Hodges.

The subjects of these images reflect a larger anomaly of the voyage itself. The central aim had been the discovery of the long-rumoured southern continent. No land had been found during three gruelling summer cruises in far southern latitudes. Instead, however, an extraordinary range of encounters with Oceanic peoples had taken place, during the two intervening winters, spent substantially in the tropics and New Zealand. The bulk of Hodges's pictures depicted these Islanders and their islands. These people were interesting, undoubtedly. But if meetings with them were extraneous, strictly speaking, to the voyage's purpose, and if the findings with respect to the great southern land were negative, how was the accomplishment of this expedition to be measured and evoked?

Similar problems had nagged at Cook during his first voyage. He had a strong sense that an explorer trod a delicate balance. He might be charged with cowardice or 'timorousness' if he failed to approach a dangerous coast but with recklessness or 'temerity' if

he was wrecked upon it.[2] He worried too that readers would make adverse judgements about his dealings with native peoples and the fatalities among his crew. During his second voyage, his concerns were mostly less defensive. He read Bougainville's *Voyage* and was impressed by it. He perhaps gained a new sense that information about native peoples – about human rather than cartographic discoveries – might loom large in a book that recounted a voyage. Above all, Cook knew that the systematic nature of his efforts to criss-cross blank spaces on maps made his predecessors over two centuries look like naïve amateurs. He was not only conscious that the definitive nature of his exploration of the southern oceans gave his voyages historic significance; he also wanted his public to be fully aware that that was so. As the second voyage progressed, he gave – his journals suggest – steadily greater thought to what was involved in making his voyage's accomplishment explicit and public. He certainly thought about the sort of book he wanted to write, and he did much work revising his journals toward publication, during the voyage itself.[3] To what extent he also thought about how the book might be illustrated, we do not know. William Hodges was not Cook's servant, but his own artist. Yet if he thought toward paintings appropriate to the Royal Academy, he must also have anticipated that some of his work would be engraved to provide a visual complement to Cook's text; at some point in the voyage, he must have thought toward those engravings.

It would be impossible and perhaps unprofitable to try to reconstruct those thoughts. But certain phases of the process – of coming to terms with the voyage's findings, and arriving at an expression of them that would convey the right messages to the *Voyage*'s public – are manifest in Hodges's extant work. This essay focuses upon two moments of that process, one attested to by a group of sketches, and one by a distinct group of the published engravings.

The first group of works need to be seen in the context of the richness, already alluded to, of the human contacts of the voyage. Cook's predecessors in the European exploration of the Pacific had generally had no more than brief or sporadic encounters with Islanders. In most cases the visitors had no linguistic competence; people were in some cases met in canoes without Europeans even landing; even when they did land stays were short and marked more by mutual incomprehension than by dialogue or the acquisition of what we might call anthropological knowledge. For example, Bougainville – though considerably more curious and sophisticated than earlier European observers – had called at Tahiti for only ten days and had no knowledge of any other Polynesian population. In contrast, even during his first voyage Cook had profited from what was already known of Tahiti and Tahitian from Wallis's visit of 1767. His crew included both officers and common seamen who had sailed either with Wallis (the European 'discover' of Tahiti) or his predecessor Byron (who had encountered other Polynesians in the Tuamotu archipelago). The *Endeavour* was at Tahiti for three months. This stay was followed up by meetings with both closely related populations elsewhere in the Society Islands and the more distantly related Maori of New Zealand. Such understandings as derived from these contacts were enriched by much discussion with the Raiatean priest Tupaia who was on the ship from July 1769 until his death at Batavia (Jakarta) in December 1770.

At the beginning of the second voyage, Cook and some of his crew thus already possessed greater – if nevertheless still limited and certainly ethnocentric – knowledge of Pacific Islanders than any previous European visitors. A mix of chance and design meant that both the depth and the range of this knowledge would be spectacularly enhanced. Tahiti, Huahine, and Raiatea would each be visited twice and, in the case of Tahiti, for extended periods. New Zealand too would be called at again; the people in Dusky Sound, in the far south, would be encountered for the first time; and people around Queen Charlotte Sound three times, where Cook had already met Maori. The Tongan islands, Easter Island or Rapanui, and Tahuata in the Marquesas Islands, that had been earlier reported by Abel Tasman, Jacob Roggeveen and Pedro de Quiros respectively, provided anchorages, supplies, and further contacts. Niue would be visited for the first time by a European. All this meant that the wider range of the Polynesian peoples – who to varying degrees had social and cultural institutions and practices such as chieftainship, hereditary rank, tattooing, and the making of barkcloth in common – were recognized for the first time as related populations, as representatives of a 'great nation' that had quite astonishingly dispersed itself across extraordinary Oceanic distances.

The decisive evidence for this relatedness was linguistic. Cook later pointed out that if one speculated about the common origins of populations on the basis of affinities in customs, one could easily be led astray by accidental similarities, but where whole series of words were identical or obviously cognate, groups of people, however geographically separated, had to have been pre-

viously connected.[4] It was this fact also that facilitated the voyagers' communication with even those Polynesians of whom they had no previous knowledge. Conversation was not necessarily more than rudimentary, since some of these languages were much closer to the one known best, Tahitian, than others, and in many cases the Europeans' grasp of Tahitian was anyway only basic. If this trawl of information generally remained remote from indigenous self-perceptions and understandings, it was nevertheless dramatically more nuanced than any earlier observation. The affinities between the peoples encountered moreover prompted less in the way of general reflection on 'the state of nature' than curiosity concerning the character and causes of particular differences, for example in the mode of life of Marquesans, Tahitians, and Tongans. Moreover, the variations among these closely related Islanders would be thrown into relief by encounters with apparently unrelated or at least physically, culturally and linguistically different peoples in the western Pacific.

The pre-eminent synthesist of 'the varieties of the human species' in the Pacific was Johann Reinhold Forster, who had replaced Joseph Banks as the second voyage's senior naturalist after Banks withdrew. Forster's *Observations made during a voyage round the world* (1778) is notable for its sustained and elaborate discussion of the range of forms of 'social union', government, religion, education and so forth observed among the peoples of the Pacific Islands. Forster did not merely describe the manners and customs that had been witnessed, but analysed them from the standpoint of Enlightenment social theory. He understood the differences between the Islanders of the east and west in progressive terms, and postulated a grand analogy between the progress of society and the development of the individual human being. Savages were like children, barbarians like passionate and unruly adolescents, and more civilized peoples were more or less mature. Maori, in Forster's eyes, were certainly passionate and prone to warrior excess; in Tahiti, he saw refinement and the feminine amelioration of masculine barbarity, but also luxury and incipient corruption. He did not precisely order or rank each society on a single progressive continuum but discoursed at length concerning their qualities, and was sometimes equivocal in his assessment of their faults, virtues, and advancement or lack thereof.

Forster's writings have been drawn upon by a number of commentators, including several of the contributors to this volume, to contextualize the work of William Hodges, and especially major paintings such as the views of Matavai Bay and Vaitepiha Bay. Both these paintings and Forster's book were of course completed after the voyage, and their analysis is thus an analysis of the ways questions that arose during the voyage were, if not answered, at least provisionally resolved, in the work that voyage participants produced after the fact. In this essay I offer a complementary discussion by focusing on a set of major sketches produced by Hodges during a critical phase of the voyage. The artist's perceptions were at this time no doubt stimulated by discussion with Johann Reinhold Forster, as well as with Forster's brilliant son George and others on board, not least Cook himself.

Yet Hodges's understanding of what he was depicting could not at this time be informed by an interpretation that was yet to encounter some of its materials, and yet to be distilled.

The works in question are a group of nine pen and wash drawings, comprising views of coasts, and in most cases bays, canoes and inhabitants at Tahuata, Tahiti, Raiatea, Niue, Tonga, Malakula, Efate, and New Caledonia.[5] They may be distinguished from other voyage sketches by Hodges, most obviously, by their impressive size. So far as I am aware no technical comparison has been undertaken, but the paper is presumably of the same stock, since in all cases the height is around 60–62 cm (24 inches), and the width around 117–119 cm (46–47 inches). Two works are panoramas consisting each of two sheets of this size.[6] Some but not all are bordered with ruled lines; in several cases titles are printed in capital letters beneath the drawing. Joppien and Smith suggest that these were prepared during the voyage's second tropical cruise, that in effect began with the visit to Easter Island of March 1774 and concluded with the return to Queen Charlotte Sound, New Zealand, in October of the same year.[7] This is uncontentious in the sense that five of the drawings depict Tahuata, Niue, Malakula, Efate, and New Caledonia,[8] none of which were visited earlier; and this second cruise was important precisely because it was this phase of the voyage that saw the knowledge of Polynesia dramatically extended, and Cook's first encounters with peoples of the western Pacific.

On arriving at previously unvisited places, Europeans immediately noticed the physical characteristics of the 'new' people, and they also had to deal, immediately, with how those people dealt with foreigners. Receptivity or hostility was not a merely pragmatic issue, however. Almost instinctively, Europeans would understand people as more or less civilized, according to the level of curiosity and openness they exhibited toward foreigners. Those who appeared devoid of interest, and uninterested in acquiring European things, were considered as the most miserable of human beings (for instance, in the case the Tierra del Fuegans), or the closest to the state of nature (in that of indigenous Australians). Conversely, people who were both interested in acquiring new things and keen to establish relationships with Europeans were thought to be civilized. Although relationships between the British and the Tahitians had not been free of violence and tension, the nature of chiefly politics in the Society Islands prompted Tahitian chiefs actively to seek alliances with the powerful visitors, to fete them, treat with them, extract goods from them, and otherwise make the most of them. Though Europeans were not oblivious of the pragmatic and strategic motivations of individual chiefs, they persistently interpreted chiefly friendship sentimentally and represented it as an uncomplicated, genuine civility rather than a response that was to some extent politically shaped.

Hodges's two-sheet panoramic view is of Matavai Bay (cat. no. 19) but is entitled simply *OTAHEITE* and can be seen as a summative view of both the bay that had provided the central theatre of European-Tahitian meetings up to that time, and the people

Fig. 9 Tahitian sculpture of a male figure. Copyright © British Museum.

encountered there. The 'face of the country' is certainly benign and opulent. The littoral is plainly densely inhabited; there are canoes on the beach, and canoe shelters and houses can be seen. The foreground is occupied by several canoes of different types – single, double, with and without shelters, and in one case with an elaborate sculpted attachment. Hodges places these canoes close to the boat or (given the apparent height of the vantage point) the ship. This is not just a compositional arrangement but one that implies a relationship between the occupants of the canoes and the occupants of the ship. The relationship is not only one of unthreatening proximity but mutual interest. The most prominent of the canoes is not simply nearby or going about its business, but is approaching the European vessel. A number of those in the canoes look toward or turn to look at the artist/viewer, who is thus struck by their lively curiosity. This might appear a banal observation, but in other drawings in this sequence, depicting other places and other

Fig. 10 William Hodges, *Mallicolo* [*Malakula*], July 1774, pen, ink and wash, 62.2 x 119.4 cm. The British Library, London.

encounters, the response and attitude that Hodges recorded, or at any rate chose to present, is quite different.

If this drawing has a single eye-catching feature, it is the carving that is central to its right-hand section. A double-canoe is carefully depicted; the viewer sees the ingeniously sewn hulls that Cook's journal describes. But if these and other aspects of the canoes shown may be technically admirable, the arresting feature is an improbably tall column that rises from the prow of one hull, that is rigid and erect but constructed of some indeterminate material, that has a substantial bundle of cloth wrapped about it half-way up, and that supports a solid, squat, loosely naturalistic, anthropomorphic figure. There is no Tahitian canoe of this sort preserved in any museum collection, but the strong proportions of the figure correspond with a type of Tahitian sculpture, examples of which were collected by Forster during the voyage. Those he obtained, now in the Pitt Rivers Museum, are around 30 cm (12 inches) in height; another example, in the British Museum, is 53 cm high (fig. 9). If one's eye moves from the carving to the seated man in the canoe, the scale looks right, if the object is at the larger end of the range. But the effect belies whatever perspectival correctness we may impute. The carving and its enigmatic support (probably of basketwork, around a pole) are given daunting prominence, commanding the scene, looming over and overseeing the landmass of Tahiti itself.

The image as a whole implies that Tahitians are 'civilized', at least to the extent that their society is differentiated and complex: the status of those in the canoes evidently varies (some exhibit the bearing, demeanour and idleness of aristocrats), while the canoes themselves display the advancement of their industry and arts. The people seem benign and friendly: though the double canoe is of the sort elsewhere described as a 'war galley', no weapons are brandished. But the carving that is given such prominence nevertheless insists on the alien remoteness of their

religion. A mysterious (and possibly barbaric) cult seems to hold sway over this landscape, which is not a natural wilderness but a humanized and cultivated terrain. Yet it is humanized exotically. It is effectively integrated with the curious customary order that the figure seems to govern.

Others of these large sketches evoke different environments and, in part by omission, quite different responses to peoples. The view of Niue (cat. no. 20), briefly visited in June 1774, aptly conveys the distinctive topography of this raised atoll. The island is fringed not by any pleasing coastal plain but by jagged coral cliffs. The ship is not far offshore and two boats are shown, sailing from the shore back to the *Resolution*. On 22 June a party had landed but was subjected by the Niueans to a barrage of stones and spears. 'The Conduct and aspect of these Islanders occasioned my giving it the Name of *Savage Island*,' Cook wrote after withdrawing.[9] Hodges may have been among the party but made no attempt to depict the action. Although there were said to be canoes on the beach that is visible, he does not show these. Perhaps neither houses nor gardens could be seen from the sea, in any event Hodges gives no indication that the island was occupied. The dense brush above the cliff suggests that if it was, it was nevertheless uncultivated. There is no impression that even a savage kind of customary order reigns over this landscape that appears rather as a topographic than a national entity.

The island of Malakula, towards the north of the archipelago called the New Hebrides by Cook, now the nation of Vanuatu, is significant to the second voyage's emerging ideas of Oceanic anthropology because it was here that darker-skinned speakers of non-Polynesian languages were first encountered. Hodges's drawing, inscribed *MALLICOLO* (fig. 10), has certain compositional parallels with *OTAHEITE* that underscore the contrasts between the two scenes. In both cases canoes occupy the foreground. The Malakulan landscape consists of low coastal hills rather than the

Fig. 11 William Hodges, [*A View of Balade Harbour*] *New Caledonia*, September 1774, pen, ink, wash and watercolour, 61.5 x 233.6 cm. The British Library, London.

grand juxtaposition of Tahitian mountain and plain. Its uniform vegetation like that of Niue suggests no particular agricultural activity. This lack of literal cultivation might connote a lack of other natural and social improvements.

The occupants of the canoes are again close but in this instance proximity does not promise friendliness. The men are armed in one case with bow and arrows, in another with a heavy and bulbous club. Though this canoe too has a sculpted prow, the bird it shows is not the image's eye-catching feature. Rather, the unambiguously central figure is that of the standing warrior. The presentation of him in profile draws attention to an aspect of dress and ornament that the mariners had not before encountered, and that they found surprising and shocking. The testicles were exposed, but the penis itself wrapped in an extended cloth that was tied up around the belt. This covering 'rather displays than conceals, and is the very opposite of modesty,' considered George Forster.[10] Cook thought that the tightness of wrapping had to be painful ('it was a wonder to us how they could endure it'); this no doubt accentuated the distastefulness of the display.[11] Whereas the imagery of Tahiti presented a voluptuous landscape, beautiful women, and male aristocrats who lived luxuriously, the vision here is of an unsocial, insensible and at least potentially belligerent masculinity. The voyage journals indicate that the Malakulans were in fact not inclined to violence but were profoundly cautious before visitors whom they may have seen as potentially malevolent ghosts or returning ancestors. They suffered Europeans to land but dissuaded them from moving beyond the immediate shoreline or venturing near women. As in the case of the Niue drawing, the information here is constrained by the limits imposed on Europeans. There were elaborate agricultural systems here, and native art forms that were no less spectacular than those mounted on Tahitian canoes. But both gardens and sculptures were out of view; Hodges could not depict what he did not know. The little he did know was inflected by the attitude that imposed the limitation in the first place. While the lively interest that the Tahitians exhibited toward Europeans manifested their civility, the caution shown by Malakulans was perforce taken to illustrate something else: a degree of barbarism that seemed consistent with their martial sociality (though the Tahitians were often enough warriors too), their black skin, their way of treating their women, and so on.

The Malakulans and the inhabitants of southern Vanuatu were puzzling in part because the islands they occupied lay between Tahiti and Tonga on the one hand and New Zealand on the other. Both New Zealand and the eastern Oceanic islands were clearly occupied by related, Polynesian speaking peoples, so it seemed anomalous that those generally in their geographic midst should not belong to the same family. After Vanuatu Cook proceeded south-west and encountered the coast of New Caledonia, not previously known to Europeans. Here the people were again somewhat cautious but less so than either those of Malakula or Tanna. Relations were generally good, the Europeans were impressed by irrigation systems, and pleased that the people did not possess the propensity to pilfer that they were generally accustomed to. While later ethnologists grouped the Kanaks (to use a modern term of indigenous self-identification) with ni-Vanuatu as 'Melanesians', these eighteenth-century visitors were probably more struck by the differences than the similarities.

Hodges produced a further panoramic view with canoes in the foreground. The implication that it represents an addition to a series is supported by a similar inscribed title, *NEW Caledonia* (fig 11). One of the canoes, to the far left is close to the vantage point of the artist. Unfortunately the face of the standing figure at the very edge of the image is smudged and partly lost, and it is not clear whether this man looked at or away from the artist and viewer. A crouching figure beside him looks away; his attitude is one of disengaged independence. Those in other canoes appear more interested by the European presence. The group in the canoe central to the right hand sheet manifests a social structure. The vessel is propelled or steered by a man with an oar; a standing figure holds a club with a star-shaped head, corresponding to a type well-known in ethnographic collections; two women and a man are seated around a small cooking-fire; they all wear cloaks, the man one of the 'Concave cylindrical stiff black caps' that Cook noted were 'a great ornament among them, and we thought only worn by men of note or Wariors.'[12] In other words a hierarchical society of something like a Tahitian type appeared to be present here, even though, in physical and other respects, the people had more in common with the Malakulans and Tannese.

These images and others in the series register the responses to 'the varieties of the human species' (Forster's term) that the second voyage encountered in the Pacific. The idea that Tahiti was an island of unusual civility, a place that uniquely excited curiosity, and one that was singularly luxurious comes through in the

Fig. 12 William Hodges, *War canoes of Otaheite [Tahiti]*, 1774, pen, ink and wash, 61.0 x 193.7 cm. The British Library, London.

Matavai Bay panorama. This work alone foregrounds a lively engagement on the part of indigenous subjects in the scene of interaction; elsewhere people seem to put up with or just witness the European intrusion, and notably do not reciprocate the Europeans' curiosity in the face of a new people. The approbation of the Tahitians had been elaborated upon in a further large sketch depicting a fleet of war canoes (fig. 12). This drew attention again to the remarkable character of native naval architecture, and to the exotic elaboration of priests' costumes and suchlike. It also showed that this was a society that mounted spectacles: a mass of what might have been called the Tahitian public line the foreshore and crowd the hill visible at the far left, behind the assembled fleet, that was evidently extraordinary to Europeans and native people alike.

Views of the Marquesas and Raiatea in the series do not evidence any similar native curiosity through the depiction of spectators, individual attention or expression, but do depict the *Resolution* surrounded by canoes presumably engaged in vigorous trade. In fundamental contrast, the Malakulans are standoffish and potentially hostile. The Niueans are not seen at all. The New Caledonians look to be more advanced in their form of government, but their country lacks the attractiveness of Tahiti, and they themselves resemble the ni-Vanuatu.

By the time Forster produced his *Observations* in 1778, these incomplete and inconsistent perceptions were to some extent resolved. It was clear to him that all the people of the western Pacific were of a distinct nation that was not as advanced as that which occupied the eastern part of the ocean. The anomaly of Niuean resistance was a detail that dropped out of the picture. Skin colour was not central to this discrimination, but it happened to be the case that the east was occupied by light skinned and the west by dark skinned people. The negative aspect of this judgement was in due course reinforced when later voyagers came to the conclusion that New Caledonians were cannibals. The understanding of human variety in the Pacific thus became increasingly moralized, racialized and straightforward.

Many of the plates engraved for Cook's *Voyage* would be portraits derived from Hodges's large red chalk sketches (cat. nos 16, 17, 21, 22). Some of the individuals depicted were named, and others were described generically ('Man of Mallicollo', 'Man of Tanna', 'Woman of Tanna', etc.). Apart from one Tongan, all the named individuals are Society Islanders and are represented essentially as aristocratic figures, and in this sense the set is consistent with the larger impressions of human variety that emerged over the course of the voyage: Tahiti occupied the zenith of Oceanic civility. Tonga was evidently also a highly advanced Oceanic society, yet one with an order and institutions somewhat different to those of the Society Islands, one that remained essentially unfamiliar to Europeans. At the other end of the spectrum, the 'Man of Christmas Sound' appeared as desperately uncivilized as Cook's narrative found the inhabitants of Tierra del Fuego to be. Yet, although a variety of physical characteristics and distinctive ornaments are depicted, in more particular senses the series of portraits does not illuminate the types of more specific assessments that Cook, Wales and the Forsters most systematically were forming of particular peoples. The facial decoration of the Tannese man for example makes him appear more remote from Europeans than the Malakulan, though those on the voyage were all more impressed by the former than the latter. The Maori woman does not appear a representative of one 'great nation' that is more advanced than another, to which the women of Tanna and New Caledonia belong. In fact she looks more like a waif from the streets of London than a member of the people that Cook rather idealized. The Marquesan and Maori are both either ornamented or disfigured by their facial tattooing; there is no sense that the former is closely affiliated with the idealized Tahitians, and the latter a representative of a disturbing warlike people whose cannibalism had been witnessed, or rather staged, in late 1773. In sum, though these images no doubt worked to stimulate the interest and curiosity of purchasers of the *Voyage*, they cannot have done much more than they claimed to do, in depicting a range of individuals.

This is notable but not surprising, because the objects of the voyage's proto-anthropological knowledge were not 'races' of the sort that would, over the decades subsequent to the voyages, unevenly in various discursive domains become the classic objects of anthropological study.[13] 'Races' could have been and in due course would commonly be exemplified by individual specimens. But the indices of human variety salient to the voyage were far more nebulous. They included the status of women, which was obliquely indicated in some of Hodges's work. They also included, as I have discussed, the level of interest that native peoples variously exhibited toward foreigners. In his major, panoramic sketches Hodges had the makings of a set of engravings which suggested this dimension of native civility. Yet these works were used to only a limited extent in the account that was published: plates appeared based on the views of Tahiti and the Marquesas, and of the war canoes of Tahiti, but the Malakula and New Caledonia images were not worked up into prints.

Possibly, Hodges made his own decisions about which pictures should be developed further, and no doubt also participated in discussions with Cook, Lord Sandwich (the First Lord of the Admiralty) and possibly also Banks as to which images were to appear in the book. These discussions cannot be reconstructed but, for whatever reasons, led to the series I have discussed being only partially represented in print: the views of Matavai, the canoe fleet (a subject that Hodges dealt with in several oils), and Tahuata appeared but no others. On the other hand, a new series of works was developed, for which there seem to have been no preparatory sketches that date from the voyage. These featured the moments of initial contact at Eua, Malakula, Erramanga and Tanna, and were entitled *The Landing at Middleburgh* (Eua), *The Landing at Mallicollo*, and so on (cat. nos 34-36).[14] The three landfalls in Vanuatu were at places unknown to Europeans until the second voyage. Although Eua had been sighted by Tasman in 1643, it had not been revisited subsequently, so the 1773 meeting there was effectively a moment of first contact too. Hodges could equally have depicted new meetings at Dusky Sound, Easter Island, Niue, New Caledonia and Tahuata, but did not, perhaps merely because he ran out of time, or because there were thought to be sufficient prints. However, the four images represent contrasting, perhaps representative, experiences of contact.

The Malakulans were shown to be armed but welcoming; the Erramangans vigorously resisting Cook's landing, as they in fact did; the Tannese awed and alarmed (some cower or flee; others brandish their weapons). In each of these cases, and despite the negative implications of native caution or hostility, both sides are represented as parties to a founding historical moment. These meetings, Cook understood, were ideally expressions of mutual friendliness and benevolence, but were prone to break down. Shortly after making contact with the Tannese, but undoubtedly with the violence at Erramanga in mind, he wrote

we found [the Tannese] people Civil and good Natured when not prompted by jealousy to a contrary conduct, a conduct one cannot blame them for when one considers the light in which they must look upon us in, its impossible for them to know our real design, we enter their Ports without their daring to make opposition, we attempt to land in a peaceable manner, if this succeeds its well, if not we land nevertheless and mentain the footing we thus got by the Superiority of our fire arms, in what other light can they than at first look on us but as invaders of their Country; time and some acquaintance with us can only convince them of their mistake.[15]

Cook understood that these moments might be subjected to intense moral scrutiny. He was concerned to vindicate his own practice. If his landings entailed an injustice, it was an unavoidable one, one that followed from an understandable but nevertheless (he presumes) false assumption on the part of Islanders, who took him and his men to be invaders. At the same time he is almost equally concerned to vindicate them: their hostility arises not from savagery but a predictable patriotic suspicion. In another version of the text I have quoted, he elaborates, 'these people are yet in a rude state . . . frequently at War not only with their Neighbours, but amongst themselves, consequently must be jealous of every new face.'[16] This contextualization is consistent with the generally dignified treatment of indigenous caution and resistance in Hodges's 'Landings', but detracts something from these peoples' advancement, even as it presents their behaviour as rational. Cook's proto-anthropological observations were less systematic than Forster's but consistent with them. For both, a key feature of society in 'a rude state' was this mutual antagonism and fragmentation. Greater civility meant a greater degree of social union and the development of government and law.

Hence the *Landing at Middleburgh* (cat. no. 41) shows that the people Cook significantly called the 'Friendly Islanders' did not possess this deep-seated suspicion of foreigners. Evidently, their dealings with each other enabled them to anticipate that Europeans might not be invaders. Their civility is manifest in the fact that one chief has clearly entered Cook's boat prior to the actual landing. He appears to have assumed the role of the Europeans' spokesman, and announces their diplomatic intentions by holding aloft the plantain or banana leaf that was an emblem of peace among most Polynesian people. Although it is not clear from the journals that Ataonga, the man that Cook did meet at this time, in fact escorted the party ashore in the manner depicted, it is entirely conceivable that he did so. It was and is a normal aspect of Polynesian sociality that a native of one place can affiliate himself with a group of visitors, in order to make signs and offerings and express respectful greetings that they, for reasons of linguistic incompetence or unfamiliarity, are unable to make and express. The Europeans were certainly familiar with somewhat similar behaviour: Society Islanders such as Tupaia (on the first voyage) and Mahine (on the second) had acted as go-betweens in a number of contexts. In any case, invented or not, Ataonga's diplomacy for Cook's party was striking for its implication that an Islander might be instantly enlisted, to help inaugurate a peaceful commerce.

If the 'Landings' underscored the historic nature of Cook's mission, they also conveyed the emergent understanding of the major distinction between the nations of the eastern and western Pacific. Though the islands visited were unevenly represented by this particular group of images, the juxtaposition between the civility of the *Landing at Middleburgh* and the violence at Erramanga could not have been starker. Yet the variations among the three landings in Vanuatu can only have deprived the viewer of these prints of any neat understanding of human variation in the Pacific. While Forster had articulated, more clearly than anyone else, the sense that there were 'two great varieties of people in the South Seas', he had proceeded to acknowledge that within each variety, there was a plethora of notable differences.[17] Although he was nothing if not a Linnean traveller, he seems nevertheless to have accepted Buffon's understanding, that variety was manifold and mutable. Varieties of people, like other life forms, changed more or less drastically or subtly as they moved into new climates — climates that were social, hence to some degree of a people's own making, as well as merely natural. People, therefore, were susceptible to description but perhaps, in the end, not to rigorous classification.

To embrace this sort of principle was perhaps to make a virtue of necessity. The observations of Oceanic peoples that participants in Cook's second voyage were able to make were extensive and various but also in many ways confusing and inconsistent. They were empowered by a novel level of familiarity and an unprecedented degree of linguistic competence, in Tahitian and closely related Polynesian dialects. But they were ultimately constrained by European assumptions, for example about the nature of 'superstition' and 'government', that precluded any but the most superficial perceptions of Polynesian ritual, and any but the most mechanical ideas of Polynesian politics and sovereignty. And the differences among peoples, from one place to the next, sometimes did not add up; whether one set was more or less civil than another was not straightforward. What makes the textual and visual archives of Cook's second voyage enduringly fascinating, is that they fully reveal the obstacles to synthesis and the uneven-

ness of cross-cultural understanding: at various times and in various ways, these travellers could not help admitting that for every moment of insight there was another of incomprehension. In what amounts to his representations of 'the varieties of people in the South Seas', William Hodges left us with a set of real problems, rather than a false solution.

[1] Cook (1777), vol. 1, xxxvi. In this essay I keep citation to a minimum, but the reader should be aware that Cook's second voyage has been extensively discussed, notably in the introduction and annotations to Cook (1955–67), vol. 2, Smith (1985) and Smith (1992). Joppien and Smith (1985) is particularly relevant for Hodges's work. For the Forsters see Forster (1778; 1996) and Forster (1777; 2000). For recent commentary see also Salmond (2003) and Thomas (2003). In the text and notes, 'Forster' means Johann Reinhold unless otherwise indicated.

[2] Cook (1955–67), vol. 1, 380.

[3] See Thomas (2003), 202–3, 217–19.

[4] Cook (1955–67), vol. 3, 462, 468.

[5] The whole group is located at Add. MS. 15743 in the British Library. These include views of Sandwich Island (Efate), a Tongan canoe, and the port of Fayal, that I do not discuss here.

[6] A third, also consisting of two sheets and showing the massing of a fleet of Tahitian war canoes, is not as wide.

[7] Joppien and Smith (1985), 78.

[8] The Tahitian view of the war canoe fleet certainly relates to the 1774 visit, and it is likely that the other does also. It is of course difficult to argue that these drawings were not prepared *later*, though in most cases they precisely record topographic and other local information, and thus are likely to have been drawn at the time or soon afterwards, with the help of field sketches.

[9] Cook (1955–67), vol. 2, 435.

[10] Cook (1777), 480: cf. 492.

[11] Cook (1955–67), vol. 2, 464.

[12] Cook (1955–67), vol. 2, 540.

[13] For further discussion, see Douglas (1999).

[14] See David Bindman's essay in this volume.

[15] Cook (1955–67), vol. 2, 493.

[16] Cook (1955–67), vol. 2, 493 n. 3.

[17] Forster (1778; 1996), 153.

Hodges's visual genealogy for colonial India, 1780–95

Natasha Eaton

Following his work for the Admiralty, Hodges aspired to find patronage from another powerful institution, turning to the East India Company. In Britain, the Company's Court of Directors maintained close links with Parliament and the Admiralty, becoming one of the most influential cultural brokers of the age. Its servants imported Indian and Chinese paintings, it officers and officials trained Indian artists in botanical drawing and sent them on diplomatic missions, its shareholders funded the decoration its London headquarters with the works of modern British artists and it permitted as many as sixty European painters to operate in its Indian settlements of Calcutta, Madras and Bombay.[1] Living in London, Hodges must have seen the exhibited pieces of the first colonial artists to travel to India, Tilly Kettle (fl. 1768–76) and George Willison (fl. 1774–80) both of whom made substantial fortunes from portraiture. In the realm of landscape painting, Captain Francis Swain Ward's views of India were on public view first at the Society of Artists and then in the Chamber of the Committee of Correspondence, East India House.[2] Mostly representations of the south Indian kingdom of the Carnatic, Ward's paintings depended on the *camera obscura* and professed few aspirations to be 'landscape as high art'.

In contrast, Hodges wanted to subordinate topography to historical narrative. Of all the painters permitted to travel to India, he was the only artist to receive a salary direct from the Company, largely due to his personal links with Warren Hastings. For his patrons in India, Hodges fashioned ambitious historic landscapes of Mughal India that aimed to capture the grandeur and the pathos of what he perceived as the 'greatest and the richest empire, perhaps of which the human annals can produce an instance'.[3]

This essay explores Hodges's relationship with Warren Hastings and their intersecting attitudes towards the representa-

tion of authority in India. It will propose that Hodges created a visual equivalent to British conceptions of Mughal and colonial history, by formulating a 'hybrid aesthetic' that negotiated with classicized landscape, *plein-air* sketching and Mughal miniatures, as well as with ideas of climatic determinism and moral philosophy. It concludes with an exploration of the ways in which Hodges became embroiled in Hastings's impeachment (1786–95), as indicated by his strategic choice of exhibition oils.

Hodges and the creation of a constitution for Company Bengal

Hodges's relationship with his greatest patron is eulogized in the anonymous verse 'Peace: An Ode To Hastings':

Thy patronage will future wonder cause,
For these sights Hodges draws.
With wondering eye will gazing Britain view,
The scenes O Hodges thy pencil drew,
 From various distances will the wandering stranger view,
The animated tents and semblance true,
The grazing sire will ken the impending rock,
That vainly dared to brave a British shock.
Will view the fort that seemed to menace fate
And drop a tear although with joy elate!
And many a scene so beautifully wild,
Thy tints will give to fame, though bold yet mild.[4]

In this most polite and most vicious age, epitomized by the cut-throat competition of the London art market, Hastings's long-standing patronage of Hodges and his family worked against the grain. In India, he organized military protection for Hodges's tours and he commissioned several oil paintings including two views of his Calcutta home. In addition to his private patronage of Hodges, he also organized a Company salary (some of which he paid personally) and he may have assisted in finding additional Company funding for Hodges's aquatint series *Select Views of India* (1785–88). Hastings introduced the artist to his circle including his future patrons Claude Martin, Robert Pott, Sir Elijah Impey and most importantly the District Collector of Bhagalpur in Bihar, Augustus Cleveland. After his return to Britain, Hastings housed the artist's ninety Indian sketches in a specially designed bookcase in the library of his new home at Daylesford and later offered them to the artist's family to pay off their debts. In 1790, Hastings commissioned a 'sublime' depiction of his wife caught in a storm at Colgong, and although it becomes increasingly difficult to determine subsequent Indian commissions, after Hodges's death in 1797 Hastings found a cadetship for Hodges's Anglo-Indian son.[5]

In reciprocation, Hodges gave Hastings several paintings that he made on his tours and on return to London, he exhibited Hastings's paintings at the Royal Academy, eight of which were later engraved as illustrations to the *Travels*. He swore an affidavit of his participation in Hastings's controversial annexation of the region of Benares, to be used in the governor's defence during his trial.[6] Whether Hodges's images maintained the 'disinterested' stance expected from classicized landscapes, or whether they were coloured by partisan interest, they did act as totemic artefacts for stimulating heterogeneous publics' ideas of India.

In spite of his controversial political career, ('sacked' by the Company in 1764, reinstated and promoted as governor, threatened with Parliamentary recall in 1776 and in constant conflict with Calcutta's Supreme Council), Hastings styled himself as a great patron of art. Even before becoming Governor General, he commissioned his likeness from the president of the recently established Royal Academy, Sir Joshua Reynolds. Elegantly posed in a chintz waistcoat with Persian letters and seal to hand, the composition conveys his self-presentation as an Orientalist scholar and statesman.[7] Ever mindful of his public image, the Governor sat to every British portraitist to visit the Company's capital at Calcutta and sent painters to Faizabad, Lucknow, Murshidabad, Arcot and Tibet.[8] Hastings also collected Mughal miniatures, favouring those from the court of Akbar (reigned 1556–1605), including a highly prized copy of the imperial chronicle, the *Akbarnama*.[9] He devised a *visual* genealogy of the Mughal Emperors, comparing their reigns with the English monarchy and writing brief, biographical notes to accompany their portraits, central being Akbar 'the first confessed emperor of Hindustan, the author of all its political and financial economies . . . a wise, great and noble prince'.[10]

Akbar's regime provided Hastings with a political constitution that he would combine with British ideas of sovereignty.[11] There was no precedent for direct British rule over non-European peoples; nor were there modern examples of European sovereignty

in Asia, forcing Hastings to devise a hybrid government for the East India Company 'state'.[12] In 1772, he was ordered by the Company's Court of Directors to assert Company authority in Bengal: in consequence, he arrested or dismissed the *nawab's* ministers, moving the machinery of government to Calcutta and subsequently carving it into separate departments dealing with revenue, justice and commerce. He also sent ambassadors to eleven Indian states so as to 'extend the influence of the British nation to every part of India not too remote from their possessions'.[13] Behind these reforms, his private papers agonize over the Company's equivocal position *en face* a concept of British political virtue that was epitomized by 'governmentality' – liberal governance that, while reliant on state surveillance, operated through limited interference into the semi-independent spheres of economy, civil society, and so on. Paraphrasing one of governmentality's principal British exponents, the Scottish moral philosopher Adam Smith, Hastings concluded that 'a company of merchants are it seems incapable of conducting themselves as sovereigns even after they have become such'.[14]

Hastings needed to extend the Company's position of power through alliances with the old Mughal ruling class who, along with a developing Company historiography, epitomized by Alexander Dow's *History of Hindustan* (1768–72), positioned Akbar at the centre of India's political constitution. The governor admired Akbar's centralized bureaucracy, his military campaigning, his extensive expansion of the Mughal Empire and his cultural cosmopolitanism. In the early 1780s when Hastings was patronizing Hodges's portrayals of north India, he commissioned an English translation of the first section of Akbar's governing edicts, the *A' in-i Akbari*, so as to 'legitimize' the British as the inheritors of 'Enlightened Despotism'.[15] Although European political thought stereotyped 'oriental despotism' as an authoritarian model, based on obedient rather than free subjects, with no right to property, the colonial system attempted to reconcile this species of rule with governmentality, believing India to be a prosperous, agricultural-commercial society, governed by laws or customs. The diversity of Indian and British interpretations of the Mughal constitution enabled Hastings to manipulate it as a rhetorical tool that would detract from the piecemeal character of his motley bureaucracy. Although he wanted to promote absolute sovereignty through a centralized government that gave him maximum authority, his plans were frustrated both by conflicting British factions and his reliance on short-term deals with Indian landholders.[16]

Under Hastings's patronage, Hodges created a cultural geography whose polar points were colonial Calcutta and Akbar's tomb at Sikandra (fig. 56). The selection of locations discloses the Governor's promotion of a history that inter-contextualized the achievements of the 'Golden Age' of the Mughal dynasty (the reigns of Akbar, Jahangir, Shah Jahan and Aurangzeb, 1556–1707) with the recent victories and government policies of the East India Company.

To meet the challenge of representing the exigencies of such a sophisticated imperial history, Hodges returned to the works of his master Richard Wilson, whom he praised for 'grandeur in the choice or invention of his scenes, felicity in the distribution of his lights and shadows, freshness and harmony in his tints'.[17] Although Wilson had depicted classical myths such as the *Destruction of the Children of Niobe* from Ovid's *Metamorphoses*, that anthropomorphized Roman sculpture in sublime settings, Hodges did not represent events from Mughal history and mythology. Instead, his landscapes are closer to Wilson's combinations of Italian or British topography with structural or rhetorical borrowings from Claude, Gaspard Dughet and Rosa. Although several of his Indian paintings cite passages from Wilson, his style is looser, his references to the Roman school more tenuous; he omitted some of the human activities, painterly details and the suggestion of depth associated with classical landscape's rendition of the ideal, in favour of a closer focus on Mughal architectural structures, which after all were new subjects for European art.[18] Through this combination of topographical observation and trains of association, Hodges wished Mughal subjects to participate in a tradition of moral landscape that rendered art and nature both didactic and poetic, as characterized by the sublime, the elegiac or the georgic and influenced by the development of Enlightenment ideas of history. The classical meaning of history related exemplary deeds as lessons towards virtuous conduct; yet, by the mid 1770s, 'history became a narrative of contexts as well as of actions', exemplified by the work of Scottish moral philosophy and Edward Gibbon's examination of the Roman Empire.[19] Manners, customs and civil society now formed the ingredients of a new 'science of morality' for understanding civilization, which had already influenced Hodges's intellectual encounters in the Pacific and that also informed Hastings's perceptions of Indian society.

Hodges's Indian views, particularly when accompanied by textual description as in *Select Views in India*, exhort the viewer to ruminate on the events of colonial and Mughal history. Additionally, human activities (such as fishing, shown in *View of the Jungle Ferry, Bengal, Moonlight*, RA 1786, private collection) connote stages of civilization: hunter-gatherer, pastoral, agricultural or commercial. Such strategies relied on a sophisticated viewing public, educated in modern and classical culture, encompassing both ancient Greece and the Roman Empire. While the Forsters had strongly criticized Hodges's superimposition of Greek drapery onto Pacific peoples, in Bengal Hodges sought naturalized comparisons, noting that wet *saris* had the effect of classical dress, by making Hindu women resemble naiads. Whereas the eastern Pacific had been popularized as an exotic Arcadia, Company officials believed that India displayed *actual* archaeological and biological links with classical civilization. At the close of Hastings's governorship, the judge and philologist Sir William Jones began to explore the entanglements of Sanskrit, Greek and Latin, interpreting ancient India's history through the lens of classical literature. Hodges's own archaeological investigations at the Hindu city of Benares [Varanasi] had already made

several analogies to Greek culture – finding mimetic connections through the scroll of a temple column, while his depiction of *sati* (the practice of burning Hindu widows on their husband's funeral pyres) portrays the widow like a mourner from a Greek *stele*. Yet his European analogies are employed cautiously without formulating a systematic orientalized classicism. After all, the model for Hastings's regime was not in the roots of ancient Hinduism but in the power structure of Mughal society.[20]

As often as classical analogies, Hodges selected Mughal, Pacific and western European cultural mediators in his construction of place. He would never visit Greece and ultimately rejected it as the critical standard for civilization. Instead he defended the 'accuracy' of his images, locating his work in the discursive context of the 'customary', as defined by commentators as various as Burke, Blackstone, Buffon and Sir Joshua Reynolds.

> Everything has a peculiar character and it is the finding out of the real and natural character which is required; should a painter be possessed of the talents of a Raphael and were he to represent a Chinese with the beauty of a Grecian character and form, however excellent his work might be, it would still have no pretensions to reputation as characteristical of that nation.[21]

Hodges selected these cultural analogies for their temporal and political resonance, describing and painting Bengali boats as possessing a 'perfect similarity' to those of Tahiti, underscoring their shared primitivism; while the nawab of Awadh's palace at Lucknow he compared to a twelfth-century European castle, consonant with the 'medieval barbarity' of 'vicious' (as opposed to 'enlightened') despotism.

If 'every thing has a peculiar character' what character did the Company state assume? In Hodges's portrayal of Calcutta (cat. no. 43), the city's neoclassical architecture signifies the sublimity of conquest over a mosquito-infested river and *nawabi* forces, in the simultaneous construction of nature and culture. The eye 'progresses' through time and space: from the 'primordial' huts in the foreground cast in darkness, where an Indian assumes a pose of melancholic contemplation, towards the modern city, its public buildings glittering in impasto against a stormy horizon. This coexistence of 'before' and 'after' Company sovereignty is underlined by Hodges's creation of an ambivalent viewer-position – either as traveller in the act of arriving in the city (invoking Wilson's views of Rome from the Ponte Molle, or Canaletto's views of Venice), or alternatively identified with the Bengali dwelling on the margins. These exchanges between artist, viewer and figure-in-the-landscape entail not the absolute division of self and other but a 'civilizational' rite of passage. In radical contrast to colonial Calcutta, Hodges represents the former provincial Mughal capital Murshidabad (fig. 13) as decadent and overgrown, pitching Bengal between a provincial Mughal regime and the visionary modernity of the Company state. He exaggerates Murshidabad's decay, making Murshid Quli Khan's still magnificent Katra Masjid (1724–25) appear overgrown, even ruinous, the

Fig. 13 William Hodges, *A View of the Cuttera built by Jaffier Cawn at Muxadavad* [*Murshid Quli Khan's Katra Masjid, Murshidabad*], 1781, pencil and wash, 48.9 x 66.0 cm. Yale Center for British Art, Paul Mellon Collection.

result being to push the *nawabi* order further into the past.[22] Here as elsewhere, Hodges maps a variety of cultures onto India's cartography, as dispersal in space reflects difference in time.

Despite being the heartland of the Company, much of Bengal lacked the natural and artistic 'curiosity' that Hodges sought. Instead he represented this British province in the form of sketches of fertile terrain, villages and farmyards, suspended in the ethos of governmentality, which was committed to pastoral care and a species of governance based on individual and collective liberty.[23] But how could this translate to Company territories where Hastings's bitter disputes with the Indian land-holding class were the norm? Bypassing such political wrangling, Hodges extolled both Hastings and Cleveland for their 'liberality' towards their subjects, as manifested by the grandeur of the city of Calcutta and the cultivation of 'beautiful, park-like country'.[24] Yet his writings stress that this was ultimately a hybrid governance, resonant of benevolent despotism, presenting the Company as protector of subjects whose property rights are never mentioned:

> From the apparent state of a country a just estimate may generally be formed of the happiness or the misery of a people. Where there is neatness in the cultivation of the land and that land tilled to the utmost of its boundaries, it may reasonably be supposed that the government is the *protector* not the oppressor of the people. Throughout the kingdom of Bengal it appears highly flourishing in tillage of every kind and abounding in cattle. The villages are neat and clean and filled with swarms of people.[25]

One of his most 'Claudean' oil compositions, *Tomb and distant view of the Rajmahal Hills* (cat. no. 47) represents cow pastures and rice paddies that stretch to the shimmering, ocean-like river,

which provided Hodges with descriptive notes for his writings: 'a beautiful scene opens itself to the view, namely the meandering of the river Ganges through the flat country and glittering through an immense pain, highly cultivated as far as the extent of the horizon'.[26] The image also visualizes the pastoral component of governmentality. The prospect invites the classically educated, Orientalist gaze of Hastings or Cleveland, leading in swiftly to the carefully mapped horizon, then returning to the shaded remains of Mughal culture, a tomb and a *dargah* (the tomb of a saint), before arriving at the signs of cultivation that punctuate the middle ground.

As elsewhere, Hodges's 'spirits of place' (orientalized shepherds, soldiers, mourning widows, conversing scholar-priests, mothers and children or travellers) facilitate his viewers' sentimental identification with the subject, but even more so with the moral aura of the prospect. Here the figure watches over his herd but also faces the tomb, invoking the viewer's melancholic contemplation of the Mughal past, as a variation on *ego fui in arcadia*, and thus referring to a primordial existence that for the region's 'aboriginal' tribes is supposedly not so distant. Additionally, Hodges's *Travels* note the lasting effects of the devastating famine of 1770 that had wiped out thirty percent of Bengal-Bihar's population (not helped by bad Company management of this disaster), which bestows added pathos to the view. Such 'imperialist nostalgia' (concern with what colonialism is simultaneously reforming and destroying) elicits a cultural difference that is not about pure otherness.[27] For Hodges, pictures should be 'connected with the history of the various countries, and . . . faithfully represent the manners of mankind' – a strategy exacerbated by his encounters with Mughal culture.[28]

Hodges's nostalgia and the 'pathos of distance' in Mughal India

Against this pacific image of Bengal, Hodges's representations of northern India continually reinforce a dialectic of past Mughal magnificence and present chaos or cruelty. Steeped in a lexicon of moral decline, Hodges condemns the 'successor states' for their neglect of Akbar's heritage, 'monuments of human greatness now dissolving to dust' before his eyes.[29] For him, the kingdom of Awadh in particular (a vast and wealthy region where the Company was directing an aggressive foreign policy) displays 'the private vices of the Mussulman princes', which he associates more with 'the *want of property* in the people than the natural sterility of the country which, on the contrary, I believe to be capable of producing the finest crops'.[30] In spite of the dry terrain of northern India, which could perhaps never match tropical Bengal, Hodges blames the nature of governance. His account pivots on the lack of 'property', a marker of liberty that he never used directly with regard to British territory.

Hodges's writings and images reach their most pathetic at the former sites infused with the 'liberality and humanity' of Akbar's reign, above all Agra (figs 20, 27), which once 'must have been a perfect garden, but now all is desolation and silence'.[31] Hodges's nostalgia pivots on the recurrent trope of the 'perfect garden', which figured as a moral trope in both English and Indo-Islamic philosophy and poetry. The Urdu *shahr-i ashob* (poetry of the ruined city), agonizes, through reference to the idea of the garden, that *inqilab*, or 'messianic' darkness, has engulfed India:

> Here where the thorn grows, spreading over mounds of dust and ruins,
> These eyes of mine once saw the gardens blooming in the spring.[32]

Although the influence of Mughal poetry on Hodges's paintings can only be surmised, Hastings courted Urdu writers, who no doubt informed his sense of place.[33] Complementing this indigenous literature, Hodges believed Mughal miniatures to be 'documents' of Akbar's India. The frontispiece to *Travels in India* was not one of Hodges's own views but a lavishly coloured engraving after a Mughal miniature of *Two Men under a Tree*. He also included an engraving of a *zenana* (the women's rooms of a Mughal palace), again after a Mughal miniature (fig. 14). His inclusion of Mughal art encourages British viewers to see through Indian images, a technique extended to his prose, as in the description of Bhagalpur:

> The care that was taken in the government and the minute attention to the happiness of the people rendered this district at this time (1781) a perfect paradise. It was not uncommon to see the manufacturer at his loom, in the cool shade, attended by his friend softening his labour by tender strains of music. There are to be met with in India many old pictures representing similar subjects in the happy times of the Mughal government.[34]

Hodges's Orientalist lens filters Mughal art into the Company's regime.[35] Although praising the Mughal depiction of a *zenana* for its 'perfect accuracy' and experiencing the 'offensive' scent of a Lucknawi flower garden 'laid out in the same manner as we see in Indian paintings', his attitude towards Mughal painting pivoted on ambivalence.[36] He deduced that Indian artists had been precluded from the portrayal of nature, retreating to the minute and the ideal, and instead exhorted that 'a constant study of simple nature . . . will produce a resemblance which is sometimes astonishing and which the painter of *ideal objects* never can arrive at'.[37] For Hodges, under Company rule, these Indian pictorial ideals are transformed into reality, as colonial government emulates and translates Mughal aesthetics into the practices of everyday life. Just as Hastings had used Indo-Persian chronicles to legitimize the Company's sovereignty, so Hodges was deploying Mughal miniatures in the construction of a temporally and culturally layered colonial idea of place.

In spite of these strategic mediators, the *Travels* participated in a bitterly contested discourse of bad government that condemned

Fig. 14 W. Skelton after Mughal artist, *A View of the Inside of a Zenanah . . . from an Indian Painting in the Possession of William Hodges R. A.*, engraving, from Hodges (1793). National Maritime Museum, London.

the successor states, especially Company Bengal. For the Bengali elites steeped in *inqilab*, this was a state of emergency. Art collector and chronicler Ghulam Hussein Khan's *Seir Mutaqherin: History of Modern Times* laments the vices of the Company:

> On comparing present times with the past, one is apt to think that the world is overspread with blindness and that the earth is totally overwhelmed with an everlasting darkness . . . If a house that has no owner is not likely to be tenanted, such a house is likely to totter for want of repair . . . and will become ruinous in a short time, so likewise a country of this immense extent, having no apparent master, must in time cease to flourish and at last must fall into decay.[38]

Ironically, his condemnation was translated into English by one of Hastings's supporters to be used in the Governor's trial for impeachment. Ultimately in the parliamentary battle over Hastings, it was not the *Seir Mutaqherin* but Hodges's *Travels* that leapt to the Governor's defence.

Distant suffering: Hastings's empire on the line

In the alternative colonial history generated by his trial, Hastings was publicly condemned for his high-handed governance: his financial corruption, his cruelty towards regional rulers and his servants' torture of Bengalis. Rejecting the lens of Hodges's sparsely populated scenes, Parliament trained its deep focus on the distant suffering of the Company's Indian subjects.

Imperialism transforms terrain to stage, quite literally in the impassioned spectacle of Hastings's trial held in the highly visible space of Westminster Hall before the metropolitan elite.[39] While

Fig. 15 James Gillray, *Blood on Thunder Fording the Red Sea*, engraving, published 1 March 1788 by S. W. Fores. Copyright © British Museum.

Fig. 16 P. A. Martini after H. Ramberg, *The Exhibition of the Royal Academy 1787*, engraving, published 1 July 1787. Copyright © British Museum.

Hodges was publishing his aquatint series *Select Views* (1785–88, dedicated to the East India Company), the Whig opposition under the influence of Edmund Burke, was becoming increasingly preoccupied with the legality and morality of empire. For Burke, Hastings, on quitting Britain, had abandoned Georgian political virtue in favour of arbitrary power, thus distorting India's constitution, which Burke believed to be based on the rule of natural law, not oriental despotism. He described pre-colonial Mughal governance as a happy equilibrium of custom and religion and which should be 'governed upon British principles, not by British forms', a position that now does not seem so very distant from the ideology of Hastings's regime.[40] Yet the differences mattered. Although he enlisted his audience's sympathies for India by portraying it as a virtuous, commercial society, for Burke, Hastings's reign of terror challenged the threshold of the legal and the moral. Burke wanted his London audiences to experience this spatially, temporally distant suffering as directly as possible. Just as his earlier philosophical treatise on the sublime had pushed aesthetic experience to its limits, now his political rhetoric, spotlighting the Company's human subjects, made Hastings's rule an object of almost unrepresentable horror that exceeded his audience's experiences and imaginations, causing its members to faint and Burke himself to collapse. He describes how the inhabitants of Rangpur in Bengal were taken by Hastings's men

> and beaten with bamboo canes upon the soles of their feet until their nails started from their toes . . . The wives of the people of the country lost their honour in the bottom of the most cruel dungeons . . . They put the nipples of the women into the sharp edges of split bamboos and tore them from their bodies.[41]

For graphic satire, such rhetoric stimulated attacks on both Hastings and Burke. James Gillray's *Blood on Thunder forging the Red Sea* (fig. 15) is neither a biblical ocean, nor the Ganges at Benares, but a dead sea of Hastings's rapacity. Although satirical images occasionally envisaged maimed Indians as victims (the mutilated bodies connote Burke's oratorical closure on the Rangpur torture), these prints never refer to Hodges's landscapes. Yet the majority of the trial charges targeted Hastings's foreign policy, events that had occurred in those sites portrayed by Hodges.

At the same time as these parliamentary debates, Hodges was showcasing his paintings at another politicized public forum, the Royal Academy.[42] From 1785 to 1788, he exhibited twenty-two views of India, several of which were the property of Hastings, and seventeen represented sites under direct Company rule. Some of these are featured on the north wall in J. H. Ramberg's view of the Academy exhibition of 1787 (fig. 16).[43] 'On the line' of the prestigious eastern wall, hangs Hodges's *View of Part of the City of Benares*, owned by Hastings. The location of this monumental subject – having the size and public importance of a history painting – demonstrated Hodges's support for Hastings, as well as the Academy's approval for both its newest member and perhaps also for his patron.[44]

In May 1787 when Hodges was being ushered into the Academy, the House of Commons was wrangling over Benares as the grounds for impeachment. Benares inspired Burke's, Grey's and Fox's greatest speeches (including Fox's rhetorical assumption of the character of Chait Singh), as well as unleashing the bitterest confrontation for both sides' 'preservation and recuperation' of Indian traditions. Benares signified Hastings's governance at its most neo-Mughal; he appointed the Indo-Muslim official Ali Ibrahim Khan as judge of the *adalat* (criminal court), effectively allowing him to act as governor.[45] Hodges's reference to the Company as Mughalized protector of Hinduism is strategically envisaged in both the *View of Part of the City of Benares* (RA 1787) and its enormous companion, *Aurangzeb's Mosque, Benares* (RA 1788; see also cat. no. 60). In the latter, the vista complies with a Company rhetoric of paternalism – of continuity with both Hinduism and the Mughal order, epitomized by the central location of the mosque, which according to local tradition, had been constructed on the site of an ancient temple. Hodges believed the Company's possessions to be of equivalent size to Aurangzeb's dominions.[46] Although Aurangzeb was widely blamed for the decline of the Mughal Empire through his religious intolerance and military ambition, at Benares Hinduism still flourished, as the ambivalence of Hastings's regime was located in the very structure of Mughal 'despotism'. Both pictures attracted critical attention:

> In view of local nature, it is difficult for those who have not visited the country to determine what effect may arise from the climate and this makes one hesitate to condemn the chemical tint of Hodges, but his buildings are more positive and in those he always displays a hardness of outline, as well as cast of colouring which strangely suggest the idea of Delft. The present piece [*View of Part of the City of Benares*] which exhibits part of the city of Benares, is executed exactly in the manner alluded to and altogether is cold and heavy.[47]

Perhaps the comparison with Delft refers to the Dutch city's involvement in eastern trade and its identity as an entrepôt dogged by religious dispute and invasion, paralleling Benares. More positively, the following year a different reviewer perceived that Hodges's *Aurangzeb's Mosque, Benares* 'brings us to the very spot and conveys some of the *inquisitiveness* of a voyage to the East Indies' – a curiosity no doubt coloured by public interest in Hastings's trial.[48]

From 1788 to the mid 1790s Hodges stopped exhibiting Indian views at the Royal Academy; likewise the number of graphic satires generated by the trial plummeted, indicative of the wane in public interest as London society sought its spectacle elsewhere. Hodges continued to support Hastings but even art critics grew weary of what they now viewed as his partisan position. Whereas in 1785 journalists praised his Indian landscapes as 'very interesting and classical', displaying 'the evident spirit of a master's pencil', when he again exhibited Indian views in 1794, one critic complained that he 'condescends even to illustrate the *dreary waste* of evidence upon the impeachment of Mr Hastings': these melancholic landscapes signified that the trial itself had become a wasteland.[49] Towards the close of the defence in 1794, (two months before the Royal Academy exhibition), Hodges published his only public representation of Hastings, in which he was not associated with Akbar but allegorized as the wronged Roman governor *Belisarius*, his full-frontal likeness resembling recent portraits and busts by Abbott and Banks. Although Hastings was acquitted in 1795, he was greatly aged and tainted by the controversy surrounding his political ideas. Likewise Hodges's reputation – also exacerbated by events that careered out of his control – was left in tatters.

Fig. 17 Thomas and William Daniell, *The Observatory at Delhi*, 1808, aquatint, from *Antiquities of India* (London, 1799-1808). The British Library, London.

Afterword

Hodges's sophisticated world-view, based on 'an almost involuntary . . . chain of reflections relating to the state of the arts', was condemned by his contemporaries as esoteric, highly personal, even as absurd.[50] In the realm of colonial landscape, he was swiftly eclipsed by Thomas and William Daniell (fl. 1786–94) who travelled as far as Mysore and the Himalayas, transforming their drawings into a massive publication of 144 aquatints, *Oriental Scenery* (1795–1810). Reliant on the *camera obscura*, they located drama not in historical narrative but in formalistic interpretations of architecture, as in their *View of the Delhi Observatory* (fig. 17), whose giddy perspective and diverging curves disclose little of its imperial context.

Like Hastings's hybrid constitution, Hodges's Indian landscapes were soon forgotten, as under the auspices of colonial modernity art split from politics. Anglicizing policies of 'improvement' supplanted the rhetoric of Mughal pasts, while colonial sketching was increasingly confined to the cosseted realm of picturesque tourism. Hodges's contemporaries and successors detected that his patient labyrinth of brushstrokes traced the lineaments of his political physiognomy – each reflecting and infusing the other – which for them was no longer fascinating: Hodges was well and truly history.

[1] See Archer (1965); Archer (1972) for the Company as an art patron. The fashion for Indian and Chinese paintings can be traced through the sales catalogues of Christie's, St James's, 1770–95.

[2] Rohatgi (1995).

[3] Hodges (1793), 149.

[4] Anon, *Peace: An Ode to Warren Hastings*, Hastings Papers, British Library, Add. MS 29,235 lines 142–53 (undated).

[5] Stuebe (1973).

6 Hastings Papers, Add. MS 29,202 volume 5 ff. 188 ff., dated 19 January 1790. This is an account of Hodges's experience of Hastings's annexation of Benares and is very similar to the description in Hodges (1793).

7 At the time he sat to Reynolds, Hastings was also trying to establish a Persian chair at Oxford University, greatly encouraged by Reynolds's friend Samuel Johnson. Marshall (1973), 255.

8 There are at least nineteen documented or surviving European portraits from Hastings's Indian career, as well as six Indian portraits deriving from these and later portraits in England.

9 Hastings's art collection included rare brush sketches of *The Death of Akbar*, *Akbar entertained by Dancers*, and many other images that derived from Akbar's court. See Marshall (1973) and Christie's (1968).

10 Hastings Papers, *Constitution of the Mughal Empire*, British Library, Add. MS 39,892 f.80.

11 Grewal (1970).

12 Marshall (1999), 3.

13 Ibid., 6.

14 Hastings Papers, Add. MS 39,892 ff.38–39.

15 Marshall (1973), 247.

16 Wilson (2000); Travers (2001).

17 Hodges (1790), 404–5.

18 His essay on Wilson praised those images by the artist that displayed a 'broad, bold and manly execution . . . [that] at all times agree with the whole'; Hodges (1790), 86.

19 Pocock (1999), 9.

20 Hastings himself knew Persian and Urdu but no Sanskrit, which as yet was not considered vital for comprehending India's past. It was only in the later 1780s that Hinduism began to rival the importance assumed by the Mughal 'constitution'. Around this date Hodges also began to shift his attention towards Hindu culture, inferring his desire to be seen as an Orientalist keeping abreast of the latest scholarship.

21 Hodges (1793), 144.

22 Murshidabad was in fact becoming an important Shi'ite centre at this time; Asher (1992).

23 On governmentality, see Foucault (1991).

24 Hodges (1793), 15–16 and 27–28.

25 Ibid., 17.

26 This description is of Terriagully, but the painting could relate to several other passages describing this area, for instance Hodges (1793), 87, which refers to a Muslim burial ground and a *dargah*, a subject listed in Cleveland's inventory.

27 Rosaldo (1989).

28 Hodges (1793), 156.

29 Hodges (1785–88), no. 35.

30 Hodges (1793), 106 (my emphasis). Hodges condemned Lucknow as the dirtiest and meanest city he had visited, yet in fact it was being transformed into a fabulous Shi'ite centre by the nawab Asaf ud-daula (1775–97), who was anxious to relieve famine by employing his subjects in such building projects: Sharar (1975).

31 Ibid., 120–21.

32 Russell and Islam (1969), 247.

33 Marshall (1973).

34 Hodges (1793), 27.

35 Ibid., 150.

36 Ibid., 22, 101.

37 Ibid., 151.

38 Ghulam Hussein Khan (1789), vol. 3, 200, 161.

39 Suleri (1991), 49.

40 Marshall (1981), 32–33.

41 Marshall (2000),

42 The same publics who bought political satire, attended the trial and visited the Royal Academy. For the political status of the Royal Academy see Hoock (2000).

43 This signalled a departure from his gift of five oils to the East India Company's court of Directors in 1783, which focused on Akbar and Company foreign policy – a view of Akbar's Tomb at Sikandra, two views of Acbarabad, views of Gwalior and of the nawab of Awadh's palace at Lucknow – and on which they refused to pay the import duties.

44 'On the line' refers to the line that ran around the Great Room at the Royal Academy on which the best pictures were hung: Solkin (2001). Hodges's diploma piece presented to the Royal Academy in 1787 (following his election as ARA in November 1786) was also *A View of the Ghats at Benares*, which was subsequently exhibited in 1788 in the Academy's Council Room.

45 Ali Ibrahim Khan's letters to Hastings mourn his departure saying that if Hastings had stayed in India a great commercial city would have grown up at Benares. He was instrumental in the construction of a rare public monument to Hastings – a ceremonial gateway with music gallery – a signifier of Mughal kingship usually associated with the entrance to a palace or great city (*naubat khana*): Hastings Papers, Add. MS 29,202. During the trial, Hastings's allies gathered petitions from the chief Brahmins and merchants of Benares which were offered in Hastings's defence.

46 Hodges (1793), 17–18.

47 Anonymous review in the press cuttings of Royal Academy reviews, Witt Library, Courtauld Institute, 1787.

48 Anonymous review in ibid., 1788.

49 *Morning Post*, 29 April 1785; *General Advertiser*, 2 May 1785; *Oracle and Public Advertiser*, 29 April 1794.

50 Hodges (1793), 150; Edwards (1808), 250 condemned Hodges's moral landscapes for 'the absurdity of attempting to lead the mind of the spectator into a train of speculative ideas, by the representation of some uninteresting object'.

The artist's 'I' in Hodges's Travels in India

BETH FOWKES TOBIN

William Hodges's *Travels in India* (1793)[1] is remarkable in being one of the earliest published travel accounts by a professional artist. Its importance lies not only in documenting key moments in the rise of the British Raj, but also in raising crucial questions about the politics of travel writing and the relationship between aesthetics and colonialism. In addition to illuminating the ways in which art and literature participate in the colonial process, Hodges's book offers insights into the tensions between those who make art and those who consume it, tensions that have to do with status and social rank.

Sprinkled throughout Hodges's account of his sojourn in India are self-revelatory passages that reveal his anxiety about his social position, his status as an artist, and his tenuous access to cultural authority. Though hired as a draughtsman to document Governor General Warren Hastings's tour through northern India, Hodges presents himself in this book as possessing a gentleman's taste, sensibility and expertise. To bolster his identity as a man of taste, he deploys a variety of means to signal his cultural sophistication, from using georgic tropes to praise British rule in Bengal to casting himself as a scenic tourist with an eye for the picturesque. He also attempts the language of connoisseurship with his dissertation on Hindu architecture and engages in an antiquarian discourse on Mughal ruins. With such verbal gestures, Hodges imitates the language of his social superiors and reveals his aspiration to be regarded less as a draughtsman and more as an artist and humanist; for he pronounces not only on the liberal arts but also on questions of morality and ethical judgment. This essay explores the way in which Hodges draws on a variety of learned and aesthetic discourses to construct an image of himself as intellectually worthy of commenting on South Asian society and cultural production.

The artist as humanist

The ideological implications of Hodges's self-fashioning in his book relate more widely to the status of artists in the eighteenth century. As historians of British culture have argued, central to this was a struggle between professional artists and gentlemen connoisseurs for the privilege of judging aesthetic value and pronouncing on the cultural significance of art and architecture. Prior to the Romantic definition of the artist as genius, painters were commonly regarded as 'mechanics', practitioners of a craft. The intellectual and aesthetic ability to discriminate on the grounds of taste was reserved for the educated connoisseur. As John Brewer has written:

> Gentlemen scholars, critics and collectors were far from ready to concede their authority to mere painters who, since they merely performed the mechanical task of transmuting ideas and theories into tangible objects, were judged of little consequence.[2]

Because professional artists, such as Hodges, often did not have a formal education other than their technical training as artists, they were perceived as less capable than connoisseurs and scholars of engaging in a sophisticated way in humanist accounts of human nature and civil history. The gentlemanly tendency to generalize from observed details and to reflect on larger issues required particular cultural competencies, derived from a combination of elite education and the informal inculcation of legitimate culture within the family.[3]

Opposed to this was the academic position espoused by Sir Joshua Reynolds, President of the Royal Academy, who insisted that the artist's role in society was to profess the liberal arts. In his *Discourses*, Reynolds argued that the artist, through educated reference to classical precepts of ideal beauty, should aspire to represent ideal forms and general human nature. This was only achievable through history painting, which unlike 'the humbler walks of painting', such as landscape or portraiture, could depict 'nature in the abstract', rather than its local or accidental forms.[4] Painting, thus elevated, would be worthy of 'the name of Liberal Art' and 'sister of Poetry'.[5]

For an artist to claim, as Hodges does in his book, that his landscapes were capable of depicting a country's manners and morals was to assert a kind of cultural authority usually reserved for gentlemen and scholars. He proposed that landscape painting should serve a 'moral purpose', similar to history painting, 'to amend the heart while the eye is gratified', as he wrote in the prospectus to his 1794 exhibition.[6] Concluding the *Travels in India*, he writes:

> Pictures are collected from their value as specimens of human excellence and genius exercised in a fine art; and justly are they so: but I cannot help thinking, that they would rise still higher in estimation, were they connected with the history of the various countries, and did they faithfully represent the manners of mankind. (155–6)

With this statement, not only does Hodges step beyond the bounds of decorum and propriety by usurping the gentlemanly discourse on the comparative history of civilizations, but he also asserts the central role of the landscape artist in informing it, and thus challenges contemporary ideas about the status of landscape painting, its purpose, and its pleasures.

The artist as a man of polite imagination

Hodges, however, is acutely aware of the conflict between his professional status as landscape painter and the man of letters that he aspires to be; and that the polite educational requirements for this are denied to him by his profession:

> It is evident that the studies absolutely requisite to any degree of proficiency in a liberal art, and the practice of that art afterwards as a profession, can leave but little leisure for the cultivation of literature; and perhaps my engagements have been even more unfavourable to this object than those of most artists. A long circumnavigation, and the professional labour required in completing the works for Captain Cook's second voyage, occupied me for several years; and a voyage to India, with my different excursions in that country, absorbed no inconsiderable portion of my time and attention. (v)

He acknowledges his debt to other more learned commentators for the information in the book, deferring to the scholarship and expertise of India specialists such as James Rennell and Robert Orme, and disclaims his competence to write on Hindu architecture, prior to launching into a dissertation on the subject.[7] Despite such disavowals, he marshals an array of aesthetic and connoisseurial discourses to mark his narrative as sufficiently

Fig. 18 W. Angus after William Hodges, *The Pass of Sicri Gully from Bengal entering into the Province of Bahar*, engraving, from Hodges (1793). National Maritime Museum, London.

authoritative and to bolster his identity as an expert on India.

In tone, *Travels in India* resembles the published tours of the English, Scottish, and Welsh countryside by Arthur Young or William Gilpin in the recourse to the term 'picturesque' and use of accompanying illustrations. He writes, for instance:

> On the top of the hill is a ruined tomb of a Mussulman sied, or saint. The whole scene appeared to me highly picturesque; a plate, therefore, is given of this view, as it marks the general character of this part of the country. (23) (fig. 18)

Similarly, he describes his travel through the landscape as a 'tour'.[8] He is just as concerned as any picturesque tourist with vantage points from which to view the 'beautiful and extensive prospects' (91). Conceiving the landscape in terms of Claudean tripartite space, attending to the foreground, middle distance, and far distance, in a manner made popular by Gilpin's tours in search of the picturesque, he describes Nawab Shuja-ud-daulah's palace at Lucknow:

> on the foreground of the pictures is one of the pavilions, and on a high bank is a mosque, with two minarets; and adjoining is a durgaw, or burial place, with a view of the river. The picture from which the print was engraved was painted on the spot.' (102) (fig. 19)

Hodges makes use of georgic and pastoral imagery to describe fertile and prosperous lands, which he implies owe their well-being to judicious British rule, concluding that the country about Colgong is 'the most beautiful I have seen in India' (25), where the Ganges 'gives the prospect inexpressible grandeur' (25–6). He praises his friend, Augustus Cleveland, the district collector of Bhagalpur, for his good management of the region: 'The care that was taken in the government, and the minute attention to the happiness of the people, rendered this district, at this time, (1781) a perfect paradise' (27). Here the industry of the peasantry was rewarded with plenty, and Bengal, under the rule of Governor

Fig. 19 J. Fittler after William Hodges, *A View of the Palace of the Nabob Asoph ul Dowlah at Lucknow*, engraving, from Hodges (1793). National Maritime Museum, London.

General Hastings, boasts of agricultural bounty and paradisiacal green: 'The periodical rains had now commenced, and every natural object presented a new face, with such a freshness of verdure, and with such vigour and fullness of foliage, that all nature appeared in the utmost luxuriance' (38). In contrast is Muslim-ruled India, particularly the country between Allahabad and Fyzabad, which Hodges depicts as a barren landscape filled with impoverished peasants:

> After leaving the flourishing district of Benares, I could not help viewing with a melancholy concern the miserable appearance of all the territories which were under the absolute direction of Mussulman tyrants. (107)

Hodges resorts to antiquarian and connoisseurial idioms to describe India's cultural landscape and built environment. Mughal architecture is described in terms of antiquarian narratives:

> The fort of Chunar is situated on the Ganges, near twenty miles above the city of Benares: it is built on a rock, which is fortified all round by a wall, and towers at various distances. At that end overlooking the river is situated the citadel, which has formerly been strong. This fort is said to be of the highest antiquity, and originally built by the Hindoos. In the citadel there is an altar, consisting of a plain black marble slab, on which the tutelary deity of the place is traditionally at all times supposed to be seated, except from sun-rise until nine o'clock in the morning, when he is at Benares, during which time, from the superstition of the Hindoos, attacks may be made with a prospect of success. In various parts of the fort there are old sculptures of the Hindoo divinities, now nearly defaced by time. There are likewise on the gates some old Persian inscriptions, mentioning in whose reign, and by whom, the fort was repaired and strengthened. (55–6)

In general, local history for Hodges usually features Mughal impe-

rial history of the seventeenth century with references to mid-eighteenth-century conflicts between British and Mughal rulers.[9]

Hodges also resorts to connoisseurship, most notably in his dissertation on Indian architecture and its relation to Greek architecture. This involves not only aesthetic evaluation but also a comparative mode of analysis, such as his comparison between the mosque at Mounheer [Maner] (cat. no. 53) and European architectural forms, above all Gothic. In his description of this 'certainly very beautiful' building, he judges Indian dome design to be aesthetically superior to European style.[10]

Though Hodges can appreciate the beauty of Mughal architecture and does not display Eurocentric chauvinism toward Hindu and Mughal building, he repeatedly remarks that Indian architecture, particularly Mughal mosques, forts, and palaces are in a state of decay and ruination. Typical is the final comment on the mosque at Mounheer: 'The whole, however, is much decayed.' (46)

Indeed, Hodges has frequent recourse to the discourse on ruins. As part of his attempt to produce for himself a cultured identity, Hodges positions himself within the powerful debate that circulated among British poets, antiquarians, connoisseurs, and admirers of the picturesque. Central to this 'cult of ruins' is the idea of the sensitive spectator.[11] Ruins not only elicited antiquarian curiosity and connoisseurial expertise, but also encouraged reflection on the mutability of the human condition and the vanity of human wishes. Hodges's description of Agra, accompanying the *View of Agra* (fig. 20), is worth considering at length:

> The whole of this spot, as far as the eye can reach, is one general scene of ruined buildings, long walls, vast arches, parts of domes, and some very large buildings, as the Cuttera, built by the great Shah Hest Khawn, in the reign of Aurungzebe; here are also several Tombs. (113–14)

Surveying Agra's ruins, Hodges anchors the city's lost vitality in the irretrievable past of the great sixteenth- and seventeenth-century Mughal emperors' reigns. Everywhere he looks are remains,

Fig. 20 J. Walker after William Hodges, *A View of Agra taken from the South West*, engraving, from Hodges (1793). National Maritime Museum, London.

confirming that Mughal power to create magnificent structures of 'eastern elegance' (114) is exhausted, dissipated by the extravagance and intemperance of its rulers.

> The whole space between these two walls is one mass of ruins. The inner wall is but in indifferent repair, and within it is easy to discern that it is chiefly composed from the ruined buildings, except, indeed, towards the Delhi gate of the fort, where is the great Musjud or Mosque, built of red stone, but greatly gone to decay. Adjacent to this spot is the Choke, or Exchange, which is now a mere ruin; and even the fort itself, from its having frequently changed masters, in the course of the last seventy years, is going rapidly to desolation . . . It was impossible to contemplate the ruins of this grand and venerable city, without feeling the deepest impressions of melancholy. I am, indeed, well informed, that the ruins extend, along the banks of the river, not less than fourteen English miles. (118)

In addition to the ancient grandeur of these ruins, Hodges emphasizes his own response of melancholy, a theme he develops in the ensuing discussion of Akbar's tomb at Sikandra, where the 'present solitude that reigns over the whole of the neglected garden, excites involuntarily a melancholy pensiveness'. His conclusion, significantly, is a moral one: 'This fine country exhibits, in its present state, a melancholy proof of the consequences of a bad government, of wild ambition, and the horrors attending civil dissentions.' (122–3)

Hodges's meditation on the use and abuse of Mughal power confirm his status as an enlightened observer of the Oriental scene, and in calling attention to his own response of melancholy, he also assumes the identity of a man of taste. He claims a kind of social distinction when he tell his readers that, upon viewing Agra and Akbar's tomb, he was moved to contemplate the vagaries of history and to indulge in a state of elevated sensibility. His melancholic reverie is, in part, his attempt to appear, as Addison would say, 'a Man of Polite Imagination', whose elite status, and consequent distinction from the vulgar crowd, is signalled by his 'capacity for aesthetic pleasure'.[12] Casting himself in this instance as a scenic tourist rather than a working painter, Hodges aspires to the role of a gentleman of taste and learning, and in the process characterizes Mughal cultural achievements in such a way as to relegate them permanently to the past and to the realm of inevitable decay.

The artist as Orientalist

Hodges's confession of melancholy not only helps to establish his credentials as a man of genius and learning, but also performs significant ideological work from an Orientalist perspective.[13] His melancholy is aroused not by regret and longing for the return of the glorious reign of Akbar, but by a nostalgia for that which is completely unrecoverable. Susan Stewart has written of the desires aroused by antiques and souvenirs: 'Nostalgia is a sadness without an object. A sadness which creates a longing that of necessity is inauthentic because it does not take part in lived experience'. For these reasons, 'the nostalgic is enamored of distance, not of the referent itself. Nostalgia cannot be sustained without loss.'[14] For Hodges as well as all those ruin enthusiasts in Britain, loss is a necessary condition for the creation of nostalgia. For those who love ruins, it is the assurance that a previous political order and social system are indeed lost that enables their pleasurable feelings of sadness. The picturesque framing of Hodges's visual and verbal views of Agra's ruins produces 'an elegiac acknowledgment of their vacated power'.[15] Likewise, Anne Janowitz contends that melancholy, the 'peculiar pleasure' of viewing ruins, 'comes from the contemplation of the absolute pastness of the past within the aesthetically controlled shape of temporal transience'. This melancholy is the result of the 'social function' of landscape having been 'evacuated' to become 'an empty world' where 'private functions and feelings can then fill it up'.[16] In this way Hodges's travel narrative, even in its meditative moments, constructs two distinct temporal frames, locating Mughal and Hindu India in the past and British India in the present. In portraying Mughal architecture as picturesque ruins, Hodges's representation of India participates in the on going construction of a British Orientalist doctrine, which, as Homi Bhabha argues, depicted 'India as a primordial fixity – as a narcissistic inverted other – that satisfies the self-fulfilling prophecy of Western progress'.[17]

Implicit in Hodges's system of cultural analysis and aesthetic evaluation is the subsistence theory of human development, which, if he had not consulted the relevant treatises himself, he would have learned at second hand through contact with the Forsters on Cook's second voyage. According to this model of human history, progress towards civilization could be divided into four stages, from the hunter-gatherer, to a pastoral, nomadic stage, to agricultural settlement, and finally to the highest stage, that of commercial society.[18] European countries, as commercial nations, comprised the highest developmental stage, while Mughal India was seen as feudal, one stage behind Europe. Other parts of India were supposedly still further behind, in the hunting and pastoral eras.[19] Hodges characterizes Hindu culture as ancient and non-evolved, and exemplified by Benares:

> [T]he same manners and customs prevail amongst these people at this day, as at the remotest period that can be traced in history . . . According to universal report, this is one of the most ancient of Hindoo cities; and if the accounts of their own antiquity may be depended upon, it is, perhaps, the oldest in the world. It certainly is curious, and highly entertaining to an inquisitive mind, to associate with a people whose manners are more than three thousand years old. (59)

For Orientalists, Hindu culture was static and unchanged since the earliest stages of human society while Mughal society, by contrast, was seen as much more evolved. According to Orientalist thought, India's glorious ruins were the product of the Mughal feudal society, which, however, had not progressed to the next developmental stage because of the ruinous influence of climate and intermarriage with less developed indigenous populations.[20] This notion of history, while depicting progress as natural, also allows for the possibility of stagnation or regression. Mughal society's progress, according to British Orientalist thinking, had halted with the death of the great Mughal emperors of the seventeenth century. Hodges's melancholy faced with Mughal ruins can be read as his acknowledgment of the potential possessed by Mughal culture to progress to the highest development stage and his regret that Mughal society was the victim of cyclical forces of decay that seemed inevitable in India, with the exception, of course, of British rule.

The artist as natural historian

Hodges's concern with architecture as a measure of a society's degree of civilization predates by more than half a century the work of James Fergusson, who argued that architecture was the only reliable means of constructing 'a scientific history of India'.[21] Hodges lays claim to a particular kind of ethnographic authority in treating architecture as a measure of a society's civility, stating that *Travels in India* is 'a work professedly dedicated, in some measure, to the history and progress of the arts in India' (63).

The way in which he secures for himself this cultural authority, bestowing on artists the ability to judge another culture's artistic productions, is through reference to 'the eye', making use of this in a manner typical of picturesque touring literature.[22]

This word 'eye' had been used throughout the century in a variety of aesthetic discourses, including pastoral, georgic, and topographical poetry as well as travel writing. Poets such as Dyer, Thomson, Cowper, and Wordsworth all refer to what the 'eye' sees when the viewer gazes on the prospect afforded by the vantage point of a place such as Grongar Hill. John Barrell has argued convincingly that this idea of the prospect is associated with privilege and in particular with the landed elite and the politics of taste.[23] Connoisseurs also used the phrase of having an 'eye' to explain their ability to respond to and evaluate a work of art. Having an 'eye' was tantamount to having good taste.

However, Hodges pushes the boundaries of this metaphor beyond evaluating art and architecture by linking having 'an eye' with a capacity for evaluating a country's social practices and national character. He extends the ability to appreciate views of a nation's cultural productions and natural landscape to include an ability to assess its state of civilization. In discussing Hindu sculpture, Hodges uses the phrase 'the eyes of the artist' to certify the excellence of his taste and to lend credence to his connoisseurial distinctions between the aesthetic merits of different societies' cultural productions:

> I am concerned I cannot pay so high a compliment to the art of sculpture among the Hindoos as is usually paid by many ingenious authors who write on the religion of Bramah. Considering these works, as I do, with the eyes of an artist, they are only to be paralleled with the rude essays of the ingenious Indians I have met with in Otaheite, and on other islands in the South Seas. The time when these sculptures were produced I believe is not easy to ascertain; but this much is certain, that the more modern works in sculpture of human figures, by the Hindoos, lay claim to very little more merit than the ancient productions. Some ornaments, however, that I have seen on Hindoo temples are beautifully carved. (26–7)

With this discursive strategy, he links ethnography with aesthetic sensibility, giving himself license to evaluate Mughal and Hindu art, architecture, design, and sculpture and to read national character into these art forms.

Hodges further aligns art with natural history through curiosity. He refers to curiosity repeatedly to signal his engagement with natural historical questions about the country's 'customs and manners' and to draw attention to the inquisitive quality of his mind. He writes, for instance, 'At a little distance from Rajemahel are the ruins of a zananah, which I went from curiosity to inspect, as they are when inhabited sacred spaces' (21–2). Having a curious mind was a sign of intelligence and willingness to explore the unknown, and was an attribute that carried great weight with travellers, explorers, and natural historians. Curiosity also licensed all sorts of inquiries into other cultures' social practices, which, as Nicholas Thomas has demonstrated, frequently ignored local customs and transgressed bounds of hospitality.[24] Curiosity led Hodges to view several "exotic" scenes, most dramatic being a sati, or widow burning, and, among the hill tribes, a ritual sacrifice of a buffalo (92–3). Curiosity also led him to seek out subjects to draw, including a 'Hindoo monk' (26), sepoys, merchants, Hindoo pallankeen bearers, bathing women, and meditating Bramins. Such 'picturesque groups' were 'valuable subjects for the painter' (31–2), and Hodges states that 'several of the subjects I had collected in my journey' were used later to produce pictures for Hastings (36). He represents himself as artist-explorer and ethnographer, using the language of natural history to cement that identity as producer of knowledge.

Linking art-making with the quest for scientific information and 'truth', he proposes that any future artists travelling to India should go from Benares to Surat, as 'this is a part of India untrodden by an artist' and 'much matter might be collected relative to the state of ancient India . . . [that] would add greatly to our stock of knowledge relative to the Eastern continent' (154). Hodges insists on the importance of the artist not only to the process of gathering information about other cultures but also to understanding national character. Whole parts of India, he says, have yet to be explored by the 'enterprizing artist', and he cites the Malabar coast as being particularly rich in 'picturesque beauty . . . how valuable would be the representation of that scenery, whether as a natural object, or as connected with the history of the country, and the manners of the people?' (155). He concludes by enumerating the three qualities in the painter requisite to such a task: 'a perfect knowledge of his art, and with powers to execute readily and correctly; judgment to chuse his subjects; and fancy to combine and dispose them to advantage' (155). However, these qualities must be carefully balanced to represent 'real and natural character':

> the imagination must be under the strict guidance of cool judgment, or we shall have fanciful representations instead of the truth, which, above all, must be the object of such researches. (155)

In 1793, Hodges summarized his thinking about art's relationship to 'truth', writing to a friend:

> truth is the base of every work of mine – and through the various countries I have passed my endeavors have unvariedly aimed, to give the manners of mankind in the varied shades from the Savage in the wilds to the highly civilized in the palace.[25]

When Hodges in his *Travels* doubles as a consumer of scenic landscapes and as a producer of landscape paintings, he alternates between connoisseurship, which assumed a leisured, amateur status associated with the English gentleman on the Grand Tour, and the artisan's need to work to support himself. In positioning himself as a connoisseur of Hindu and Mughal architecture, he reaches for a social standing hitherto reserved for the educated upper classes. Yet as a paid producer of picturesque images he had to labour, which threatened his tenuous grip on the role of gentleman scholar to which he aspires in this text. At the same time as he uses the language of aesthetics in his *Travels* to consolidate his identity as a gentleman and a professional expert, he also uses it ethnographically to characterize the peoples and cultures of the northern sub-continent. In this activity, Hodges falls into the Orientalist practice, which men like Warren Hastings and Sir William Jones encouraged, that simultaneously created India as decayed, luxuriant and timeless, and England as vigorous, rational, and an agent of history. National identity and class position are subtexts in Hodges's *Travels*, and it is the language of aesthetics that enables him, in part, to create for himself and his fellow

Britons an imperialist identity grounded in the idea of expertise that would serve these British sojourners well in this colonial context.

[1] Page references to this text are given in parenthesis in the main body of the essay, following the citation.

[2] Brewer (1997), 259.

[3] Bourdieu (1984), 28.

[4] Reynolds (1975), 57.

[5] Ibid., 50.

[6] See Appendix, below.

[7] Rennell (1778) and Orme (1782). See Hodges (1793), 19, 59, 63, 100.

[8] For example, his excursion through the Jungleterry: Hodges (1793), 87.

[9] Exemplary is the description of the fort of Allahabad: ibid., 98–9.

[10] Ibid., 45–6.

[11] Andrews (1989).

[12] Joseph Addison, *The Spectator*, no. 411 (21 June 1712).

[13] See Said (1978) and Said (1993).

[14] Stewart (1993), 23, 145.

[15] See Suleri (1992), 83.

[16] Janowitz (1990), 1, 62.

[17] Bhabha (1994), 98. India's present is Britain's past, or as the Daniells wrote, 'the present inhabitants . . . present the image of a remote and almost obsolete antiquity': Daniell (1810), i.

[18] See Bindman (2002) and his essay in this catalogue.

[19] See Wheeler (2000).

[20] See Cohn (1996), 79, 92.

[21] Ibid., 92.

[22] See, for instance, his description of arriving in India to be confronted by new and pleasant sights, by which 'the eye being thus gratified, the mind soon assumes a gay and tranquil habit, analogous to the pleasing objects with which it is surrounded': Hodges (1793), 2.

[23] Barrell (1992).

[24] For curiosity as a concept, see Benedict (1990); Chard (1999), 26–30; Thomas (1994).

[25] William Hodges to William Hayley, 27 April 1793, cited in Steube (1979), 2.

Hodges and Indian architecture

GILES TILLOTSON

There are five curious Pagodas [i.e. temples] here [at Deogarh], of perhaps the very oldest construction to be found in India. They are simply pyramids, formed by piling stone on stone, the apex is cut off at about one seventh of the whole height of the complete pyramid, and four of them have small ornamental buildings on the top, evidently of more modern work, which are finished by an ornament made of copper, and gilt, perfectly resembling the trident of the Greek Neptune.

William Hodges, *Travels in India*

Vimanas [towered shrines] are of three sorts, distinguished one from another by the principal materials of which they are formed, as *sud'ha*, pure; *misra*, mixed; and *sancirna*, anomalous. An edifice is called *sud'ha* which is composed of but one kind of material, as stone, brick &c., and this is considered the best of all. *Misra* is that which is composed of two kinds of material, as brick and stone, or stone and metals; and *sancirna* is that which is composed of three or more kinds of materials, as timber, stone, brick, metal, &c.

Ram Raz, *Essay on the Architecture of the Hindus*

These two passages both describe aspects of Indian temple construction, but they reveal somewhat different approaches to the subject. The first forms part of Hodges's description of the pilgrimage centre at Deogarh in Bihar (cat. no. 63).[1] It exemplifies his interest in what might be called architecture's genealogy: his chief concern is to place the temples correctly within a chronological development, assigning to them an early date, in spite of their modern-looking tops. He is also interested in their outer form, and in whatever connections they may suggest with western civilization (however specious). The second passage by contrast is not concerned with developments over time at all. It does not even describe specific temples. Its purpose is rather to define a system of classification, and to establish a hierarchy, that will guide the reader's understanding of temples in general, both actual and those yet unbuilt.

The second passage is taken from a famous ancient Sanskrit work on architecture, the *Manasara*, as translated by the early nineteenth-century scholar Ram Raz. With its focus on paradigms rather than particulars, the passage is typical of the genre of literature to which the text belongs, namely the *shilpa shastras* (or 'design treatises'). Such texts cover a range of topics from the units of measurement to the planning and social organization of cities; and together they articulate in writing the theoretical basis that underpins India's developed practical architectural traditions.

During the period of Western hegemony, foreign control over public building and changing fashions in domestic styles tended to eclipse traditional Indian architectural practices, and Indian theoretical ideas in the field correspondingly were gradually marginalized and fragmented.[2] The efforts of Ram Raz did not prevent the *shilpa shastras* from becoming lost to scholarly view. Consequently, when the modern historiography of Indian architecture was undertaken in the nineteenth century, the mostly English authors drew not on this obscured indigenous intellectual tradition but on the legacy of an earlier phase of foreign study.[3] They looked particularly to the work of the topographical artists of the previous century such as Thomas and William Daniell and – the pioneer – William Hodges. How Hodges represented India's architecture in his pictures and in his writing can therefore be regarded as having been a major force in shaping contemporary and future perceptions of it. But the character of Hodges's vision can still be thrown into relief by contrasting it with indigenous understandings of the subject, because Indian ideas – though fragmented – are not altogether lost: they are capable of being reconstructed through both texts and images that can be set alongside those produced by Hodges.[4] Pursuing this exercise in comparisons will serve to illustrate a wider point. As we seek with hindsight to describe and explain European understandings and representations of Asia during the colonial era, we may be assisted if we have some answers to the obvious question: how else might things have been done? How, for example, did Asians themselves understand and represent their own cultural traditions? European agency – even when it was supported by colonial power, and even when unaware of local intellectual traditions (as Hodges was) – did not operate in a void, for the material it sought to order was (in Asian minds) already ordered. Is it possible that exploring Indian representations of his subjects will refine our perception of Hodges?

Shahdara and Sikandra

A large late-eighteenth-century Indian painting on cloth (fig. 21)[5] depicts the tomb of the Mughal Emperor Jahangir at Shahdara, just north of Lahore. Begun in 1628, the tomb is one in a sequence of Mughal imperial mausolea, being preceded by the tombs of Humayun in Delhi (1560s) and of Akbar at Sikandra (1606–12), and followed by the Taj Mahal in Agra (1630s). Like all of the others in the sequence it stands within a formal garden, which is bounded by a wall with pavilions and is entered through a gate and a forecourt. To include all of these parts within a single image, the artist has used a variety of different points of view at once. Thus the garden and the forecourt are shown in plan, while the walls, the pavilions and the gates are shown in elevation, and the tomb itself is shown in a sort of aerial perspective.

This amalgamation of many viewpoints is not arbitrary or naïve, but carefully considered. The choice of angle from which each component part is seen relates to the role the part plays in the architectural ensemble. Thus the garden is shown in plan to reveal more clearly that it is a *chahar bagh* (a Persian paradise garden). It is the plan – the subdivision into squares by water channels – that gives the *chahar bagh* its meaning as a reflection of the heavenly paradise, a meaning of direct relevance to its purpose in a tomb complex. Around this garden, the walls, the pavilions and the gate are points of entry and enclosure. The artist has shown them in elevation because that is how a visitor to the site experiences them: they are boundaries of which we normally only see one side. The tomb building alone is shown three-dimensionally because it is the only part that the visitor walks around, and because this view draws our attention to the sarcophagus on the top.

This style of representation seems to be focused more on the meanings of the building complex and its parts than on their appearance. The painting does not show us what Jahangir's tomb looks like from one single given place; rather, it assumes and reinforces our understanding of its constituent elements and the roles they play in the ensemble. A telling detail in this regard is the

Fig. 21 Anonymous Indian artist, *Jahangir's tomb at Shahdara*, 146 x 130 cm, gouache on cloth (framed under glass), Royal Asiatic Society.

coincidence between the garden wall and the picture's border. A paradise garden creates an inward-looking and self-contained world: it is not a passage in a landscape, its surrounding wall is a barrier raised against the environment. The artist has reflected that idea by making the wall define the picture's edge.

To suggest that the complex is shown conceptually is not to say that the image is not also visual. The point is rather that the painting does not reproduce one particular sight but brings together a collection of sights and ideas, the composite of our experiences as we move around the complex. Again there is a telling detail: while the garden is shown in plan for the reason suggested, the trees within it are shown in elevation, in accordance with our common mental image of trees. In our mind's eye we see a *chahar bagh* as a plan and trees as upright, and the artist has sought to unite these two mental images in one.

This painting is unusual but it is far from unique. A similar treatment of a similar subject can be observed in a painting on

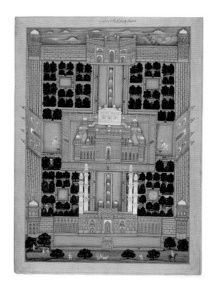

Fig. 22 Jaipur artist, *The Tomb of the Mughal Emperor Akbar at Sikandra*, c.1780, water-colour, 53.7 x 37.2cm. The British Library, London.

Fig. 23 J. Brown after William Hodges, *A View of the Gate of the Tomb of the Emperor Akbar at Secundrii*, 1786, engraving. Copyright © British Museum.

Fig. 24 Thomas and William Daniell, *The Gate of Akbar's Tomb at Sikandra*, 1789, water-colour. Christie's Images.

paper depicting Akbar's tomb at Sikandra (fig. 22).[6] Here again the main tomb building is shown from an aerial perspective, and the garden is shown in plan, but the trees are shown in elevation, as are the gates and the wall, the latter defining the picture's edge. The very close similarity between this painting and another (now in a private collection)[7] suggests that such pictures were copied, and thus were once produced in large quantities.

English depictions of the same site, by Hodges and by the Daniells (figs 23 and 24) reveal a markedly different approach not only to picture-making but even to architecture itself. The use of single-point perspective has the effect not only of situating buildings in space; it also situates us as observers in relation to them. In the Indian painting our eye is not fixed in one place, but both Hodges and the Daniells tether us securely in the south-east corner of the complex, outside the main gate. They therefore show us only part of the whole, only as much as we can see from this single spot. Each of their pictures is a record not of our experience and knowledge of a complex site, but of one act of seeing it. They imply an approach to architecture as an object of vision more than as something to be understood.

So the English pictures are more about seeing, about appearances, but this is not to suggest that they are naturalistic, or that they replicate our visual experience. Both are highly charged with aesthetic conventions – though they differ from each other in this regard. Hodges (fig. 23)[8] has distorted some of the architectural forms to make them more accessible to his European audience, for example by adding a Gothic ogee pinch to the gate's arches, and by introducing an entirely fictitious ruined Gothic abbey porch as a foreground object. The scattering of rather classical-seeming fragments on the ground suggests that he is trying to give Sikandra the Piranesi treatment and thus to compare it with Rome.

At first sight, the watercolour by the Daniells (fig. 24)[9] appears more immediate and spontaneous. Indeed the detail and clutter included here – the tents and some of the officers and the sepoys of the artists' military escort – far from de-historicizing the scene, place it very specifically in time as well as in space. For this is not merely the view as you see it from this particular spot, but as it was seen on 25 January 1789, the day that this particular group of people stopped by. Even more emphatically than Hodges's image, this is a record of an act of seeing. But even here, aesthetics intrude: the shadow in the foreground is cast by convention, not by any real object or unevenness in the ground. Its purpose is to project our eye into the picture's middle ground, to create a sense of scale, and so to enhance the impression of the building as a sculptural object of visual contemplation.

When Hodges and the Daniells travelled through it, the region around Agra and Sikandra was under the control of the Marathas – hence the need for the military escort. After the Mughal cities were taken by the British in 1803, they became more accessible

Fig. 25 Delhi or Agra artist, *The Gate of Akbar's Tomb at Sikandra*, c.1808, water-colour, 64.1 x 81.9 cm. The British Library, London.

Fig. 26 Anonymous Indian artist, *Red Fort at Agra*, 54 x 37 cm, gouache on paper. V&A Picture Library.

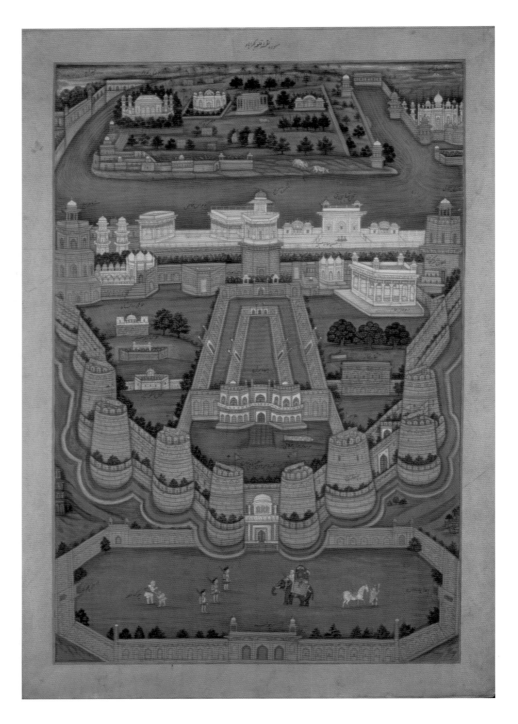

Fig. 27. William Hodges, *Agra Fort from the North East*, 1783, pencil and wash, 47.7 x 100.3 cm. Yale Center for British Art, Paul Mellon Collection.

to European visitors and this early tourist trade gave rise to a genre of so-called Company painting in the form of images of Mughal monuments made by local artists for European consumption. Such paintings seek to reconcile, but actually highlight, the differences between the earlier Indian and English depictions of the same subjects. In a typical image of the gateway at Sikandra, made in Delhi or Agra about 1808 (fig. 25),[10] the artist has adopted something approaching single-point perspective and thus like an English artist focuses our attention on one part of the complex rather than the whole. But the point of view is also shifted to a frontal location so as to eliminate the symmetry-distorting effect of the angled view.

The introduction of perspective marks one step towards reproducing a visual experience. But it is not accompanied by the introduction of naturalistic light effects, as the scene is evenly lit from all directions. The decision to include all of the details of the gateway's stone inlay decoration similarly militates against any illusion of light and space. It is as though the artist wished to remain faithful to all that could be shown.

The conceptual habits that are characteristic of an Indian artist are revealed in two important details. Standing in front of this gateway, one cannot in fact see any part of the actual tomb, concealed behind. But the artist knew it to be there and in the space below the central arch has depicted the all-important interior of the tomb's uppermost enclosure around the sarcophagus, thus re-introducing the (invisible) focus of the whole site. Secondly, in the years before and after 1800, the gateway's corner minarets

lacked their crowning *chhatris* (pavilions), as the views by Hodges and the Daniells attest (they were not restored until a hundred years later, on the orders of Lord Curzon). But the Indian artist has corrected this imperfection to show the building not as it was but as it ought to be. And so in spite of the desire to appeal to a European clientele, the artist has depicted the building with an Indian eye, having a view to its meaning and its wholeness, rather than merely reproducing appearances.

Agra and Fatehpur Sikri

A view of Agra Fort dating to around 1803 (fig. 26)[11] shows a similar treatment to the pre-Company views of Shahdara and Sikandra with multiple perspectives contained within a generally aerial view. In this case, though, structures have been relocated and the line of the fort wall has been redrawn to suit the picture's ordered scheme. The two previous subjects, the tomb complexes, both follow Mughal conceptions of symmetry and order, and in representing them the Indian artists have respected those principles. But the fort at Agra and the structures within it were built over three successive reigns from Akbar to Shah Jahan, and although their sequence makes perfect sense in terms of court ritual they are not disposed symmetrically. And so the artist has considerably imposed this lacking order. The perimeter wall has been made into a perfect 'D' shape when in fact it is quite irregular; and the main western gate has been aligned with the bastion

Fig. 28 Delhi or Agra artist, *Panorama of the Agra Fort* (detail), c.1815, water-colour. Royal Asiatic Society, London.

Fig. 29 Delhi or Agra artist, *Gateway at Futtypoor Sicri [Fatehpur Sikri]*, c.1808, water-colour, 68.7 x 77.5 cm. The British Library, London.

known as the Mussaman Burj, which has been made to project inwards to face the viewer rather than outwards over the river. On the far bank, the tomb of Itimad-ud-daulah and the Chini ka Rauza have been compressed into a space immediately opposite the fort (they should be out of view to the north, or left), and the bend in the river is truncated to allow the Taj Mahal to appear at the far right (it is much further away to the south-east).

There can be little doubt that this image is intended to be a visual record of Agra – that it is in that sense a topographical picture – but the intention has been mediated by a variety of forces: by the artist's desire to show all of the components that contribute to the whole; by the principles of Indian architectural composition, not always carried through in practice but respected and enforced by the artist; and by the conventions of Indian painting that stress wholeness.

No such concerns constrained Hodges, whose drawing of Agra Fort (fig. 27)[12] is mediated by quite different preoccupations. Obliged by European convention to select one point of view, Hodges chose a view of what he took to be the fort's most distinctive feature, its river front. The one common factor was the desire to include the Taj Mahal, though the angle chosen by Hodges permitted him to do this without distortion.[13] It is perhaps ironic that his picturesque aesthetic would have sanctioned a measure of relocation for the sake of the composition. The difference is that while the picturesque promotes irregularity and asymmetry, the Indian artist has relocated buildings in order to impose a non-existent regularity. They were pursuing opposed aesthetics.

A typical Company period scroll painting (fig. 28)[14] again highlights these differences even as it attempts to negotiate a middle path. The artist has selected the riverside view that was favoured by European patrons, but in order to include every structure, clearly labelled, has adopted a sort of rolling perspective. The eye moves in a continuous line across the fort wall, so that each apartment is viewed in the same perspective, and the picture has an ever-receding vanishing point rather than one fixed in the centre.

On 23 March 1783, Hodges reached Fatehpur Sikri. Already an admirer of the Emperor Akbar and his works, he began to explore the imperial complex, and he was particularly struck by the great mosque and by the Buland Darwaza, the vast portal attached to its southern side. 'On the summit of the highest hill', he wrote later, 'is a large mosque, which was built by Acbar. The building is in a high style of Moorish architecture. The ascent from the foot of the hill is by a flight of broad steps, extending to the principal entrance, which is through a portal of great magnificence.'[15] The drawing that Hodges made on the spot (fig. 59) illustrates the extent to which his picturesque aesthetic can be in conflict both with his desire to reveal Indian topography as accurately as possible, and with the Indian aesthetics of his architectural subjects. His rock-strewn uneven ground, overhanging ruin and distant monument are all textbook picturesque, but scarcely convey the spirit of the place. The area is dominated by the Buland Darwaza, which stands over 130 feet high and is one of the proudest statements of Mughal architecture. It is rather more Timurid than 'Moorish' in style; but it hardly matters at this distance: Hodges's view shows it obliquely from behind, dwarfed by lesser buildings, and barely recognizable.

Perhaps it was because of such tensions with Indian aesthetics that the picturesque did not appeal greatly to Indian artists. Even when they were working for European customers, they were slow to adopt the full range of picturesque conventions. An interesting exception to this – and one which might be said to prove the rule, given the method of transmission involved – is the pair of Indian drawings that are copies of two of Hodges's aquatints. One of these (fig. 60)[16] is based on Hodges's aquatint version of the drawing just discussed. This diminished version of the Buland Darwaza

Fig. 30 William Hodges, *The Taj Mahal*, c.1783, oil on canvas, 90.2 x 152.4 cm. National Gallery of Modern Art, New Delhi.

hardly accords with Indian artists' more usual treatment of Mughal architecture and could only have been achieved by copying. A more typical Company rendering of this subject (fig. 29)[17] restores the gate's scale, splendour and symmetry.

The most challenging subject for an artist depicting Mughal architecture is no doubt its most famous monument, the Taj Mahal. Hodges was perhaps a little daunted: at an early stage of the production of *Select Views* he promised his customers an aquatint devoted to it, but he did not deliver, in spite of having sketched it on site.[18] He did however produce a fine work in oils (fig. 30),[19] which shows it from what he said he considered the best point of view:

> When this building is viewed from the opposite side of the river, it possesses a degree of beauty, from the perfection of the materials and from the excellence of the workmanship, which is only surpassed by its grandeur, extent, and general magnificence. The basest material that enters into this center part of it is white marble, and the ornaments are of various coloured marbles, in which there is no glitter: the whole together appears like a most perfect pearl on an azure ground. The effect is such as, I confess, I never experienced from any work of art.[20]

The Taj Mahal of course became a favourite subject among Company artists and their customers. Views of the monument and details of its ornament account for more than half of all Company paintings of Mughal architecture. A typical view that was frequently copied shows it obliquely and with an attention to perspective that would appease the most demanding European eye (fig. 31).[21] The treatment of the paving on the podium in particular reveals a dazzling dexterity in the handling of perspective that surpasses that of many European artists, including Hodges. But emulating Western art was not the Company painters' only – or even chief – concern. The absence of a landscape context and of strong light effects from their images implies a continuing resistance to the picturesque. Even more telling is the inclusion of all of the details of the tomb's surface ornament. If one stands sufficiently far back from the Taj Mahal to have such a perspective view then the details of the *pietra dura* are obscured; one can only appreciate its colour and precision by approaching. But the Company artist gives us both outline and detail, so that here too (as in the pre-Company paintings) there is more than a single point of view: the near and the far.[22]

Fig. 31 Delhi or Agra artist, *West Side of the Taaj Mahl at Agra*, c.1808, water-colour, 68.7 x 99.7 cm. The British Library, London.

Hodges and architectural theory

All of the subjects that have been mentioned so far are examples of Mughal architecture, but the pre-Company style of painting was applied equally – indeed perhaps primarily – to Hindu temples, including for example the great temple complexes at Srirangam and Madurai in south India (fig. 32).[23] In such images the emphasis is placed on the path of the pilgrim and on the encounter with the divine, in the form of the *murti* or sacred idol. Mughal buildings are of course inspired by a very different aesthetic from Hindu temples, even when they are contemporary in date.[24] That they received the same pictorial treatment in eighteenth-century Indian painting is an indication firstly of the closer interconnections between late Mughal and Hindu courtly painting traditions, and also of areas of common ground about how architecture was understood. This makes it pertinent to discuss the Indic theoretical or *shastric* literature, and to contrast it with Hodges's theoretical ideas about architecture as articulated in his *Dissertation on the Prototypes of Architecture* of 1787 and other writings.

Indian ideas about architecture were first formalised in texts composed in the late Gupta period (6th century AD). This scholarly and literary tradition flourished under the patronage of medieval Hindu kings and survived until as late as the mid-twentieth century, even though (as already suggested) in later times it became fragmented and was less widely understood, as European methods came to dominate architecture in the public sphere. In the late eighteenth century, *shastric* ideas were still relatively strong, but they were strongest in regions such as the southern interior and western India where Hodges did not venture. In spite of his professed interest in Hindu learning when visiting Benares, Hodges makes no mention of this intellectual tradition and he was clearly unaware of it.

In his own theorizing about Indian architecture, Hodges therefore starts from what he does know, drawing direct comparisons between particular buildings that he encounters and European styles. For example, the visual resemblance between the pointed arch of Islamic architecture and of Gothic leads him to assume a connection and to revive a theory of diffusion, which had earlier attracted the attention of Christopher Wren and others. In the letterpress accompanying his aquatint of 'A Mosque at Chunar

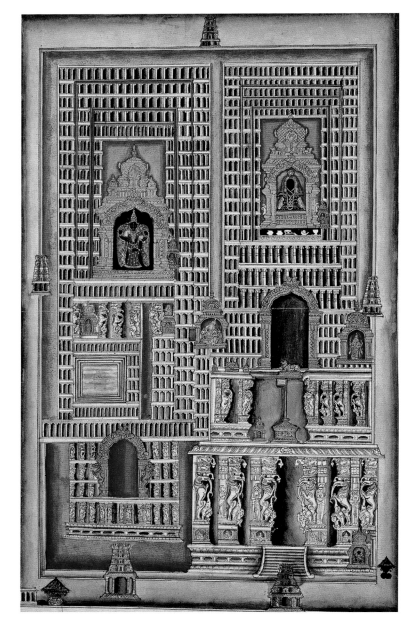

Fig. 32 South Indian artist, *The Minakshi-Sundareshwara Temple at Madurai*, late 18th-century, water-colour. V&A Picture Library.

Gur' he suggests that the view affords:

> A remarkable instance of the perfect similarity between the Architecture of India, brought there from Persia by the descendants of Timur, and that brought into Europe by the Moors seated in Spain, and which afterwards spread itself through all the Western parts of Europe, known by the name of Gothic architecture. The general forms of this building, as well as many others in India, are the same as those we see in Europe.[25]

But Europe's classical tradition apparently has its counterparts too: Hodges remarks of a mosque in Ghazipur that 'the minarets are curious in their form, particularly as we see the Corinthian capital lengthened and formed into the shaft of a column, and decorated with the same leaves.'[26] And emerging from the Vishveshvara temple in Benares, 'I was surprised to discover ornaments upon it which were familiar to my eyes'. He believes these details to be classical and declares that 'it is certainly curious to observe most of the ornamental parts of Grecian architecture appearing in a building erected on the plains of Hindostan'.[27] Whether he has observed them correctly his readers may judge for themselves as he helpfully illustrates the point with a drawing of one of the temple's columns.

Suggesting such links with European traditions was prompted in part by Hodges's desire to render Indian architecture accessible to his English readers. Though assuming that they would acknowledge an 'intimate connexion' with India, he also knew that they had been afforded few opportunities to learn anything of 'the face of the country, of its arts and natural productions'.[28] Hodges was therefore on a mission to persuade, to promote understanding of architecture and landscape that he himself had learned to admire.

The column in Benares prompted a set of reflections that led to the writing of the *Dissertation* in pursuit of that mission. The primacy afforded to the column in his discussion of the Vishveshvara betrays the influence on Hodges of western classicism and forewarns us about the nature of the *Dissertation*, in which Hodges engages with some prevailing classical thought. Certain ideas in Vitruvius had been taken up in eighteenth-century France to formulate a rationalist and functionalist approach to the tradition. Initiated by Abbé Cordomoy's *Nouveau Traité* of 1706, this approach had been developed by Abbé Laugier's *Essai sur l'Architecture* of 1753, and then introduced into England with modifications by William Chambers in his *Treatise on Civil Architecture* of 1759.[29] It was an approach that insisted on the primacy of the column and claimed for the classical tradition a natural genealogy. The columns, pediments and other forms of the classical tradition, it asserted, were derived from those of a primitive wooden hut, from humanity's first habitation, indeed almost from nature itself, and this accounted for the tradition's eminence. Classical architecture was superior to all other forms because it was rational and natural.

How much of this Hodges had studied in detail we cannot say, but it is plain that he was familiar with the outlines of the argument, because his starting point was to take as given the idea that a primitive, quasi-natural prototype provided the source and the justification for a developed architecture. Thus he begins by defining his subject as a study of 'the prototypes, or first models of architecture', and he is happy to allow 'what must be allowed, that the Greek columns, as they are drawn and applied by genius, are the most beautiful stone representations of the wooden props or supports of their original hut'.[30]

His contribution was to argue that the prototypes were many, not one; that the differences in climate, terrain and materials between regions must have given rise to a diversity of primitive dwellings; and the classical hut must therefore acknowledge the existence of its foreign cousins:

However partial I must feel, from habit and education, to the Greeks, whose free and unfettered genius, in a long series of ages, improved the original hut of a woody country into the incomparable beauties of a marble temple or palace; yet I freely avow that this by no means prevents my entertaining a similar partiality for countries, where different models have been brought to an equal perfection. The forms of the first habitation have differed, as the respective countries, climates, and manners of the builders, and as the nature, abundance, or scantiness of materials have directed.[31]

To add detail to this argument, Hodges drew on his own experience, citing amongst other things 'the wigwams of the torpid, wretched, unsettled Pecherais on the frozen coast of Terra del Fuego' and 'the various thatches and huts which I have seen in the South-sea Islands'.[32] Chinese buildings, he proposes, can be understood as developed 'imitations of the tent made of bamboo', while the prototype of Indian architecture is the cave. Indian temples, for example, are 'evident copies' of 'caverns, cool grottos and excavations.'[33]

This argument has the effect of de-throning classical architecture from its assumed primary position by furnishing other traditions with a comparable genealogy or rationale. The idea that 'the Grecian architecture comprizes all that is excellent in the art', Hodges dismisses as 'erroneous and servile', since a cave has at least as many advantages as a model as does the hut. Another effect of the argument is to challenge the importance attached to the hut's primary support, namely the column. Indeed Hodges seems to be addressing Abbé Laugier directly when he urges his readers to reject the idea that 'the whole excellence of architecture depends on the column alone.'[34]

Hodges argued that the cave should be considered as the prototype not only of Indian but also of Islamic, Egyptian and even Gothic architecture. These traditions no doubt drew their inspiration from the prototype in a variety of ways, as the interiors of Hindu and Egyptian temples are imitations of the cave interior, while the Gothic spire and the Islamic minaret imitate the towering rocks enclosing it. But what they have in common is their source in natural rock formations rather than the wooden hut. Thus these 'several species of stone buildings, which have been brought more or less to perfection, (I mean the Egyptian, Hindoo, Moorish, and Gothic architecture) instead of being copies of each other, are actually and essentially the same'.[35] And so in spite of Hodges's pluralistic intention, his argument also has the effect of justifying the kind of cross-cultural connections that he was often tempted to make by the apparent resemblances he detected in buildings that he encountered.

Another European intellectual fashion to which Hodges was plainly indebted was the rise of archaeology. What was known about classical architecture in the eighteenth century was considerably expanded by the explorations of men such as James Stuart and Nicholas Revett who went to Greece in 1751 and published the two volumes of *Antiquities of Athens* in 1762 and 1789.

Containing measured drawings of great classical monuments, these volumes were of immediate practical utility to contemporary architects. Hodges's plates are conceived in a picturesque rather than an archaeological style, but they similarly presented European audiences with their first detailed images of Indian architecture, and so could be seen as a kind of 'Antiquities of India'. No less a figure than Sir Joshua Reynolds even suggested that they could provide inspiration to architects.[36]

Ram Raz and the *shastras*

For an Indian perspective on these more abstract and theoretical matters we must return to the *shastric* tradition mentioned above. This literature was not accessible to Hodges because the first modern study and translation of it was not undertaken until the 1820s. The scholar concerned, Ram Raz, had been born into a poor family in Tanjore about 1790, but he studied English as a child and so gained employment as a clerk in the Madras Infantry, and later in the office of the Military Auditor General. His translation of a work on the revenue regulations of Tipu Sultan brought him to the attention of one Richard Clarke, who recommended him for a post in the college at Fort St. George (Madras). Later, it was the same Richard Clarke who suggested to the Royal Asiatic Society in London that they should sponsor Ram Raz (who was by now a Judge and Magistrate at Bangalore) to investigate whatever could be rediscovered about *shastric* texts. The fruit of several years of painstaking study was published by the Society as an *Essay on the Architecture of the Hindus*, in 1834.

In letters to Clarke that are included in the preface to this book, Ram Raz describes some of the difficulties that he encountered in pursuing this research. His first problem was that *shilpa shastras* had become 'very scarce in this part of the country'. When he did manage to locate some 'shattered remains' of texts he encountered a second problem in an apparent divergence between theory and practice. The learned *pandits* who were normally so helpful in interpreting Sanskrit texts were completely baffled by the architectural technicalities contained in these, while the expert builders either could not or would not even read them. It is significant that these problems arose in the British Madras Presidency, and Ram Raz himself provides the explanation when he comments that 'the best of our workmen have been so long disused to their own ancient style of building durable public edifices, that it is not to be wondered at they should now ascribe their ignorance of the art . . . to the want of encouragement, which appears indeed to have ceased on the decline of native rule.' Fortunately, in time Ram Raz met 'a good sculptor of the Cammata tribe, a native of Tanjore, who is well acquainted with the practical part of the Hindu architecture, and with most of the terms used in the art'. With this man's help he was able to make progress.[37]

Ram Raz's list of the contents of the *Manasara* – the principal

Fig. 33   Ram Raz, *Portico of Four Columns*, c.1834, wash, 34.0 x 54.0 cm. Royal Asiatic Society, London.

text that he studied – gives a good indication of the ground that is covered by *shastric* literature. It includes chapters on such topics as the units of measurement, the education of architects, the qualities of different types of soil, the method for making a gnomon, the definition of the parts of a ground plan, and the rites for consecrating ground. It also includes longer discussions of village, town and city planning, and definitions of the relative proportions of the parts and the storeys of different types of building.

In his more detailed account of these contents, however, Ram Raz gets as far as the gnomon and then skips over the chapters on planning in order to deal with the material that he supposes to be of greater interest to his English readers, the building's parts. His discussion of bases, pedestals and columns occupies one quarter of his entire text. This distorted emphasis and his frequent reference to the 'orders' of Indian architecture[38] indicate that he is trying to fit the *shilpa shastras* into the mould of a classical treatise, to make Hindu architecture sane for Westerners. He does at last get back to the chapter on planning, but he dismisses the chapter on the *vastu purusha mandala* as 'not immediately connected with the main purpose of this essay', when in fact it describes the fundamental conceptual tool of Indian design.[39]

In spite of this serious shortcoming (a consequence of the intellectual influence of his intended audience), even Ram Raz's version of the *shilpa shastras* presents a distinctive approach to architecture that is quite unlike anything conceived by Hodges. In the first place, *shastric* texts are not at all concerned with tracing connections between different cultures. They do not, like Hodges, draw up family trees of the civilizations. Ram Raz indeed seems to have Hodges in mind when he explicitly rules out any such connections. 'Some of the Western authors have traced a certain resemblance in the leading features of the buildings in Egypt and India', he comments, but goes on to dismiss this resemblance as 'merely owing to accident'.[40]

More importantly, it is not the purpose of a *shastric* text to explore architecture's origins or evolution. This is not because architecture is deemed not to have such attributes – as if it were static or eternal – but because the emphasis of the texts is to focus on a level that transcends and accommodates historical change. The texts define architectural paradigms that may be deployed in a variety of materials and styles. They do not look backwards to trace a genealogy or to find a justification for a given style in a natural prototype; they look forward, to equip architects with organizing principles that will prove to be adaptable to any circumstances and conditions.

The drawings that Ram Raz provided to illustrate his text accordingly present a very different vision of Indian architecture from what we see in the works of Hodges. Though some are based on details of particular and actual buildings, and all of them draw to some degree on the south Indian temple tradition, most of them present images not of specific monuments but of ideal or typical components. We are shown a portico of four columns, for example (fig. 33),[41] or a *gopura* (temple gateway) of twelve storeys, and the information that we receive will enable us not so much to write the history of Indian architecture as to build it.

English artists working in India in the late eighteenth century by and large were not influenced by local painting styles, much less by Indian ideas on technical topics like architecture. But Hodges is known to have looked at Indian painting – he even owned one or two examples (fig. 14) – and his intellectual engagement with the region went deeper than most. Even so, comparing his pictures and writings with those made by some of his Indian contemporaries has revealed some wide divergences. Hodges's approach to architecture tended to be more formalist and historical, where theirs was conceptual and atemporal. For them a building was defined primarily by its purpose, whereas for Hodges a building provided a scene and marked a point in time. Whether we are therefore inclined to regard Hodges as having been in some sense in error about his Indian subject matter will depend on the view we take more generally about cross-cultural representation. Hodges himself tended to be rather severe on this point, notably arguing that 'should a painter be possessed of the talents of a Raphael, and were he to represent a Chinese with the beauty of a Grecian character and form, however excellent his work might be, it would still have no pretensions to reputation as characteristical of that nation'. But as he makes clear, this argument rests on the premise that a culture has a single 'real and natural character' to be found out, that what is 'characteristical' is incapable of change.[42] The premise is questionable, especially in relation to India where there have always been many traditions, which often interacted. Starting from the perspective of the Indian material that has been explored here, one might turn the argument around and suggest that Hodges's pioneering application of the picturesque aesthetic and of classical thought to Indian architecture helped to reveal qualities that might not otherwise have been discovered. He shows us ways of seeing that could not have been reached from earlier Indian perspectives alone.

[1] The Deogarh (near Bhagalpur) visited by Hodges should not be confused with the now more famous Gupta temple site of the same name in central India.

[2] This complex process is described in greater detail in Sachdev and Tillotson (2002), 149–52.

[3] Apart from Ram Raz, the most celebrated of the Indian contributors to this exercise included Syed Ahmed Khan and Rajendralal Mitra. But even Indian scholars such as these were not equipped or disposed to employ *shastric* ideas any more than British writers such as James Fergusson and Alexander Cunningham.

[4] This essay builds on some preliminary work in this field by the present author: Tillotson (1998), 59–79; and Tillotson (2000), 78–86.

[5] Royal Asiatic Society, RAS 056.001; see Head (1991), 148, where the painting is attributed to a Mughal artist working in Lahore around 1770, and the patron is presumed to have been Indian. However, the work has also been catalogued as early nineteenth-century 'Company school' from Rajasthan: Arts Council of Great Britain, *In the Image of Man* (London, 1982), no. 250. More remains to be discovered about the circumstances of the painting's production.

[6] OIOC, Add. Or. 4202. I am grateful to Jerry Losty for drawing my attention to this painting, and for our discussions of it.

[7] See Welch (1978), 134–5; and Victoria & Albert Museum (1982), no. 88. While both sources agree on a late eighteenth-century date, the first catalogues the work as from Jaipur, the second as Mughal. The production and patronage of both paintings require further study.

[8] The view engraved by J. Brown is one of two plates prepared to illustrate Hodges's *Dissertation* of 1787: see Stuebe (1979), no. 403.

[9] Formerly in the P&O Collection; see Christie's, Auction 5664 (24 September 1996), no. 51.

[10] OIOC, Add. Or. 933; see Archer (1972), 173.

[11] V&A IS 153–1984; see Archer (1992), no. 101, which includes a discussion of the date. The inclusion of English sepoys points to a date around 1803, but it is clear that the painting draws on a previously established tradition and may even be an imitation of an eighteenth-century work.

[12] Yale Center for British Art, Paul Mellon Collection, B1978.43.1802; Stuebe (1979), no. 167.

[13] The course of the river has changed since Hodges was there and now flows some distance away from the fort walls. The aquatint based on this drawing (*Select Views* no. 15) was dismissed by William Daniell as 'exceedingly faulty': see Tillotson (2000), 42.

[14] RAS 092.004a: Head (1991), 215. The work is dated *circa* 1815.

[15] Hodges (1794), 128–9.

[16] OIOC, Add. Or. 1134: Archer (1972), 79. It is based on *Select Views*, no. 11. The companion piece (Add. Or. 1133) is based on *Select Views*, no. 12.

[17] OIOC, Add. Or. 935; Archer (1972), 174.

[18] The promise of an aquatint view of the Taj Mahal 'in a subsequent number' is made in the letterpress accompanying *Select Views*, no. 15 (the aquatint based on the drawing reproduced here as fig. 27, in which the Taj Mahal appears in the background). Hodges's drawing of the subject is in the Yale Center for British Art, Paul Mellon Collection B1978.43.1735; Stuebe (1979), no. 178.

[19] National Gallery of Modern Art, New Delhi, no. 1388; Stuebe (1979), no. 179.

[20] Hodges (1794), 124.

[21] OIOC, Add. Or. 922; Archer (1972), 172.

Fig. 34 Thornton after Richard Westall, *William Hodges Esqr. R. A. Landscape Painter to the Prince of Wales*, engraving, from *The Literary and Biographical Magazine*, June 1792. The British Library, London.

jects', and whom the conservative Farington castigated in January 1795 as a 'violent Republican', perhaps because he was about to publish a poem celebrating Erskine's conduct of the defence in the treason trials that dominated the newspapers in late 1794.[9] But nothing in Hodges's catalogue, or in Farington's second-hand account of the progress of his exhibition, suggests that he intended to produce images which unmistakably 'proceeded from Democratic principles', as his outraged Royal visitors apparently believed, or which seemed to offer direct commentary on the daily events of the winter of 1794–95.[10] If in the summer of 1794, when Hodges began the two paintings, he intended to reflect in general terms on what he, like many of the Whigs of his circle, might then have seen as an unnecessary war, and to exercise a 'slight' and unacknowledged influence on the views of their audience, the events of the autumn and winter sharpened the focus of his visual 'lessons', and made them more urgently politicized, and more legible as a commentary on immediate issues and debates, than he could easily have foreseen earlier in the year. By then, British troops had been forced by a series of ignominious retreats to withdraw from northern Europe, and the failure from drought

of what had been a promising harvest threatened serious food shortages.

In autumn 1794 the government succeeded in delaying the opening of parliament until 30 December, when the session opened with a firm restatement, in the king's speech, of 'the necessity of persisting in a vigorous prosecution of the just and necessary war in which we are engaged.'[11] Parliament had initially been prorogued only until 19 August, and successive delays were variously attributed to the need to wait for the conclusion of the treason trials, to the progress of the war, and even, by some satirists, to Pitt's poor memory.[12] The *Morning Post* commented on 28 November that had parliament reconvened earlier, as had been expected,

> Ministers foresaw the consequences, that they could be scarcely able to retain their places, while news of some mortifying disaster would arrive daily, that must urge the People not to squander more money in the hopeless projects of Ministers. By proroguing the Parliament, they conceive that both armies will go into winter quarters, and that then they may amuse the People with the brilliant prospects that offer themselves, should they approve of another Campaign.[13]

Following the king's speech, amendments urging him to 'take the earliest means of concluding a peace', put forward by the Earl of Guildford in the Lords, and William Wilberforce in the Commons, were debated with heat and urgency.[14] These debates on the soundness of the case for war must have been enormously significant in shaping the way Hodges's paintings were viewed, and it is therefore worth exploring the possible intersections of parliamentary arguments and newspaper comments with Hodges's catalogue descriptions.

It is significant, first of all, that Wilberforce, like the *Morning Post* in November, felt that the precise timing was important. During the debate of 28 January 1795, on Grey's motion respecting peace and the aims of the war, Wilberforce argued that had parliament met 'on the day on which had been originally summoned', allowing him to put forward his motion when Britain was in a position of relative strength, peace would have seemed a more attractive possibility.[15] He denies, of course, that there is any humiliation in suing for peace in the current situation, but the implication of his preference for an earlier opportunity to speak out against the war, the suggestion that arguments for peace have been made more controversial by the disasters of the campaigns of the autumn and winter, is unmistakable. It suggests that the anti-war lesson of Hodges's contrasting images would have been more palatable during the period when they were designed and executed, than it was by the time they were on display. In July 1794, for example, the *Oracle*, which strongly supported government policy, reported favourably and in some detail on the progress of Hodges's contrast, praising him as 'the great *moral* painter of landscape'.[16] Peace could seem an attractive option to the government's supporters as late in the day as 28 November 1794, when *The Times* argued, in its 'Political Observations', that 'A wish for Peace is general throughout Europe', and commented hopefully that 'the sudden prorogation of Parliament, at a moment when it was least expected, has excited the attention of everyone to overtures of Peace'. But on the same day the paper's news column argued that peace would be 'a very serious misfortune to this country', because 'We then indeed could be overrun with French principles, and have more to dread from internal foes than open enemies'.[17]

The principal points of the debates on Wilberforce's and Guildford's amendments turned on the extent to which Britain could be seen as justified in continuing a war which they were understood to have provoked the French into declaring and which could no longer be understood in terms of the original *casus belli*, to support the resistance of the Netherlands, which had now entered into negotiations with France. The war now appeared to be about hostility to republican politics, and the desire to impose regime change on France in order to preempt the arrival of hordes of proselytizing revolutionaries in Britain. The government argued that despite the fall of Robespierre, they could not enter into negotiations with French republicans, who posed 'the greatest danger with which [Europe] has been threatened since the establishment of civilized society.'[18] Lord Mulgrave urged his fellow peers to recollect 'that not only our lives, our laws, and our liberties are at stake, but even the national character of our posterity'.[19] Windham, the Secretary at War, also insisted that the war was about political principle, and that 'The advantages of war or peace were not to be estimated by the territory or the trade we might gain or lose'.[20] This high-minded attitude must have come more easily to him as a result of his belief that the costs of war 'were now so lightly to be born as hardly to be felt', a persuasion he grounded in the 'maxim, that if the rich felt no suffering, the poor also were not likely to feel any.'[21] Where the government did acknowledge that the war was costing Britain dear, they urged that French resources would be drained even faster; and concluded that the effects of peace would be far more alarming and devastating than any possible consequences of continued war.

The arguments of the Foxite opposition to the war, to which Wilberforce uneasily found himself allied, emphasized that the recent campaign had been 'unparalleled for disaster',[22] and 'calamitous beyond example'.[23] In the Lords it was pointed out that because there was nothing in the king's speech that 'in the smallest measure determined what the object of the war really was', the conflict was potentially a 'war of mutual destruction'.[24] Fox ridiculed Windham's arguments by paraphrasing them to suggest that this was a contest 'the issue of which involved, not territory or commerce, not victory or defeat in the common acceptation of the words, but our constitution, our country, our existence as a nation.'[25] These arguments, stressing the indeterminacy of the aims of the war and the consequent difficulty of bringing it to any conclusion, and emphasizing its enormous cost, were repeated at meetings up and down the country, and summarized in the numerous petitions reported in the newspapers, and particularly of course in the opposition press, for

January 1795. A letter from 'A DEMOCRAT' to the *Morning Post*, for example, warned of the imminence of famine:

> We should relinquish all further mad notions of prosecuting a Continental War, and keep our provisions at home to feed our own Countrymen, instead of sending it abroad to feed Foreignors . . . let Ministers look to it – for we must apprize these weak and ignorant men, that while they revel in riot and luxury, Famine *is at our doors*, and all its attendant horrors![26]

Hodges's representations of peace and war directly addressed the economic consequences of conflict. Peace, in his account of the paintings, is characterized by abundant evidence of commercial prosperity in the business and conspicuous affluence of the port, and the organization and productivity of the countryside. The 'vigorous executive government' that encourages commerce also nurtures 'the high state of agriculture in the country.' In Hodges's narrative on the companion piece, the 'same scene' is shown 'under the most melancholy difference – the city on fire – ships burning in the harbour . . . Batteries of cannon now occupy the rich fields of husbandry'.[27] The Duke of York commented, according to Edwards, that

> he thought no artist should employ himself on works of that kind, the effects of which might tend to impress the mind of the inferior classes of society with sentiments not suited to the public tranquillity; that the effects of war were at all times to be deplored, and therefore need not be exemplified in a way which could only serve to increase public clamour without redressing the evil.[28]

As the price of entry to Hodges's exhibition was one shilling, it seems unlikely that the paintings would have been able to impress the minds of the inferior classes with any lessons. Evidently Hodges's contrast did represent the obvious point mentioned by the Duke: war 'at all times' damages commercial and agricultural prosperity somewhere. But what made the image a threat to 'public tranquillity', in the Duke's eyes, may have been the specificity of the location for this damage, the emphasis on the effects of continental war in Britain, and on the cherished notion of the familial content and 'happy state of the peasantry'.

In the foreground of his image of peace, Hodges paints a domestic and familial idyll, which is unmistakeably British, even in the Virgilian details of the vine and fig, naturalized by the conventions of patriotic georgic. In the contrasting image, he shows 'The same scene', but 'once happy cottagers are destroyed or dispersed . . . soldiers of a distant region now usurp the happy retreat of the peasant'.[29] The contrast does not simply represent the devastating consequences of war in general; it brings them home to the British countryside and to family life in a manner that was strongly associated with opposition to the war with France, and with rejection of the foolish or cynical complacency exemplified by Windham's remarks. Sir George Beaumont told Farington that 'Wilberforce has done much mischief by his conduct in Parliament, and that it certainly appears as if the solicitation of the Dissenters had strongly operated on his mind.'[30] The arguments of Wilberforce and Fox followed those of prominent dissenters in stressing the domestic consequences of the war, and insisting that though the scenes of bloodshed and devastation might seem comfortably distant from mainland Britain, both their effects and the responsibility for them inevitably came home, and potentially violated the domestic intimacies of 'once happy cottagers', disrupting the ties of familial affection and the mutual dependence of the generations.

In her influential Discourse for the Fast of 19 April 1793, *Sins of Government, Sins of the Nation*, which lucidly articulated the misgivings of many dissenters, Anna Laetitia Barbauld had argued that though in recent years 'we have known none of the calamities of war in our own country but the wasteful expence of it', and have 'calmly voted slaughter and merchandized destruction', private individuals should never the less '*translate* this word war into language more intelligible to us', and reckon the cost in human terms: 'so much for killing, so much for maiming, so much for making widows and orphans, so much for bringing famine upon a district, so much for corrupting citizens and subjects into spies and traitors'. She details the effects of war on family life and personal integrity in Britain as well as on the Continent, and concludes that 'Every good man owes it to his country and to his own character, to lift his voice against a ruinous war'.[31] Coleridge's *Religious Musings* (written in 1794–96) refer to the parliamentary debates of 1794 on peace, and echo Barbauld's Discourse in their condemnation of the war:

> Mistrust and Enmity have burst the bands
> Of social peace; and listening Treachery lurks
> With pious fraud to snare a brother's life;
> And childless widows o'er the groaning land
> Wail numberless; and orphans weep for bread![32]

Joseph Fawcet, in his *The Art of War: A Poem* (1795), similarly emphasised the responsibility of private individuals for the devastation war effected on the battlefield, and for its domestic consequences in the grief and economic distress of the bereaved and wounded, detailing how 'complicated traffic's trembling web' carries the reverberations of war to the 'domestic scene':

> The city feels the strife that's in the field.
> To the connected, sympathising scene
> The battle's blows their dire vibrations send.
> In other ruins rages there the war;
> There falling fortunes answer falling lives,
> And broken hearts to broken limbs reply[33]

The *Morning Chronicle*, which was consistently critical of government policy in the winter of 1794, expressed enthusiastic admiration for the 'imagination and execution' of Hodges's work, and negotiated the implications of their representations of contrasting British scenes with conspicuous delicacy. Peace, it argued emphatically, showed 'the present glorious and happy internal state of Great Britain at this moment', whereas the contrasting image showed 'what would, and what must be the inevitably consequence of disunion in this great Empire', without the support of its present 'glorious Constitution'. The journalist was able to support his praise on the basis of the 'testimony . . . by that most upright and amiable Nobleman' the second Earl of Dartmouth and his family. The Earl, known for his piety and sympathy for Calvinistic dissent, probably shared the disquiet about the war common among evangelical associates of Wilberforce.[34]

Nathaniel Marchant noted, when he saw the paintings at the end of November 1794, that 'the pictures are liable to criticism, the first scene, *peace*, exhibiting an English Country and people, – the second, *War*, the same scene under circumstances of devastation, with *Turkish* soldiers only in the front.'[35] Marchant's doubts turn on Hodges's decision to represent an unambiguously English scene in both paintings, and Hodges's own comments suggest that depiction of England as the scene of invasion and pillage had been intended to shock. He wrote to Hayley that 'I declare I revolt at the picture myself.'[36] Hodges presumably chose to represent the 'soldiers of a distant region [who] now usurp the happy retreat of the peasant' as recognizably Turkish because while Islamic religion and a reputation for Francophilia made the Ottoman empire an obvious candidate for animosity, the empire was also sufficiently remote to pose an unlikely threat of invasion to mainland Britain. But by the winter of 1794–95, the image of the Turks had acquired a sharper definition, which might have been in conflict with the potential appropriation of his contrast to the campaign for peace as well as with the direction of government policy. For Hodges's exhibition coincided with the arrival of the new Turkish ambassador in London as a feted guest. On 29 January 1795, at least a month after his arrival in the country, the ambassador made his public entry, journeying through London to St James's Palace in the king's state coach at the head of a splendid cavalcade, which 'afforded a pleasing sight to a great number of spectators.'[37]

The representatives of the fading Ottoman empire were welcomed so warmly, despite the empire's tradition of friendship with the French, because it was perceived to be increasingly necessary to support the Turks as a check on the power and ambition of Russia. Suvarov, the Russian general responsible for the brutal defeat of Ottoman forces at Ismael in 1790, at which Russian troops were reported to have behaved like cannibals, succeeded in crushing the Polish rebellion in November 1794 in a 'horrible massacre' which led a correspondent to the *Courier* to remark that 'Had we the accounts complete, I am of opinion we could not bear to read the dreadful narrative.' This defeat of Poland significantly increased the possibility that 'the Turkish empire in Europe [might] be annihilated' by Russia 'before the European powers, interested in its preservation, could have time to prepare for its defence', giving Russia access to the Mediterranean and seriously destabilizing the balance of power in Europe.[38] By the winter of 1794–95 the fate of Poland reinvigorated memories of the massacre at Ismael, and reinforced the perceived need to check the Russians, which had brought Britain to the brink of

Fig.35 Mather Brown, *Lord Howe on the Deck of the 'Queen Charlotte', 1 June 1794*, c.1794, oil on canvas, 259.1 x 365.8 cm. National Maritime Museum, London.

war in 1791. The *Courier*, for example, published a poetical 'Farewell to the Year 1794', on 31 December, reiterating the link between the Turkish and Polish massacres. The poem begins by lamenting that 1794 has been a 'long year of Massacre', before praising the Polish revolutionary leader, Koscuisko:

> Illustrious Chief! – *sure 'tis no treason here*
> To pay an heartfelt tribute to thy worth;
> O'er suff'ring Liberty to drop a tear,
> *And curse the bloody Tygress of the North.*
> Lo! Ismael's brutal Conqu'ror from afar
> Leads on his myrmidons in scent of prey;
> Train'd up to all the cruelties of war,
> To age, to sex, they no distinction pay!
>
> Ill-fated Praga yielded to their rage,
> And, oh! the massacre that there ensued!
> In blood of blooming youth, and hoary age,
> Their savage hands were wickedly imbrued![39]

Pitt's government found itself in the awkward position of balancing its desire to maintain the Ottoman empire as a bulwark against the expansive ambitions of Russia, at the same time as negotiating the treaty with Russia which Catherine the Great signed on 7 February 1795.[40] The opposition press in particular emphasized the link between Polish and Turkish oppression by Russia in order to increase the government's difficulties. A 'Friend

to Peace and Humanity' wrote to the *Courier*, for example, expressing revulsion at the possibility of a British alliance with 'the cruel and detestable Catherine':

> That scourge of mankind, the Empress of Russia, with whom we were not long since on the very point of entering into a War, *to preserve the balance of Europe*, (but whose powerful co-operation we are now so frequently told of) has been most basely employing her power in enslaving the virtuous and unfortunate Poles.

The Friend went on explicitly to compare the atrocities of Russian action at Ismael and Warsaw.[41] Hodges's depiction of 'an English Country and people' suffering under invasion by '*Turkish* soldiers only' might have seemed 'liable to criticism' by the time it was exhibited because it reawakened memories of antagonism towards Turkey that were out of tune in slightly different ways with both opposition sympathies and government policy.

The reception of Hodges's ambitious paintings was further complicated by the immediate circumstances of the exhibition. Hodges, as I have mentioned, paid for his exhibition space in Orme's Gallery, but he did not have exclusive use of the rooms. Since 2 April 1794 (and perhaps earlier), Daniel Orme had also been exhibiting Mather Brown's massive 17 foot painting of *The Attack on Famars*, and on 1 January 1795 this was joined by Brown's equally enormous companion-piece, *Lord Howe on the Deck of the 'Queen Charlotte'* (fig. 35). It was presumably the desire

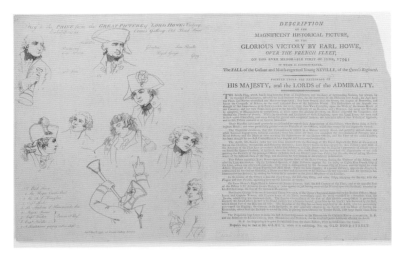

Fig. 36 Mather Brown, *Key to the Print from the Great Picture,* engraving, 1795. National Maritime Museum, London.

to admire the heroic representation of himself leading the attack at Famars, in the hills near Valenciennes, in juxtaposition with Howe's celebrated (but ambiguous) victory of the Glorious First of June, that attracted the Duke of York to make his fateful visit to Orme's Gallery. Hodges's paintings were viewed not only in contrast with each other, but in contrast with Brown's celebratory visions of all-too-scarce recent British triumphs. The styles of painting and the attitudes to war on display in the gallery could hardly have been more different.

Mather Brown's career as an artist in the 1780s and 90s has been fully documented by Dorinda Evans in her valuable study. It followed a very different trajectory to Hodges's. Hodges seems to have sacrificed personal fortune to his lofty ambitions for his art, as Edwards reported without much sympathy, sinking such riches as he gained from his years in India in the lavish publication of his *Select Views in India* and the costs of his final exhibition, whereas Brown, having arrived in London as an unknown American disciple of Benjamin West, rapidly secured commercial success at the expense of artistic prestige. By 1790, Brown was able to style himself 'Painter to their Royal Highnesses the Dukes of York and Clarence', and, having entered into a financial arrangement with Daniel Orme, the engraver, he became 'the first major history painter to have his topical subjects immediately engraved and published so as to capitalize on sustained public interest.'[42] His paintings of the 1790s displayed what Evans aptly describes as 'that strange mixture of contemporary reportage and grandiosity that characterized the genre' in that decade, and functioned as loss-leaders for Orme's prints, a role which seems to have driven, for example, the decision to display *The Attack on Famars* before it had been completed. Brown's later reputation inevitably paid the price for his commercial success. Farington commented rather acidly on Loutherbourg's topical painting of Valenciennes that 'When the novelty is over these pictures appear very deficient', and Brown's work was subject to a similar deflation of respect.[43] His friend C. R. Leslie, who visited his studio

after he had become able to retire on his profits, lamented that 'a more melancholy display of imbecility I never saw.'[44]

Evans notes that 'Unlike earlier engraved pictures, beginning in the 1790s, the topical print was usually advertised in the newspapers, and this publicity at times bordered on the sensational.'[45] Small uniform advertisements for Hodges's exhibition were published in a range of newspapers, stating baldly that at Orme's Gallery 'Amongst many others, will be exhibited the MAGNIFICENT PICTURES, painted by WILLIAM HODGES, R. A. Elucidating the Effects of Peace, and the Consequences of War.' The first series of advertisements, in the *Oracle,* were headed with the address of the gallery, but in later versions they carried the more provocative heading 'PEACE and WAR', echoing the headline used for the announcement of anti-war petitions.[46] Hodges's notices are modestly restrained in contrast to Brown's sensational publicity. Advertisements for Brown's celebration of Howe's victory were large, and took a number of forms, often including lengthy descriptions of the painting spread across substantial areas of the page. But in Brown's advertisements (as in Loutherbourg's), the name of the artist did not figure prominently. The topicality of the subject, the documentary accuracy of its depiction, and the authority of those who sanctioned or approved it, were more important selling points. Hodges's paintings in his later years were not known for high finish or exact detail: it was the 'slightly painted' character of his Yorkshire landscapes, as well as their high-handed approach to topographical fidelity, that led Fawkes to claim they were not worth the price he charged for them, as Farington reported with perhaps some degree of *schadenfreude.*[47] Hodges's work was praised instead for 'brilliancy and effect', the 'conception of grand and poetic scenery; where the minor excellencies of execution and detail are unattended to in the broad expansion of the *idea.*'[48]

The advertisements claimed that Brown's picture was 'entirely novel' as a result of its 'introduction of Portraits into a Naval Picture', and as a result of this practice, which was of course already characteristic of the work of West and Copley, *The Times* concluded that 'Out of the multitude of Pictures commemorating that glorious action on the First of June, that sanctioned by the Admiralty, in Old Bond-street, is the only one deserving the Public attention'.[49] It was these portraits that most obviously supported the claim of the key to the print, which Orme issued on 1 January 1795 (fig. 36), that though 'the most brilliant Scenes, for the Executions of the Historian and the Artist' had been afforded by earlier British naval victories, 'never was Triumph so complete, or Magananimity so conspicuous, as when upon this glorious Occasion, an Howe despensed the Vengeance, and directed the *Thunders of Britain*'. Brown's use of portraiture represents the officers as men of sensibility, but their humanity is not expressed in compassion for the suffering inflicted on the French, or on ordinary seamen. This is a portrait of group sympathy, of fellow feeling in loss as well as in victory. The death of Neville, and the wounding of Sir Andrew Snape Douglas, do not detract from the sense in which this is a triumphant and celebratory image, but

Fig. 37 Isaac Cruikshank, *Lord Howe they run, or, The British Tars giving the Carmignols a Dressing on the Memorable 1st of June 1794*, engraving, published 25 June 1794 by S. W. Fores. Copyright © British Museum.

suggest that victory is an occasion for magnanimity, an occasion on which it is appropriate to temper glory with humanity. The representation of the small group of Frenchmen apparently caught by cannon fire in the centre of the image is most obviously in line with the way popular prints had represented the victory soon after news of it reached London. Cruikshank, for example, in a print of 25 June 1794 (fig. 37), represented the victory as a bout of fisticuffs between stout British tars and emaciated half-naked Frenchmen, with the caption 'Lord Howe they run, or the British Tars giving the Carmignols a Dressing on Memorable 1st of June 1794.' By the time Brown's painting went on display, in January 1795, glee at French suffering may have seemed less appropriate, certainly to more elevated genres.

Loutherbourg's representation of the victory, which was on display in Pall Mall from 2 March, emphasized the devastating human cost of the battle, as did the paintings by Robert Cleveley, which were on display as advertisements for Anthony Poggi's prints from 21 February 1795.[50] In Orme's print after Brown, the distressed Frenchmen prominent in Brown's canvas are no longer the centre of the composition, in fact their presence is barely suggested.

This emphasis on sensibility and even compassion does not seem to be about a new sympathy for the French. Both Loutherbourg and Brown exhibited their representations of Howe's victory as companion pieces to scenes of the Duke of York's triumph at Valenciennes, scenes I have suggested the Duke might well have wished to dwell on. In early December 1794, the Duke had returned to Britain with his tail between his legs, hastening back to the comforts of London and abandoning his defeated army to find its own way in the retreat from Flanders. The *Oracle* reported on December 8 that 'The DUKE . . . to the joy of every British subject, possesses the most perfect state of health', noting, in the adjacent column, that 'A mortality pervades

the BRITISH ARMY'.[51] Neither the Duke nor the patriotic public wished to be reminded of the contrast between the successes enjoyed by the Navy, and the disasters of the land campaign, or the miseries the retreating army were then enduring. The emphasis on death and the display of group sympathy in Brown's image may have had the effect of tactfully smoothing over the contrast been land and sea, triumph and catastrophe, as well as humanizing the face of the navy. Hodges's representation of *The Consequences of War*, in contrast to Brown's vision of Howe's victory, offered an unforgiving evocation of the appalling effects of defeat on land, without any mitigating display of sentimental heroism, or (in all probability) that attention to detail that served to displace viewers' attention from the theatrical improbablities of Brown's image. Hodges's contrast was dragged into an immediate topicality by the retreat of the army, and by the circumstances in which it was exhibited. In juxtaposition with Brown's documentary realism, it acquired by the infection of comparison a potentially sensational appearance of reportage which would have made it seriously offensive to the Duke and his supporters, and set it at odds with Hodges's own ambitions to emulate the status of academic history painting.

It was this infection of reportage that made Hodges's grandly ambitious paintings available for appropriation by James Gillray, in his unashamedly topical contrast of *The Blessings of Peace/ The Curses of War* (fig. 38). In 1794, Gillray lived at 18 Old Bond Street, moving to 37 New Bond Street later in the year and staying there till 1797.[52] He first issued his contrast on 12 January 1795, and, as several critics have pointed out, the print seems at least to echo Hodges's account of his paintings, which were on display at 14 Old Bond Street. In Gillray's print, the roundel representing 'the Blessings of PEACE, Prosperity & Domestick-Happiness' portrays a scene of rural domestic felicity; the hale and hearty father returned from his bucolic labours to the greeting of his infant children, his wife and his well-fed dog, while an older girl places a great side of roast beef on the table. The contrasting image of 'the Curses of WAR, Invasion, Massacre & Desolation' shows the same family: the three children cluster horrified around the bayonnetted body of the father, while the mother, dishevelled by rape, flings her arms wide in a gesture of despair. Behind them is a scene that might aptly be described in Hodges's words – the 'city on fire . . . the building dismantled, and the last remnant of the wood is the scathed tree – soldiers of a distant region now usurp the happy retreat of the peasant'.[53] Across the top of the plate, the line 'Such BRITAIN was! – Such FLANDERS, SPAIN, HOLLAND, now is!', with the centrally positioned prayer 'from such a sad reverse O Gracious God, preserve Our Country!!', might be taken to suggest that Peace represents a British scene, and War a continental landscape. But the fact that the same family appears in both roundels suggests that the image of War is a prophetic vision of the 'sad reverse' threatening the rural British family.

Gillray's image was produced on commission for John Reeves's loyalist Association for the Preservation of Liberty and Property

against Republicans and Levellers, also known as the Crown and Anchor Society, and its content would have been monitored by them, but as Diana Donald has persuasively argued, 'Gillray's scenes of country life make one aware of the slipperiness of the visual signs available to the ideologists of the revolutionary period'. Gillray certainly could produce unequivocal condemnations of the opposition's case for peace. He published on 2 February 1795, for example, his print of 'The Genius of France triumphant, or – BRITANNIA petitioning for PEACE, – Vide, The Proposals of Opposition' (fig. 39), which depicted the leading parliamentary proponents of peace – Fox, Sheridan and Stanhope – cowering behind the grovelling and dishevelled figure of Britannia as she kneels in abject supplication before the monstrous seated figure representing French republicanism. The posture of Britannia is reminiscent of that of the despairing mother in 'The Curses of War'. But Donald points out that in his image of Peace, the depiction of 'the independent cottager living well off his own livestock and produce' suggests 'a golden past' rather than the 'perceived realities' of grain shortages and 'near beggary'.[54] The proof impression bore the inscription 'of the truth of ye representation an appeal is made and submitted to the feelings of ye

internal Enemies of Gt. Britain', which seems to invite the viewer to perceive the image of peace as provocatively idealized, and the scene of war not as an avoidable future prospect, but as closer to Foxite depictions of the country ravaged by famine and war-inflicted bereavement.

Hodges's landscape of peace had been designed during the summer of 1794, when fine weather, not yet become a drought, seemed to promise a bumper harvest, which might have made the depiction of rural prosperity seem cheerfully optimistic, and only mildly provocative. But the political implications of visual contrasts or rural scenes were extraordinarily volatile and unstable in the early 1790s. Depictions of emaciated and desperate Frenchmen set in contrast to fat British farmers gorging on roast beef and plum pudding were subject to the risk that their audience – 'the poor starving, and the middle class unable to live as they were accustomed to live'[55] – might identify with the starving French rather than with the fantasy of British plenty (fig. 40). In Gillray's contrast of war and peace the relation between the two sides of the image, in time and in place, seems indeterminably elusive and available to different political appropriations. The savagery of war perhaps highlights the complacency of peaceful prosperity, or the

Fig. 39 James Gillray, *The Genius of France triumphant, or - BRITANNIA petitioning for PEACE, - Vide, The Proposals of Opposition*, aquatint, published 2 February 1795 by H. Humphry. Copyright © British Museum.

Fig. 40 Isaac Cruikshank, *French Happiness English Misery*, engraving, published 3 January 1793 by S. W. Fores. Copyright © British Museum.

scene of war may represent distanced continental misery, as opposed to the comforts politicians such as Windham wished to believe British labourers enjoyed. Or Peace may represent what many saw as the rights of British labourers to independence, beef and pudding, of which oppressive government and continued war deprived them. The contrast between the vision of prosperity and the reality of violence, poverty and despair might suggest the need for radical constitutional change.

Gillray's relationship with Reeves and the Crown and Anchor Society was uneven, and he sometimes satirized the Society for their failure to employ or pay him.[56] It is possible that the indeterminate meanings of his war and peace are at least partly the result of this difficult relationship. Under one version of the print there is an inscription: 'Curs'd be the Man, who owes his Greatness to his Country's Ruin!!!!!', which John Barrell has argued might have applied to Pitt or to Fox or to Reeves himself.[57] The line might also plausibly have been taken to refer to the Duke of York, who was to be promoted to the rank of field-marshal in February 1795 although he was widely blamed for the failures of the previous year's campaign.[58] Certainly, the close relation between Gillray's print and Hodges's paintings would have worked to confirm the topical reference of Hodges's work, and to enmesh his contrast inextricably in the political controversies of the day.

By late January 1795, when Hodges's exhibition closed, his grand historical landscapes had lost the power to exercise an oblique influence through subtle moral lessons. They had become a commentary on the ongoing debates and immediate circumstances that now shaped the lessons they could impart. In the context of parliamentary and newspaper discussions of war and peace in late 1794 and early 1795, they seemed to endorse the Foxite argument for peace, emphasizing the economic consequences of war, and their impact on domestic and familial life in

Britain. But the presence of the Turkish ambassador as a guest at court complicated their alignment with the policies of the opposition. Gillray's version of the contrast, as it might have appeared to members of Reeves's Association, offered an alternative interpretation of the iconography of peace not as a past golden age of plenty, but as the present which members of the administration wished to affirm was threatened by revolutionary government in France. Hodges's image of the plenty and domestic harmony resulting from good government could be read as a rebuke to the current policy of the nation, his vision of war as the horror that bad government called down on itself; but of course peaceful prosperity could also be seen as what the government waged war to defend, rather than as the price of reckless warmongering. The theory of historical landscape painting which Hodges's paintings were designed to exemplify was undermined by juxtaposition with Mather Brown's sensational and journalistic brand of history painting. Brown's huge canvasses claimed to represent the definitive account of recent events, building that claim on detailed documentary accuracy and the approval of leading naval and military authorities and the court. Hodges's work, with its emphasis on 'the broad expansion of the *idea*' and the indirect formation of '*juster* habits of thought', appealed to notions of art and of truth that Brown's work, in which 'not one single idea, nor any one beauty of art' appeared, did not even attempt to engage.[59] The theatrical jingoism of Brown's paintings attracted large crowds who, as they debated the convenience of hammock stowage and the direction of the decking, must have been nonplussed by Hodges's grand ambitions to amend their hearts and serve humanity.[60]

[1] Farington (1978–98), vol. 1, 248 (5 October 1794). See also entries for 29–30 November and, for example, the *Oracle and Public Advertiser*, 29 November 1794. For a fuller account, see Stuebe (1979).

2 See Appendix, below.

3 See Farington (1978–98), vol. 1, 271, 275 (7, 14 December 1794), and vol. 2, 296 (26 January 1795).

4 Ibid., vol. 2, 296 (25 January 1795).

5 Ibid., vol. 2, 302 (7 February 1795).

6 Hayley reported on Hodges's state to Nathaniel Marchant, who was Farington's principle source of news about the painter. Farington recorded Hayley's remarks on 3 February 1795: ibid., vol. 2, 301. Farington reports, on 20 June 1796 (vol. 2, 587), that Hodges intends to exhibit the following year, but on 2 March 1797 (vol. 3, 783), he records that 'Hodges is likely to do very well at Dartmouth; He has bought a House there in a beautiful situation. He has never painted since He went there.'

7 See Stuebe (1979), 350, 352–3.

8 See Appendix, below.

9 'Biographical Anecdotes of William Hodges, Esq. with an elegant portrait', *Literary and Biographical Magazine, and British Review*, vol. 8 (May, 1792). On Hotham and Fawkes see Stuebe (1979), 68, and DNB (Hotham in vol. of Missing Persons). Farington (1978–98) on Hayley: vol. 2, 289 (6 January 1795). For the date of publication of Hayley's *The National Advocates*, see Johnson (1823), vol. 1, 467.

10 Farington (1978–98), vol. 2, 301 (3 February 1795).

11 *Parliamentary History*, vol. 31, 959.

12 See Barrell (2000), 374–5.

13 The *Morning Post and Fashionable World*, 28 November 1794.

14 I quote from Guildford's amendment, *Parliamentary History*, vol. 31, 970.

15 Ibid., 1231.

16 *Oracle and Public Advertiser*, 22 July 1794.

17 *The Times*, 28 November 1794.

18 Sir Edward Knatchbull's speech, *Parliamentary History*, vol. 31, 1008.

19 Ibid., 984.

20 Ibid., 1029.

21 Ibid., 1031.

22 Earl of Lauderdale's speech: ibid., 988.

23 C. J. Fox: ibid., 1052–3.

24 Duke of Bedford's speech: ibid., 993.

25 Ibid., 1047.

26 *Morning Post and Fashionable World*, 2 February 1795.

27 Appendix, below.

28 Edwards (1808), 251.

29 Ibid., 249–50.

30 Farington (1978–98), vol. 2, 302 (5 February 1795).

31 [Barbauld] (1793), 27, 28, 36–7.

32 'Religious Musings: A desultory poem, written on the Christmas Eve of 1794', lines 163–7, in Coleridge (1969). On the parliamentary debates, see Coleridge's note to line 159.

33 Fawcet (1795), 36–7.

34 *Morning Chronicle*, 5 January 1795. See Stott (2003), 199, and for Dartmouth's connections with Wilberforce's circle, 82, 87, 177.

35 Farington (1978–98), vol. 1, 266–7 (30 November 1794).

36 In Stuebe (1979), 354.

37 *Morning Post and Fashionable World*, 29 and 30 January 1795; *The Times*, 30 January 1795. The Turkish ambassador arrived in London in 1794. Evans (1982), 130, 189 n.19, cites the *Pocket Magazine*, 1, 5 (Dec. 1794): 290, on the Turkish ambassador's residence at the Adelphi in London in December 1794.

38 'The History of Europe', in *The Annual Register, or a View of the History, Politics, and Literature, for the year 1795* (2nd edn, London 1807), 31. Letter from 'A friend to peace and humanity', in the *Courier and Evening Gazette*, 2 January 1795. 'The History of Europe', *The Annual Register, or a View of the History, Politics, and Literature for the year 1794* (2nd edn, London, 1806), 221. See Christie (1982), 197, and Pope (1999), 'Poland', 'Ottoman Empire', 'Russia'. One of Gillray's series of prints on *The Consequences of a Successful French Invasion* (1798) shows Turkish mutes supporting the French, in allusion to French/Turkish friendship.

39 The *Courier and Evening Gazetter*, 23 January 1795. See also S. T. Coleridge, 'Ode to the Departing Year' (1796), lines 38–61, and notes.

40 On the treaty, see Alexander (1989), 318.

41 Letter from 'A friend to peace and humanity', in the *Courier and Evening Gazette*, 2 January 1795. On Turkish links with the Polish rebels, see Alexander (1989), 315.

42 Evans (1982), 87, 115.

43 Farington (1978–98), vol. 2, 312 (3 March 1795). Farington never thought highly of Brown, commenting on 7 October 1794 that his was one of 'two names I certainly would not vote for' in elections to the Royal Academy (vol. 1, 251).

44 The W. T. Whitley Papers, vol. 2, 'Mather Brown'.

45 Evans (1982), 114.

46 See, for example, the *Oracle and Public Advertiser*, 29 November, 2, 3, 4, 5, 9, 13, 27 December 1794; the *Morning Chronicle*, 15, 17, 23, 25 December 1794; the *Morning Post*, 13, 15 December 1794, and *The Times*, 13, 16 December 1794. I quote from the advertisements that appeared in the *Oracle* and *The Times*. See, for example, the petition announced in the *Courier and Evening Gazette*, 12 January 1795, under the headline 'WAR OR PEACE'.

47 Farington (1978–98), vol. 2, p. 270 (6 December 1794).

48 Cited in Stuebe (1979), 68. *Morning Post*, 24 May 1794.

49 *True Briton*, 2 February 1795, 655; *The Times*, 8 January 1795.

50 See Farington (1978–98), vol. 2, 307 (21 February 1795). Farington reported on 5 May 1795 that Poggi worried that 'if the Prints of the naval engagement do not answer He shall be ruined' (vol. 2, 339). For the 1 June paintings, see also van der Merwe (2001).

51 The *Oracle and Public Advertiser*, 8 December 1794.

52 Hill (1965), 38–9.

53 See Appendix, below.

54 Donald (1996), 156–7. My discussion of Gillray is indebted to Donald's chapter '"John Bull bother'd": The French Revolution and the Propaganda War of the 1790s', 142–83.

55 Marquis of Lansdowne's speech, *Parliamentary History*, 31, 1272.

56 Hill (1965), 54–5.

57 Barrell (2000), 640–1. Barrell identifies the line as from the first scene of Addison's *Cato*, I, i. 24.

58 See, for example, the *Morning Post*, 10 December 1794, which reported: 'The profilgate prints, in the pay of the Treasury, are opening the batteries of calumny against the Duke of YORK. To him they attribute all the misfortunes and blunders of the Campaign, when it is well known that the Duke acted strictly agreeable to plans of the Cabinet.'

59 C. R. Leslie, in W. T. Whitley Papers, vol. 2, 'Mather Brown'.

60 Evans (1982), 126.

Part One
Making Pacific History

The maritime context, 1768-75

PIETER VAN DER MERWE

On 13 July 1771, three years out from England, the weather-beaten *Endeavour* anchored in the Downs off Deal, Kent. With his charts and journals, her forty-two-year-old commander, Lieutenant James Cook, posted to London to report to the Admiralty. Although his own claims for the voyage's success were modest, even apologetic given its length, it was quickly recognized as marking an epoch in the history of discovery. The prime aim, in which the Navy had lent means to the Royal Society, was to observe the transit of Venus across the Sun from the southern Pacific – one of several international observations of this rare event, intended to help calculate the size of the solar system. Cook's vantage point had been Tahiti, an exotic paradise only discovered and accurately positioned in 1766 by Captain Samuel Wallis of the *Dolphin*, two years before *Endeavour* sailed. However, some of Wallis's men also reported glimpses of high, cloud-capped land south of Tahiti, prolonging ancient hopes that an inhabitable unknown continent – *terra australis incognita* – hung just beyond the southern horizon, with rich potential for whichever of the rival European powers could find it. Cook also carried secret instructions to check these sightings. Should they prove illusory, as they did, he was to sail west to investigate New Zealand, of which the western side only had been partially discovered but poorly recorded by Abel Tasman in 1642.

Finding New Zealand, in October 1769, proved almost routine: far less so was Cook's complete survey of its coastline, which revealed that it was in fact two islands, both of which he surveyed with remarkable accuracy in a single, figure-of-eight pass. Almost at the intersection of this course he discovered the safe harbour of Ship Cove, Queen Charlotte Sound, in what is now the Cook Strait. With *Endeavour*'s transit-observation base at Matavai Bay, Tahiti, the Sound was to be the principal way-station of his later voyages.

Cook's subsequent flexibility in interpreting his orders crowned his achievement in *Endeavour*. Rather than sail directly home via Cape Horn or the East Indies, he took an indirect course southwest for the latter, hoping to clarify whether Van Diemen's Land (Tasmania) was connected to New Holland (Australia), whose southern coastline was then barely known. Weather condemned him never to learn that Tasmania was an island but he became the first European to discover and report on the eastern Australian coast, from whose outlying shoals Bougainville had wisely turned away, much further north, in June 1768. As with New Zealand, he surveyed its full extent from south of his first landing point at Botany Bay to Cape York, narrowly escaping the loss of *Endeavour* in his hazardous, months-long passage through the unsuspected Great Barrier Reef. He then confirmed the separation of Australia from New Guinea by passing through the Torres Strait, the first European to do so since Torres in 1607, and had the battered *Endeavour* repaired in the Dutch dockyard at Batavia (Jakarta) for homeward passage via the Cape of Good Hope.

Thanks to Cook's firm regime of shipboard hygiene and an insistence on fresh food and greens, he did not lose a man to shipboard illness until that point, itself an unheard-of achievement. Thereafter he lost thirty from the malarial fevers contracted at Batavia, including Samuel Green, its official astronomer, and the principal artist of the voyage, the likeable Sydney Parkinson. The latter, of course, was one of the private-enterprise element which also made the *Endeavour* voyage unprecedented, and its mix of naval surveyors with a civilian astronomer, artists and botanists the pattern for those which followed. For the Navy had allowed Cook to take a wealthy young volunteer, Joseph Banks FRS, to collect and study botanical and other specimens on the voyage, and with Banks came his personal salaried entourage of eight. These included the learned disciple of Linnaeus, Daniel Carl Solander, Parkinson as botanical artist and Alexander Buchan as

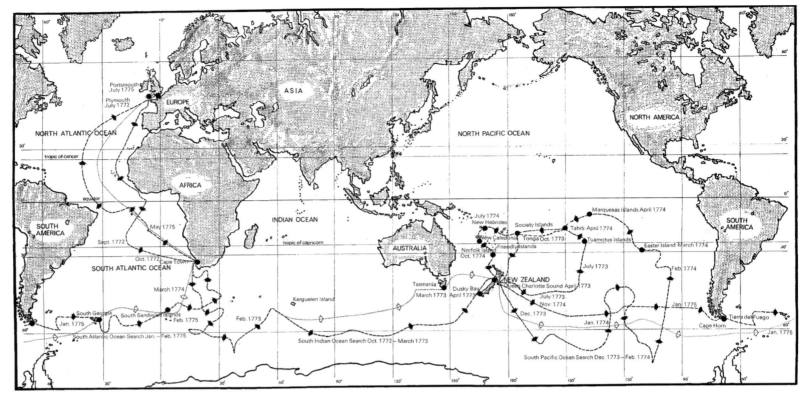

Fig. 41 Cook's second voyage, 1772–75. The bolder line and arrows show the track of *Resolution*; the dotted line shows the track of *Adventure*.

topographical artist, the last being an epileptic who died just after arrival at Tahiti. The collections and information that Banks brought home laid the foundations on which he rose to become President of the Royal Society and an arbiter of national scientific matters until his death in 1820. It was to be his only voyage with Cook, however; for when the second was prepared, the Navy refused to allow *Resolution* to sail with the additional top-hamper needed to accommodate his even larger party, and Banks went off in temporary dudgeon to Iceland instead.

A second voyage was itself never in doubt, given Spanish insistence on old Pacific claims and news that the French had in fact preceded Cook on Tahiti. Nine months after Wallis, Louis-Antoine de Bougainville landed there during his voyage of 1766–69, which first accurately measured the width of the South Pacific and brought back the first Tahitian to Paris. Bougainville's account (1771) was translated into English by Johann Reinhold Forster in 1772, one of this learned but problematic German naturalist's recommendations to replace Banks on Cook's new expedition. The national importance of establishing Pacific claims was also heightened by publication of an *Historical Collection of Voyages . . . in the South Pacific Ocean* by Alexander Dalrymple in 1770–71. A much-travelled East India Company official and later first Hydrographer of the Navy, Dalrymple was a leading champion of the existence of a Southern Continent and had himself been a keen but unsuccessful early candidate to lead the *Endeavour* voyage. In its latter stages Cook and Banks clearly discussed this vexed question, both concluding that such a continent

could only exist at a high latitude, south of 40°, with Cook being even more sceptical than Banks. To resolve the point, and probably before *Endeavour* reached home, Cook evolved the plan that the Admiralty accepted as template for a new voyage.

After the near loss of *Endeavour* on the Barrier Reef, safety this time dictated two ships. At Cook's insistence these were, like *Endeavour*, the specially purchased cat-bark colliers *Marquis of Rockingham* and *Marquis of Granby*, soon renamed *Resolution* and *Adventure*. Of 462 and 340 tons, he took the former (now in the rank of Commander) while the latter was placed under a veteran of Wallis's voyage, Lieutenant Tobias Furneaux. The talented George Forster accompanied his father in *Resolution* as botanical draughtsman, with William Hodges as official 'landskip painter' and the astronomer William Wales. The last, and his colleague William Bayly in *Adventure*, were appointed by the Board of Longitude rather than the Admiralty, with orders to test several experimental timepieces embarked as aids to finding the longitude. Of these the only successful one, making its sea-going debut, was Larcum Kendall's first official copy ('K1') of John Harrison's great 'H4' prototype of 1759, though it was not until 1779 that Dalrymple proposed the name 'chronometer' for such devices.

When the expedition left Plymouth on 13 July 1772, Cook overturned a tradition of European entry to the Pacific via Cape Horn, sailing instead for Cape Town. From there, and knowing he could use the prevailing westerly winds to bring him to safe harbour, water and fresh provisions in New Zealand, he probed southeast in November for an Indian Ocean landfall on the elusive

Southern Continent. He instead found gale-force wind, cold, ice and the first sightings of floating 'ice islands' some 200 feet high. On 17 January 1773 his party became the first men to cross the Antarctic Circle (66°33' south) before conditions drove them north once more in longitude 40° east of Greenwich. A long sweep south-east then brought them to New Zealand, where *Resolution* arrived alone in Dusky Sound, South Island, on 26 March. In *Adventure*, Furneaux became separated six weeks earlier in fog and made landfall on Tasmania before reaching the rendezvous at Queen Charlotte Sound. Cook joined him there at the end of April and, with the southern winter beginning, both sailed west and north to a friendly reunion with the Tahitians at Vaitepiha and Matavai Bay, before visiting the adjacent Society Islands. Oddidy (O-Hedidee) who joined Cook from Raiatea was returned there in 1774: Omai (Mai), whom Furneaux embarked at Huahine, was to cut a figure in London society before coming home on Cook's third voyage.

The ships then sailed west, to locate and investigate what Cook later called the Friendly Islands – Tonga – two of which had been discovered by Tasman 130 years earlier. After a week there in early October they resumed a course south for New Zealand but were finally separated by a storm off its east coast and *Resolution* spent three weeks at Ship Cove (3–25 November) without her consort reappearing. Cook therefore left Furneaux a buried message before heading south-east once more towards the Antarctic, using the southern summer as window for a last attempt to find the fabled continent. From the endless stream of north-floating ice he eventually concluded that land was there but that it could only be an immemorially frozen waste. His view that it was forever beyond reach and exploration was less prescient but understandable, given that his two last plunges beyond the Antarctic Circle found nothing but fog, intense cold and impenetrable ice. The second, on the eastern side of the Pacific (in longitude 106°54' west) on 30 January 1774, took *Resolution* to latitude 71°10', the furthest south ever reached. Ironically perhaps, this point of ocean is in fact hundreds of miles within the northern sweep of the mountainous Antarctic Peninsula, not far to the east.

Resolution could then have honourably sailed home, as *Adventure* had already done from the New Zealand rendezvous. Instead, with a view to further 'improvements to navigation and geography as well as other sciences', Cook took advantage of the sound state of his ship and the willingness of his crew to make a second Pacific sweep, with results which would have done credit to an entirely separate voyage.

Heading far north he landed briefly on isolated Easter Island in March, relocated the Marquesas Islands to the north-west for the first time since their Spanish discovery in 1595, and then dipped west back through the Tuamoto group to Tahiti, Huahine and Raiatea once more. He had already decided to probe even further west for the islands of Austrialia del Espiritu Santo, discovered by Pedro de Quiros in 1606 and more recently visited by Bougainville. After other minor landfalls and a stop at Nomuka, Tonga, he reached and surveyed them in July 1774, renaming them the New Hebrides (Vanuatu). The Melanesian inhabitants, however, were culturally and linguistically different from the Polynesians, and proved almost uniformly unfriendly.

From there he was heading south again, to approach New Zealand from the north-west, when on 4 September 1774 he sighted the unknown, 300-mile-long island he was to call New Caledonia, fourth largest in the Pacific. Mountainous, well cultivated and with a friendly people, Cook's survey of its eastern side delayed him most of the month, the wind and reefs preventing him reaching the west coast despite near shipwreck in trying to do so. On 18 October, back at Queen Charlotte Sound, he found evidence of Furneaux's passage there and on 10 November finally sailed east for Cape Horn, roughly along latitude 55° south, to cross the tracks of his earlier Antarctic forays and check for any land missed in between. Having spent Christmas on the coast of Tierra del Fuego, *Resolution* continued to survey her way east round Cape Horn into the Atlantic, and made a final attempt to locate a continental coastline predicted there by Dalrymple in latitude 60° south. That, too, proved a fiction but in turning north and west Cook's last discoveries of the voyage were the mountainous, icy fastness of South Georgia, where he briefly landed at Possession Bay, and the even more desolate South Sandwich group.

From Cape Town, via Ascension and Fernando de Norohna, off the Brazilian coast, *Resolution* returned to Portsmouth on 30 July 1775. The voyage of over 70,000 miles – more than twice round the world – was Cook's greatest in navigational and sea-keeping terms, an achievement partly acknowledged in his rapid election as Fellow of the Royal Society and the award of its prestigious Copley Medal. In practice and the negative, he had also answered the long-standing Southern Continent question, while the extraordinary reliability of the Kendall chronometer had vindicated John Harrison's claim to have solved 'the longitude problem' by mechanical means. Again, only four men on *Resolution* had died, three by accidents and none from scurvy – the usual long-voyage killer which Cook's healthy regime completely conquered. Above all, his additions to cartography had largely completed the geographic picture of the Southern Pacific. By contrast, although Cook's third voyage (1776–80) also started via New Zealand, Tahiti and Tonga, its objects lay on the American north-west coast, while his fateful discovery of Hawaii was also well north of the Equator.

Among his passengers Wales (and Bayly in *Adventure*) had data which helped fill several printed volumes of astronomical observations from the three voyages, while the Forsters substantially added to the Pacific botanical record begun by Banks. Both were also to produce independent accounts of the voyage, and George to become a distinguished writer on Pacific subjects following his later return to Germany. Hodges, the offical artist, was quickly re-engaged by the Admiralty to convert his three-year experience of the South Seas into images for engraving in Cook's published account of the voyage (1777) and to execute other official commissions for them. What that experience was, and how he interpreted it both during the voyage and later, is the first major topic considered here.

Hodges and Cook's second voyage

JOHN BONEHILL

On 30 June 1772, shortly before he was to sail from Plymouth on the start of his second circumnavigation of the globe, James Cook was issued an Admiralty order finalizing instructions for the forthcoming voyage. This included details of the late appointment of William Hodges to Cook's ship *Resolution* as the expedition's official artist:

> Whereas we have engaged Mr. William Hodges, a Landskip Painter to proceed in his Majesty's Sloop under your Command on her present intended Voyage in order to make Drawings and Paintings as may be proper to give a more perfect idea thereof than can be formed from written descriptions only; You are hereby required and directed to receive the said Mr. William Hodges on board giving him all proper accomodation and assistance, victualling him as the Ship's Company and taking care that he does diligently employ himself in making Drawings or Paintings of such Places as you may touch at that may be worthy of notice in the course of your Voyage as also of such other Objects and things as may fall within the Compass of his Abilities.[1]

It is more than likely that Hodges secured his appointment to Cook's second voyage on the recommendation of Henry Temple, the second Viscount Palmerston, one of the signatories of this communiqué.[2] Originally, the post was to have been filled by the Swiss artist Johann Zoffany, but he had withdrawn from the voyage a month earlier, along with the naturalists Joseph Banks and Daniel Solander, following a dispute with the Admiralty. Palmerston had included Hodges among his retinue on a trip to the Continent a couple of years before, and as a member of the Board of the Admiralty he was able to determine Zoffany's replacement.

Cook's first voyage to the Pacific in the *Endeavour* (1768–71) had established the value of taking a professional artist.[3] Sydney Parkinson had been employed by Banks on that occasion to make studies of plant and animal specimens, but he was to also produce a number of drawings that took Pacific peoples and landscapes as their subjects. These works were probably very much guided by Banks's interests in the natural sciences. However, Hodges's fieldwork might be more readily identified with the observational practices of the voyage's scientific personnel and ordinary seamen. Travelling on the *Resolution* Hodges came into contact with both companies. Cook's ship carried most of the scientific equipment and scientific community, for instance; the latter comprising William Wales, Johann Reinhold Forster and his son, George, and Anders Sparrman, who joined the ship as assistant botanist at the Cape of Good Hope. Hodges appears to have enjoyed a cordial relationship with all of these figures, as well as the rest of the crew. John Elliott, a midshipman serving on the *Resolution*, who spent three years living in close proximity to Hodges, considered him a 'Clever good man', while Wales thought him the model of 'politeness and affability'.[4] As these remarks suggest, Hodges seems to have remained on genial terms with all parties, even when splits began to appear in the ranks and the Forsters separated themselves from both the crew and the scientific party alike. This is interesting, given the degree of collaboration and exchange of ideas that surely took place over the course of three years. Published accounts of the voyage, together with surviving journals, provide ample evidence of the close working relationships developed between these 'experimental gentlemen'.[5] There are a number of suggestions that Hodges discussed the pictorial record of the voyage with Cook, with instances of the artist making copies of the explorer's own account of events. Further, both the Forsters and Wales appear to have suggested specific sites or subjects as likely to be of interest to the artist. Consequently, as

David Bindman and Nicholas Thomas have suggested in their contributions to this catalogue, it is not difficult to draw cross-connections and parallels between Hodges's field studies and investigations of his colleagues into meteorological conditions, or observations on the geological formation of the earth, speculation on climatic determinism or conjecture on the progress of human society.

In all this, there is considerable faith placed in the explanatory value of visual images. That Hodges's pictures might allow, in the words of the Admiralty's instructions, 'a more perfect idea than can be formed by written descriptions only' is an injunction repeated on numerous occasions throughout the textual record of the voyage. This belief in the emphatic, unambiguous quality of visual documentation is part of a more general cultural conviction current in the late eighteenth century, which saw pictorial forms occupy a privileged position in the communication of knowledge.[6] Such a belief was at odds, of course, with the generalizing or ideal art being promoted by academic theory, which concerned itself with the abstraction of particularized nature. In Hodges's work these two imperatives operate in some tension, however. Whilst this is most evident in the works he was to produce on his return to London, where the specific topographies documented by his on-location studies are filtered through a classicizing, Claudean framework, it is also apparent in the views painted in the South Seas. For in these works Hodges might be seen as adapting the lessons of Wilson's studio to both the demands for accuracy signaled by the Admiralty's order and interests cultivated through contact with the *Resolution*'s scientific company. This kind of adaptation was also necessitated by the sheer diversity of landscape and peoples Hodges was to encounter in the Pacific.

During the course of their three year journey, the crews of Cook's *Resolution* and its consort, *Adventure*, were exposed to a kaleidoscopic gamut of climatic change, extreme weather conditions, environments and peoples. These ranged from the icy wastes of Antarctic waters to the first Pacific landfall in the dense rain forest of New Zealand's Dusky Sound; from the complex, hierarchical cultures of the cluster of Society Islands to the most remote of all Polynesian societies, Easter Island. While some of these lands and peoples had experienced visitors before, Cook having stayed, for example, among the Maori of New Zealand's Queen Charlotte Sound and the people of Tahiti on his first voyage, in other cases, such as at New Caledonia, this expedition saw the very first encounters between Europeans and islanders. Contact was sometimes welcomed and amiable, at other times anxious and violent.

This medley of incidents, locales and peoples led the expedition's artist to improvise a range of pictorial strategies to cope with the unusual visual phenomena encountered. Hodges was required to respond to a staggering range of subjects, from the fantastical shapes of sea-worn ice to panoramic renderings of island cliffs and shores, and asked to produce drawings of specific plant specimens or portrait studies of local peoples.

Many of these works were more than likely determined in conjunction or collaboration with Cook or the Forsters. However, as has already been suggested, the more practical demands of navigation and seamanship were an equally strong influence.

Given the ostensible purpose of the voyage, it is hardly surprising that much importance was placed on the production of detailed navigational aids. To this end, Cook's Admiralty instructions required him to engage in 'making Charts & taking views of such Bays, Harbours and different parts of the Coast, & making such Notations thereon, as may be useful either to Navigation or Commerce'.[7] By this period, the production of charts, maps and drawings of coastal areas for such purposes had become commonplace naval practice, albeit that their publication still only took place on a private rather than official basis.[8] Hodges began making coastal profiles early in the voyage (cat. no. 2). By engaging in this kind of visual documentation Hodges was departing from his training in the classical landscape tradition. Nevertheless, he was evidently able to adapt his skills to the demands of nautical draughtsmanship, and the kind of topographical precision such views required came to inform his work on a more general level. Indeed, many of the artist's more elaborate paintings of harbours and shorelines he was to produce in the course of the voyage also observe the strict accuracy of naval practice. Still, such views demonstrate Hodges undertaking the kind of direct observation more regularly practised by naval officers. This 'influence' was a two-way street, however, with Hodges overseeing the drawings of several members of the *Resolution*'s crew. Many of the coastal profiles subsequently produced by warrant officers like Henry Roberts, Joseph Gilbert and Isaac Smith bear distinct traces of the artist's instruction. This is confirmed by Elliott's *Memoirs* which recall '. . . myself, Mr Roberts, and Mr Smith, (Cook's Nephew) were when off Watch, employed in Capt Cook's Cabbin either copying drawings for him, or drawing for ourselves, under the eye of Mr Hodges'.[9] Roberts, in particular, proved an accomplished draughtsman and especially adept at assimilating Hodges's lessons. In fact, it is probable that some coastal profiles produced during the voyage are collaborative works, with Hodges perhaps adding deft touches of colour over another's outline.

These drawings and the aesthetic of precision they demanded fed into the oil paintings Hodges was to make in the South Seas. And it is those works, especially the series of remarkably direct oil sketches made in the Society Isles during late August and September 1773 that are the most celebrated and much discussed of the artist's voyage pictures (cat. nos. 10-15). Indeed, it is with these works, as Bernard Smith has maintained, that Hodges's claims to being 'a pioneer of English *plein-air* painting must largely rest'.[10] Painting from the great cabin of Cook's ship, with the commanding views aft, and to port and starboard, it allowed, Hodges produced several island views, topographically accurate but characterized as well by an unusual attentiveness to the peculiar atmospheric conditions of a tropical climate. Smith has traced the origins of this oil sketching in the open air to the lessons of

Hodges's former master, Wilson. There is certainly evidence that Hodges's fellow pupils, Joseph Farington and more particularly Thomas Jones, actively pursued the practice, in imitation of a way of working Wilson had commenced when in Italy.[11] Faced with the singular demands of recording the bays and shorelines of the *Resolution*'s Pacific landfalls, Hodges fell back on this instruction. Whether Hodges worked directly from his subjects or from preliminary studies is unclear, but the paintings he produced in the Society Islands are certainly notable for their directness and apparent spontaneity, lacking as they are in *repoussoir* elements or incidental detail. They are also characterized by a close attentiveness to the effects of tropical sunlight, a quality Hodges was to retain in his post-voyage works, based upon these *in-situ* studies.

In those later works, Hodges is remarkably successful in recapturing the freshness and immediacy of his original observations. This has resulted in some degree of uncertainty in deciding which works were in fact produced during the voyage and which the artist made on returning to London. There is an added complication in this, in that it seems Hodges produced few works in oil on the voyage after September 1773. It has been supposed therefore that Hodges's stock of paint was exhausted well before it ended.[12] However, this is questionable, given that *A View of Resolution* [*Vaitahu*] *Bay in the Marquesas*, a painting which shares many of the stylistic traits of the Society Island works, cannot have been painted earlier than April 1774, when the *Resolution* made its visit.[13] It might therefore be suggested that it was the oil and turpentine Hodges used that was the problem, rather than the pigment. This may also explain how the artist was able to execute the two large pendant pieces, *A View of the Province of Oparee* and the *Monuments of Easter Island*, which were probably produced on the voyage home (cat. nos 24, 25).

These two pictures bridge the period in the South Seas and the work the artist was to undertake in London. Their combination of immediacy and idealization, topographical acuity and classicizing portent, effectively demonstrate Hodges's mix of conventional pictorial formula and novel pictorial solutions to the exotic and unfamiliar that so characterize his work on Cook's second voyage. That encounter with a strange, previously largely unknown world had required Hodges to constantly move between coastal profiling and landscape painting, botanical studies and portraiture. This interplay between different modes of representation is nowhere better illustrated than in another work produced during the final stages of the voyage, Cook's *Chart of the Southern Hemisphere* (fig. 42). This elaborate celebration of the cartographic, navigational and scientific attainments of the voyage was very much a collaborative piece, as an entry in J. R. Forster's journal for 8 February 1775 confirms: 'To the Map representing the Southern Hemisphere & our Ships track on it, *Mr Hodges* added the figures of *Labour & Science* supporting the Globe, to which I added the motto from *Virgils Aeneis*'.[14] Hodges's contribution of two Atlas-like or Herculean personifications of abstract civic ideals, clearly intended as Pacific islanders, allied with Forster's erudite reference and Cook's map, resulted in a work

Fig. 42 James Cook/Henry Roberts and William Hodges, *Chart of the Southern Hemisphere Shewing the track through the Pacific and southern ocean*, c. 1772–75. Public Record Office, London.

that commemorated the achievements of the previous three years in the most succinct manner. This joint product of artist, seaman and scientist, conceived with such evident awareness of the historical importance of the voyage, exemplifies the rich collaborative enterprise that characterized the voyage. Its combination of mapping and navigational knowledge, classicizing figures and quotation also neatly encapsulates the interplay of forces that so shaped the work of the voyage's official artist, Hodges.

1 TNA: PRO ADM, 2/97, ff. 542–3.

2 This is confirmed by Edwards (1808), 242; see also Charles Greig's essay in this volume.

3 For the art of this earlier voyage, see Joppien and Smith (1985a).

4 Holmes (1984); Wales [1778], vol. 2, 747.

5 This memorable description is from Sparrman (1953), 26.

6 Smiles (2000).

7 Cook (1955–67), vol. 2, clxviii.

8 David *et al.* (1988), xxxviii–xli. Cf. also Sands (1990).

9 Holmes (1984), 30.

10 Smith (1992), 123.

11 Ibid., and most recently Sumner and Smith (2003).

12 Joppien and Smith (1985b), 58.

13 Joppien and Smith (1985b), no. 2, 101.

14 Forster (1982), vol. 4, 723.

Note: unless otherwise indicated, all works were displayed at both venues. All catalogue entries in this section are by John Bonehill.

I *View of Funchal* [*Madeira*], 1772

Oil on canvas, 36.9 × 48.9 cm

Provenance: Sir Hickman Bacon; Sir Nicholas Bacon;
Sir Edmund Bacon.

Literature: Stuebe (1979), no. 22; Joppien and Smith (1985b), no. 2.2,
pp. 6–10, 134; Smith (1992), 119.

Exhibited: Free Society of Artists 1774 (384); Ferens Art Gallery,
Hull 1936, as by Richard Wilson.

Private collection.

Greenwich only.

On 29 July 1772 the *Adventure* and *Resolution* were granted safe harbour
at Funchal, Madeira, by the Spanish Governor of the island. The tense
commercial and colonial rivalry between Britain and Spain meant that
'no Plans or drawings might be made of any Fortifications'. While Cook
regarded this 'a very reasonable restriction and very readily promised on
my part', a number of views of the bay were still taken.[1] During the
three-day stay to take on provisions, Hodges produced at least one
detailed pen and wash study of the town and its coastline, and there may

well have been several more, which were then presumably developed
into oil paintings during the voyage to the Cape of Good Hope. This
picture was probably among a parcel of works left with Christoffel
Brand at the Cape for forwarding to the Admiralty and shown at the
1774 Free Society of Artists exhibition as *A View of Fonchial in the island
of Madeira*, along with two further views of the island.[2]

 This small, detailed painting of the town's buildings, set against the rising slope of the surrounding hills, must derive from studies made from the
security of Cook's cabin on the *Resolution* (or *Adventure*) while moored in
Funchal harbour. To the left, rising above the main town, is Pico Fort,
with the Convent of Santa Clara just to the right, the tall tower of the
Cathedral to the far right, and the gleaming white Governor's Palace
dominating the shoreline. Originally oval, the corners of the composition
have been filled out at some later date in another hand.

[1] Cook (1955–67), vol. 2, 21.

[2] Cook and the Forsters stayed with Brand while at the Cape. On 18 November
1772, Cook wrote to Philip Stephens, Secretary of the Admiralty, giving details
of the expedition's progress. This letter also details the contents of the parcel
Brand was to send on to London: ibid., vol. 2, 686–7. Another work, a *capriccio* of the island's interior, long thought lost, is now in the collection of the
Captain Cook Memorial Museum, Whitby (fig. 7).

2 *A view of the Cape of Good Hope, taken on the Spot, from on board the* Resolution, *Capt. Cooke,* November 1772

Oil on canvas, 96.5 × 125.7 cm

Provenance: painted for the Lords Commissioners of the Admiralty.

Literature: Stuebe (1979), no. 2, pp.18, 96–7; Joppien and Smith (1985b), no. 2.4; Smith (1985), 58–9; Smith (1992), 119–20.

Exhibited: Free Society of Artists 1774 (342).

National Maritime Museum, London, MoD Art Collection.

On the afternoon of 30 October 1772, the *Resolution* sighted Table Mountain and the Cape of Good Hope. 'In a moment' J. R. Forster noted in his journal, 'a drawing of the Land as it appeared, was made by several hands'.[1] Several of the views made by Cook's men on this occasion survive, including a watercolour of the shoreline by Hodges's hand, which was surely a study for this large, elaborate oil.[2] This painting must have been executed during the first three weeks of November 1772, as Cook's ships made provision for the first of their lengthy surveys of Antarctic waters. Cook's journal documents his artist's activities precisely: 'Mr Hodges employed himself here in Drawing a View of the Town and Port adjacent in Oyle Colours, which was properly packed up with some others and left with Mr Brand, in order to be forwarded to the Admiralty, by the first Ship that should [sail] for England'[3]. There seems little doubt that this is the painting described by Cook, and subse-

Fig. 43   George Lambert and Samuel Scott, *The Cape of Good Hope*, c.1731–32, oil on canvas, 78.5 x 117.0 cm. The British Library, London

quently exhibited at the Free Society of Artists in 1774 with the above title.

Hodges's painting is of the southern shore of Table Bay with the brilliant white buildings of Cape Town at the water's edge. Flanking Table Mountain is Devil Berg to the left and Lion's Head to the right. Superficially, the transcription of this most distinctive of landscapes accords with an earlier tradition of topographical draughtsmanship. In 1731, for instance, George Lambert and Samuel Scott were commissioned by the East India Company to supply six views of key trading posts or ports of call, including Calcutta, St. Helena and the Cape of Good Hope (fig 43).[4] Clearly intended to foster the image of a modern, global trading concern, much of the compositional emphasis of these paintings is on the Company ships in the foreground, as emblems of commercial expansionism. These were painted by Scott onto Lambert's cityscapes; views that demonstrate considerable topographical verisimilitude, depicting specific individual features in a relatively even focus. However, Lambert worked from drawings or engravings made by other artists, never actually seeing this landscape. While Hodges's painting might be placed within this mode of landscape depiction, combined with that of naval coastal profiling, it departs from their conventions in several striking ways. There is far less of a concern with the commercial activities and traffic of the harbour. Furthermore, Hodges records not only a specific topography but fleeting impressions of light and atmosphere. The storm clouds lifting from the flat top of the mountain and the dramatic light effects diffused across the canvas accord, as both Smith and Stuebe have noted, with the turbulent, squally conditions recorded by the astronomer Wales: 'It is not uncommon to see the Top of this mountain, alternately, clear and covered with thick Clouds five or six times a day'.[5] Hodges's concern to depict very specific meteorological conditions, observed from either the deck or cabin of Cook's ship, would also inform his views of Antarctic waters.

[1] Forster (1982), vol. 1, 180.

[2] For details of these works, see David *et al.* (1992), 40–4.

[3] Cook (1955–67), vol. 2, 51.

[4] Allen (1995).

[5] Wales MS Journal, Mitchell Library, Sydney. Quoted in Joppien and Smith (1985b), p. 11.

now lost. Cook noted that 'Mr Hodges has drawn a very accurate view both of the North and South entrance as well as several other parts of this Bay, and in them hath delineated the face of the country with such judgement as will at once convey a better idea of it than can be expressed by words'.[1]

Such views complemented the surveying activities of other crew members. In making several drawings of the bay from various angles, Hodges offered a means of orientation to parallel the charts produced by Cook's officers.[2] The careful delineation of the coastline's serrated edges, with the simple overlaying of gradated tonal washes suggesting the maze-like grouping of inlets, islands and rocky outcrops, picks out the principal topographical features in a way that complements the officers' planimetric views.

Hodges's earliest-known coastal profiles, such as those detailing the shoreline of the small north Atlantic island of Maio, established the basic principles of the technique he would employ later and pass onto those officers under his tutelage.[3] He began by tracing the contours of the passing coastline in pencil, then added three or four overlapping shades of wash to create a sense of depth. This simple but effective method differed from, and created a sense of spatial complexity often lacking in, the more usual linear style employed by seamen for coastal mapping. Hodges's watercolour of Dusky Sound also introduces a con-cern for atmospheric effects, generally eschewed in those earlier profile studies, recording the turbulent, trying weather on which several crewmembers remarked.

There were no explicit instructions governing the practice of coastal profiling. Accuracy depended upon careful measurement of the angular distances between features along the coastline, usually achieved on Cook's voyages with the aid of a sextant or azimuth compass. This presented a particular problem, however, for accurate vertical recording, since the breadth of a coastline was invariably greater than its height. Coasts characterized by high, rising features might produce an unacceptably long drawing. Thus, areas of the drawing were often slightly compressed or exaggerated in the interests of legibility. These technical difficulties must have been amplified by the close, cramped quarters in which Hodges had to work. His method of rapidly applying broad expanses of unmodulated colour is an ingenious solution to the difficulties of producing large-scale views under such circumstances.

[1] Cook (1955–67), vol. 2, 133.

[2] These are reproduced in David, et al. (1992).

[3] For the views of Maio, see David, et al. (1992), nos. 2.21–2.

5 *View in Pickersgill Harbour, Dusky Bay [Sound],
New Zealand,* April 1773

Oil on canvas, 65.4 × 73.1 cm

Provenance: painted for the Lords Commissioners of the Admiralty.

Literature: Stuebe (1979), no. 36, pp. 23, 117–18; Joppien and Smith
(1985b), no. 2.18, pp. 22, 145; Smith (1992), 122–3.

Exhibited: possibly RA 1776 (cat. add.) or 1777 (168); RA 1951–2
(44); Alexander Turnbull Library, Auckland 1959 (2); Auckland City
Art Gallery 1964 (11).

National Maritime Museum, London, MoD Art Collection.

On entering Dusky Bay the *Resolution* found a safe, convenient moor-
ing at Pickersgill Harbour, named after Richard Pickersgill, the third
lieutenant. Cook's journal records that they were able to anchor 'so near
the Shore as to reach it with a Brow or stage which nature had in a

manner prepared for us by a large tree which growed in a horizontal direction over the Water so long that the Top of it reached our gunwale'.[1] Following their ordeals in the Antarctic Ocean, the abundant, forested location offered 'the luxuries of life', providing a welcome respite, and an opportunity to replenish the ship's supplies.[2] Several commentators described it in lyrical but notably pictorial terms, George Forster comparing the primeval forest to 'rude sceneries in the style of *Rosa*'.[3]

However, while this untouched and largely uninhabited location provided shelter, a bountiful supply of produce, as well as an occasion for poetic reflection, such a dense, even claustrophobic, environment presented problems for the expedition's scientific community. Wales, the *Resolution*'s astronomer, required open sky for his observations, which entailed clearing the thickly wooded undergrowth, a task that occupied most of the crew for several days. George Forster's *A Voyage Round the World* offers a particularly vivid account of this activity:

> The superiority of a state of civilization over that of barbarism could not be more clearly stated, than by the alterations and improvements we had made in this place. In the course of a few days, a small part of us had cleared away the woods from a surface of more than an acre, which fifty New Zeelanders, with their tools of stone, could not have performed in three months. This spot, where immense numbers of plants left to themselves lived and decayed by turns, in one confused inanimate heap; this spot, we had converted into an active scene, where a hundred and twenty men pursued various branches of employment with unremitted ardour[4]

Forster's stark contrast between 'civilized' and 'barbaric' states underpins the voyagers' understanding of the landscape and peoples of Dusky Bay. Central to this evaluation is the capacity of a people to transform their surroundings. Throughout their voyage accounts, both Forsters assess various cultures according to their relative ability to adapt or usefully alter their physical environment. Like other contemporary theorists, Forster saw possession of the requisite technological abilities to 'improve' the landscape as crucial markers of difference between peoples.[5]

For Forster, 'civilization', as represented by the *Resolution*, had cultivated this previously unproductive landscape, and produced order from disorder. Once labour had modified the locale to meet basic human needs then it might allow the pursuit of art and science:

> Already the polite arts began to flourish in this new settlement; the various tribes of animals and vegetables, which dwelt in the unfrequented woods, were imitated by an artist in his noviciate; and the romantic prospects of this shaggy country, lived on the canvas in the glowing tints of nature, who was amazed to see herself so closely copied. Nor had science disdained to visit us in this solitary spot: an observatory arose in the centre of our works, filled with the most accurate instruments, where the attentive eye of the astronomer contemplated the motions of the celestial bodies. The plants which clothed the ground, and the wonders of the animal creation, both in the forests and the seas, likewise attracted the notice of philosophers, whose time was devoted to mark their differences and uses. In a

word, all around us we perceived the rise of arts, and the dawn of science, in a country which had hitherto lain plunged in one long night of ignorance and barbarism![6]

Forster is presumably distinguishing between his own artistic attempts to record the 'various tribes of animals and vegetables', and Hodges's descriptions of the 'romantic prospects of this shaggy country', since Hodges was hardly in his 'noviciate'. However, the latter's understanding of the landscape's rich possibilities is clear from *View in Pickersgill Harbour*. The immediacy of the brushwork, the novel, improvised composition, and the correspondence to Forster's description suggest painting on the spot, possibly from *Resolution*'s quarter gallery. X-rays also now show it was painted over Hodges's only known oil study of Antarctic icebergs, compositionally similar to a drawing that George Forster made under his influence.[7] This at least tends to support execution on the voyage.

It centres on a single figure trudging over the makeshift gangplank noted by Cook. Wales's tent, along with the ship's laundry and cauldron, are clearly visible in the clearing beyond. A dark frame of luxuriant bracken, ferns, creepers and heavy-laden branches encloses this pool of light, almost engulfing Wales's observation tent. Vivid highlights illuminate patches of wet undergrowth, while other areas are half lost in shadow. The composition opens to the right, with the ship's spars and gunwale silhouetted against a distant mountain range veiled in cloud, rain and mist. These abrupt contrasts of near and far, light and dark, together with variations in brushwork and thickness of paint, convey the optical confusion, spatial uncertainties and visual surprises that are features of such densely forested areas. The startling juxtapositions of improved and untamed nature, forest and ship, also clearly echo Forster's description.[8]

Forster's account offers a condensed history of human advancement, moving from a state of barbarism to the emergence of civil society. This was again a recurrent concern of both Forsters, which Hodges treated in his post-voyage works. However, he seems to have begun to explore similar conceptions of history in this painting executed in April 1773, in commemorating a particular place visited on the voyage, but also a significant historical moment that saw the first attempts to 'improve' that landscape. *View in Pickersgill Harbour* records the marks history left on nature.[9]

[1] Cook (1955–67), vol. 2, 112.

[2] Ibid.

[3] Forster [1777], vol. 1, 79.

[4] Ibid., 105.

[5] For an invaluable summary of these ideas, see Gascoigne (1994).

[6] Forster [1777], vol. 2, 105–6.

[7] Joppien and Smith (1985b) no. 2.10. The title *Dusky Bay/New Zealand* is also on the back of Hodges's canvas.

[8] Hodges was possibly familiar with the description of the clearing activities in J. R. Forster's journal, on which the account in the younger Forster's narrative was clearly dependent. Cf. Forster (1982), vol. 2, 265–6.

[9] The traces of the clearing cut by the *Resolution*'s crew can still be seen: Adams and Thomas (1999), 15–21.

6 *Dusky Bay, New Zealand*, April 1773

Oil on panel, 14.2 × 17.5 cm

Provenance: in a private collection since the early nineteenth century.

Private collection.

This small oil study of Dusky Bay has only recently come to light, and forces reassessment of Hodges's working practices on the voyage. Similar to the coastal profiles executed in wash, it also anticipates the *plein-air* oil sketches of September 1773 on the first visit to the Society Islands (cat. nos 10–15). The close delineation of the rises and falls of this complex configuration of small islands is accompanied by an attentive description of the atmospheric conditions. All the accounts of the voyage record the weather as showery and overcast, and Hodges's picture replicates the gloomy effects of those squalls. He also refers to encounters with the local Maori, in the form of two small canoes in the foreground. These possibly refer to a brief sighting of two such craft shortly after the *Resolution* anchored at Pickersgill Harbour. Alternatively, they might allude to the 'family' that was the subject of Hodges's epic painting of Cascade Cove (cat. no. 26): a standing figure in the foremost canoe appears to wear a red baize cloak, such as Cook presented to the old man of that group.[1] Hodges probably conflated these various incidents of contact. This became a recurrent feature of his fieldwork on the voyage, as well as the post-voyage works for the Admiralty. By including such incidental, ethnographic detail in his topographical studies, Hodges was able to relate information concerning the material circumstances of the environments he encountered, as well as their physical state.

[1] See Cook (1955–67), vol. 2, 117.

7 [*Maoris in a Canoe*], *c.* June 1773

Pen and wash, 8.9 × 33.0 cm

Provenance: probably de Loutherbourg sale, Peter Coxe, 18–20 June 1812; Colnaghi, 28 March 1868.

Literature: Joppien (1976), 28; Stuebe (1979), no. 51; Joppien and Smith (1985b), no. 2.33, pp. 49–50, 153.

Copyright © British Museum, London.

Greenwich only.

8 [*A Tongan(?) Canoe*], *c.* June 1774

Wash, 5.1 × 17.8 cm

Provenance: de Loutherbourg sale, Peter Coxe, 18–20 June 1812; Colnaghi, 28 March 1868.

Literature: Joppien (1979), 75; Joppien and Smith (1985b), no. 2.80.

Copyright © British Museum, London

Greenwich only.

These sketches were formerly attributed to Philippe-Jacques de Loutherbourg, who designed the spectacular Pacific-based pantomime *Omai, or a Trip around the World*, first produced at Covent Garden in December 1785.[1] However, their fluency and immediacy suggest that they are by Hodges, and were consulted by Loutherbourg when preparing his stage designs. They are now pasted into an album of drawings with a de Loutherbourg provenance, together with a sketch of more uncertain origin. This is an assemblage of various weapons – arrows, bows, clubs and spears – that, according to the labelling, originate from the Americas, Friendly Isles, New Zealand, the Sandwich Isles, and Tahiti. No other comparable drawing by Hodges survives, but the technique and materials are consistent with those he employed on Cook's second voyage, as in the little-known botanical sketches now in the Alexander Turnbull library. Whatever its derivation, it testifies to the voyagers' eagerness to acquire local artefacts and curiosities, not least for what they were held to reveal of the societies that produced them.[2] This interest in native manufactures is equally apparent in Hodges's sketches of a Maori and (probably) Tongan canoe, rapidly rendered with a blot-like immediacy reminiscent of the contemporary artist, Alexander Cozens. The first is datable to 4 June 1773 when the *Resolution*, anchored in Queen Charlotte Sound, was approached by a large double canoe, manned by twenty-eight men.[3]

[1] Joppien (1979).

[2] On this activity, see Thomas (1991), 125–84. Interestingly, given the voyagers' evident fascination with the martial capabilities of the islanders encountered, weapons such as those illustrated here were by far the most numerous objects collected on Cook's three voyages. See Kaeppler (1978).

[3] This sketch was later worked up into a more finished drawing: Joppien and Smith (1985b), no. 2.34. Cf. also Forster (1982), vol. 2, 291.

9 *A View in the Island of Otaheite*, 1773

Pen and indian ink wash, tinted with watercolour, 36.2 × 54 cm

Inscribed: 'A View in the Island of Otaheite from the Land looking towards the reef & Sea, and which has much the appearance of the Low coral reef Islands, the Plants ar[e] coco Nut Tree & Plantains which are Indigenous Drawn from Nature by W. Hodges in Year 1773' (verso).

Provenance: Alexander Trotter Collection; Dr. John Percy sale, Christie's (18 April 1890).

Literature: Stuebe (1979), no. 95; Joppien and Smith (1985b), no. 2.50.

Exhibited: 'Royal Academy Draughtsmen 1769–1969', British Museum (1969), no. 235.

Copyright © British Museum, London.

Greenwich only.

On 16 August 1773, Cook moored in Vaitepiha Bay on the southern side of Tahiti. He weighed anchor within the week, however, when it became evident that the provisions he badly required for his crew were not readily available. Sailing for the north side of the island, the *Resolution* made the first of its visits to Matavai Bay. After the wastes of Antarctic waters and the dank environs of New Zealand, the rich, open landscapes of the Society Islands elicited the warmest panegyrics. In his *Observations*, Forster wrote:

> nature and art have united their efforts in the Society Isles, to strike the beholder with the magnificence of prospects, and to awaken every idea of beauty, by the variety of harmonious forms and colours . . . we find them inhabited by a numerous race, in a higher state of civilization than any of their neighbours; we enter a country improved by art, and from the rough walks of uncultivated nature, pass into the lovely variety of a flourishing and well kept garden.[1]

Hodges addressed the same concern with the sheer luxuriance of the Society Islands' landscapes, with their mixture of the improved and the uncultivated. This low-lying scene with palm trees swaying in the breeze, executed in black ink with grey wash highlights of pale orange and green in the foliage, demonstrates these concerns most economically. The viewpoint, from the coast looking outward towards the sea, attends to the rich, tangled vegetation of Tahiti's shoreline, as well as referring to the transformation of such raw material into the canoe in the middle distance. These interests were further explored in the series of oil studies Hodges carried out during the *Resolution*'s first sojourn in the Society Islands (cat. nos 10-15).

[1] Forster [1778], 114–15.

10 [*A View of Vaitepeha Bay, Tahiti*], August 1773

Oil on canvas, 35.0 × 51.0 cm

Provenance: purchased from Hodges by George Woodward towards the end of the artist's life; Jenny Aldridge by descent; Phillips, 28 April 1992.

© The Kelton Foundation, 2003.

Yale only.

Which works Hodges executed on the voyage and which he painted on his return to London has long been the subject of debate. It is virtually certain, however, that this recently rediscovered view of Vaitepeha Bay dates from the *Resolution*'s brief visit there in mid-August 1773. Comparable in size and in the type of canvas to accepted voyage pictures, it is executed in a fluent, swiftly brushed manner. Similarly, its brilliant, contrasting tones of blue, green and umber, with white impasto highlights, are characteristic of the other oil studies Hodges made during the first weeks spent in the Society Islands. However, the difficulties sur-

rounding the identification of other such pieces is demonstrated by the existence of another, compositionally very similar, oil sketch of this bay.[1] Opinion on the dating of this second view is divided but the paint application and panel support suggest it was done in London, after the present work, as a preliminary study for the two large views of Vaitepiha Bay Hodges painted in 1776 (cat. nos 32, 33).

Comparison with those ambitious, polished and overtly classicizing post-voyage paintings sheds some light on what was involved in translating studies into finished paintings. The later works retain many topographical features from the view made on the spot, such as the grove of trees, the path followed by the river and the profile of the island's volcanic peaks, but also dramatically exaggerate the perspective. The concern to recapture atmospheric qualities is a conspicuous feature of all Hodges's voyage works. In this initial study Hodges bathes the landscape in a tropical sun, highlighted in the glinting spears carried by the warriors in the middle ground. However, their presence, together with the reed hut framed by the swaying palms, also displays a concern with the islanders' material social circumstances.

[1] See Stuebe (1979), no. 77, and Joppien and Smith (1985b), no. 2.41.

II [*A view of Point Venus and Matavai Bay, looking east*], August 1773

Oil on canvas, 34.3 × 51.4 cm

Provenance: painted for the Lords Commissioners of the Admiralty.

Literature: Stuebe (1979), no. 80, pp. 29–30, 142; Joppien and Smith (1985b), no. 2.44, pp. 53, 161; Smith (1992), 123–4.

National Maritime Museum, London, MoD Art Collection.

Recalling the *Resolution*'s approach to Tahiti-nui on the evening of 26 August 1773, George Forster remembered: 'We now discerned that long projecting point, which from the observation made upon it, had been named Point Venus, and easily agreed, that this was by far the most beau-

tiful part of the island'.[1] This small oil sketch of that headland, stretching out across the natural harbour of Matavai Bay, with One Tree Hill to the right, was probably painted some time during the next few days on that first visit to the north side of the island.[2] Working presumably from the cabin of Cook's ship, anchored in the bay, Hodges's picture records the effects of tropical sunlight, as well as the precise contours of the peninsula. Facing east into an early morning sun, he captures the deep shadows cast on the hillside and the vaporous humidity already beginning to cover the hilltops. The sky, suffused with rose-pinks and magenta blues, is streaked by sun rays emerging from dark clouds just above the horizon and reflected on the surface of the water.

[1] Forster [1777], vol. 1, 175.
[2] Formerly titled *View Taken in the Bay of Oaitepeha*, the subject was identified as the northern side of the island by Stuebe (1979).

12 [*A View of Matavai Bay, Tahiti*], *c.*1773

Oil on canvas, 48.3 x 60.1 cm

Provenance: Sotheby's, 14 December 2000.

© The Kelton Foundation, 2003.

Yale only.

This view of Matavai Bay has only recently come to light and, like cat. no. 10, complicates our understanding of Hodges's painterly practice on the voyage. He painted this harbour several times, with this probably a study for the two large views in the National Maritime Museum and the Yale Center for British Art (cat. nos 28, 31). However, exactly when this sketch was executed is unclear, and it further demonstrates the difficulties in determining which works were painted in the Pacific and which Hodges undertook on his return. It is painted on thickly woven canvas similar to undisputed voyage paintings but differs from those works in certain technical aspects. While it has the immediacy of the undoubted voyage paintings, the tonal contrasts are less sharp and the palette more monochromatic. Analysis of works known to have been painted on the spot shows Hodges's range of pigments probably consisted of light and dark ochre, burnt siena, Naples yellow, vermilion, lake (and probably yellow lake), Prussian blue, ultramarine, terre verte, ivory black and white.[1] The limited colour range here might be ascribed to difficulties with mixing the pigments or to the artist's 'want of proper colours'. Either suggestion implies, however, that this is a painting from the voyage itself.

[1] I am indebted here to Charles Greig, for his careful inspection of the pictures.

13 *View of Owharre* [Fare] *Harbour, Island of Huaheine* [Huahine], *September 1773*

Oil on canvas, 34.3 × 51.5 cm

Provenance: painted for the Lords Commissioners of the Admiralty.

Literature: Stuebe (1979), no. 14; Joppien and Smith (1985b), no. 2.62, pp. 53, 173; Smith (1992), 124.

National Maritime Museum, London, MoD Art Collection.

Like the view of Matavai Bay (cat. no. 12), this small oil study must date from the expedition's first visit to the Society Islands. Cook anchored in Fare harbour on the west of Huahine on 2 September 1773, staying for some five days. Hodges's picture of the bay, overlooked by a towering, craggy peak, silhouetted against a vast sky and becalmed ocean, must have been painted during this period, once more from the ship's cabin. The uneven paint application indicates a fairly hasty execution. Whereas the sky is painted with the thinnest layer of oil, showing the grain of the canvas, heavy impasto marks the native craft, the rocky outcrops of the shoreline, and the water breaking over the reef. Further variety is provided by the stark contrast of sunlit outcrops and shadow on the mountainside, and the more intricate variation of light and dark areas in the island's lush vegetation.

14 *A View of part of the Island of Ulietea* [Raiatea], September 1773

Oil on canvas, 33 × 48.9 cm

Provenance: painted for the Lords Commissioners of the Admiralty.

Literature: Stuebe (1979), no. 61; Joppien and Smith (1985b), no. 2.66, pp. 53–4, 176; Smith (1992), 124.

Exhibited: Alexander Turnbull Library, Wellington, June–September 1959 (7); Auckland City Art Gallery, 1964 (19).

National Maritime Museum, London, MoD Art Collection.

On leaving Huahine, the *Resolution* made for the neighbouring island of Ulietea (Raiatea), anchoring in Haamanino Harbour on 8 September 1773. This view looking north-east along the reef off the west coast was probably made from the ship during its nine-day stay. Hodges's response to the prospect and environmental conditions was inventive and novel,

though not unstructured; for all its apparent spontaneity, this sketch has a strong sense of compositional pattern. However, it departs from the classical landscape tradition in being structured diagonally rather than at right angles to the picture plane. Hodges is attentive here to the peculiar atmospheric properties of a salubrious climate, rendering the effects of glaring sunlight and sultry humidity with the sparest of means. A limited palette of cool blues and ochres, applied thinly and evenly, evoke hazy, reflective light, while a few marks in liquid impasto convey the shimmering sun beating down on the water. This attempt to capture the visual experience of intense tropical sun and heat was later echoed by Forster:

> the setting sun commonly gilds all the sky and clouds near the horizon, with a lively gold-yellow or orange; it is, therefore, by no means extraordinary to see, at sun-setting, a greenish sky or cloud, and it may be observed frequently in Europe. But, as the rising and setting sun causes, between and about the tropics, the tincts of the sky and clouds to be infinitely brighter than any where else, it happens now and then, that all the appearances of the sky and clouds, are more striking and brilliant, and therefore more noticed.[1]

[1] Forster [1778], 86.

15 *A View of the Islands of Otaha* [Taaha] *and Bola Bola* [Bora Bora] *with part of the Island of Ulietea* [Raiatea], September 1773

Oil on canvas, 33 × 48.9 cm

Provenance: painted for the Lords Commissioners of the Admiralty.

Literature: Stuebe (1979), no. 62; Joppien and Smith (1985b), no. 2.67, pp. 54, 177; Smith (1992), 124–7.

Exhibited: Alexander Turnbull Library, Wellington, June-September, 1959 (8); Auckland City Art Gallery, 1964 (20).

National Maritime Museum, London, MoD Art Collection.

This oil study might be seen as the pendant to the view of Raiatea (cat. no. 14), this time looking west from Haamanino Harbour. The mountainous island of Taaha, silhouetted against a rose-pink sky, almost obscures the distant prospect of neighbouring Borabora. Land, sea and sky are evenly balanced, and Hodges's restrained palette again captures the limpid, hazy sunlight and humid atmosphere. If the European classical landscape tradition evoked eternal qualities, topographical depiction serves to fix a specific temporal state. Whether by representing terrain through a limited range of colour harmonies independent of any characteristics stemming from specific climatic conditions or time of day, or by compositional frameworks which visually assert stability in the face of changing weather, the tendency is towards fixing a singular set of conditions.

16 *Otoo* [Tu] *King of Otaheite* [Tahiti], August 1773?

Red chalk, 54 × 36.8 cm

Provenance: drawn for the Lords Commissioners of the Admiralty; formerly in the collection of the Royal Naval Museum, Greenwich, 1873–1936; on indefinite loan from the National Maritime Museum, London.

Literature: Stuebe (1979), no. 140; Joppien and Smith (1985b), no. 2.54, pp. 59, 168.

Engraved: by J. Hall, in Cook (1777), vol. 1, plate XXXVIII.

National Library of Australia, Canberra.

Otoo (or more properly Tu) was the *arii nui* or leading chieftain of the Pare region, adjacent to Matavai Bay. Following Cook's visit, he successfully united the whole of the Society Islands as King Pomare I, in the process establishing the Pomare dynasty, which lasted well into the nineteenth century. George Forster offered a vivid appraisal of him:

> O-Too was the tallest man whom we saw on the whole island which he governs, measuring six feet and three inches in height. His whole body was proportionately strong and well-made, without any tendency to corpulence. His head, not withstanding a certain gloominess which seemed to express a fearful disposition, had a majestic and intelligent air, and there was a great expression in his full black eyes He wore strong whiskers, which with his beard, and a prodigious growth of curled hair, were all of a jetty black.[1]

Hodges's red chalk drawing fits well with this description, the uncertain expression capturing something of the sitter's reported timidity. John Hall's later engraving after it renders the features more heavily and forfeits that facial cast for something less personalized.

Hodges's first such portraits date from the *Resolution*'s month-long sojourn at Queen Charlotte Sound, and these drawings established his subsequent approach.[2] From an outline study in pencil, to establish also the main areas light and shade, he built up the drawing in red chalk, which enabled a subtle, varied gradation of tone.

---

[1] Forster [1777].
[2] For these works, see Joppien and Smith (1985b), 41–6, 152–3, 155.

17 [*Tynai-mai*], September 1773

Red chalk, 54 × 37.5 cm

Provenance: drawn for the Lords Commissioners of the Admiralty; formerly in the collection of the Royal Naval Museum, Greenwich, 1873-1936; on indefinite loan from the National Maritime Museum, London.

Literature: Stuebe (1979), no. 139; Joppien and Smith (1985b), no. 2.71.

Engraved: by J. K. Sherwin, for Cook (1777), vol. 1, plate XLI.

National Library of Australia, Canberra.

On 11 September 1773, as the *Resolution* lay at anchor off the southern coast of Raiatea, a party of local dignitaries led by the island's chief, Oreo, was welcomed on board. Amongst them was Oreo's daughter, Tynai-mai, who attracted the attention of several of the voyagers and was singled out in George Forster's account:

> In the afternoon Oo-òoroo, the king of the isle of Raietea, came on board with Orèa and several ladies, to visit captain Cook . . . Among the ladies was one of the dancers, named Teina or Teinamai, who had performed in the morning, and whose complexion we had much admired. She now appeared to much greater advantage than in the cumbrous dress which she wore during the ceremony. Her own hair, which fortunately was not cut, formed finer ebon ringlets than ever the luxuriant fancy of a painting produced, and a narrow fillet of white cloth was carelessly passed between them. Her eyes were full of fire and expression, and an agreeable smile sat in her round face. Mr. Hodges took the opportunity of drawing a sketch of her portrait, which her vivacity and restless disposition rendered almost impossible.[1]

Sherwin's later engraving for Cook's *A Voyage towards the South Pole* (fig. 44) was dismissed by Forster as 'infinitely below the delicacy of the orig-

Fig. 44 John Keyes Sherwin after William Hodges, *Tynai-Mai*, engraving, from Cook (1777). National Maritime Museum, London.

inal'. Far from an accurate likeness of Tynai-mai, Forster considered the image no more than 'a specimen of the generality of features in this and the neighbouring islands, and gives a tolerable idea of a Tahitian boy about ten years old'.[2] In defence of Hodges's work, Wales countered these dismissive remarks by finding it neither 'a national or particular likeness', since '*Tinamai* differed from every one else of her country-women'.[3] This exchange of views as to the veracity of Hodges's portraiture was part of an extended dispute between the Forsters and the Admiralty that commenced once the voyagers returned to London (see below pp. 109-10), and points to the dual function of such images. On one hand, they were meant as likenesses of specific individuals, and on the other as representative 'types'. The tension between these twin demands is still more evident in Hodges's drawings of the Melanesian people of the western Pacific (see cat. nos 21, 22).

[1] Forster [1777], vol. 1, 217–19.
[2] Ibid., 219.
[3] Wales [1778], vol. 2, 712.

18 [*The* Resolution *in the Marquesas*], April 1774

Pen, ink and wash, 28.9 × 23.1 cm

Provenance: Colnaghi's, 1957; purchased for the Museum by the Society for Nautical Research (Macpherson Fund).

Literature: Joppien and Smith (1985b), no. 2.104.

National Maritime Museum London.

On 8 April 1774, the *Resolution* moored in the entrance to Vaitahu Bay on the west of Tahuatu, one of Marquesas island group, weighing anchor

some four days later. During this brief visit, which was marred by a series of disputes with the native population, Hodges made, besides a fine oil sketch, several drawings of the coastline,[1] including this ink and wash study of the *Resolution* at anchor with the distinct form of a Marquesan canoe beyond. Set against a broadly brushed sky evoking raking sunlight and the rippled reflections of the water, the two vessels are delineated with considerable attention to detail. Hodges may have intended a comparison between the design and size of these craft; a compositional device he developed in later works that reflected on the voyage's achievements (see cat. no. 28).

[1] Joppien and Smith (1985b), nos. 2.101–4.

19 [*Matavai Bay*] OTAHEITE, April 1774

Pen and indian-ink wash with watercolour, on two sheets adjoined and mounted on card, 61.6 × 231.8 cm

Provenance: Sir Joseph Banks bequest.

Literature: Stuebe (1979), no. 81; Joppien and Smith (1985b), no. 2.107; David et al (1992), no. 2.169.

The British Library, London.

Greenwich only.

After Dusky Sound, Hodges appears not to have attempted any further coastal profiles, leaving such views to the officers who benefited from his tuition. It was only towards the end of the voyage that he resumed the practice. Unlike his earlier coastal views, executed in broad expanses of wash, these later images place greater emphasis on line with sparing use of colour. This is apparent in this large panorama of Tahiti's Matavai Bay, probably datable from the *Resolution*'s second visit of April 1774. On two joined pieces of paper, it is mainly done in pen and ink, with sparse washes of brown, rose and yellow confined to the left half of the composition. This suggests that the two sheets were brushed separately. It shows the rises and falls of the Tahitian peninsula, but also incorporates several detailed studies of indigenous sailing craft, most obviously those framing the central peak of Mount Orofena. These examples of native manufacture, navigation and trade are perhaps indicative of the expedition's increased awareness by this point of the complexity, differentiation and advancement of Tahitian society.[1]

[1] See Nicholas Thomas' essay in this volume.

20 *Savage Island* [Niue], June 1774

Ink and wash with colour tinting, 59 × 119.4 cm

Inscribed: 'Savage Island' (l.c.).

Provenance: Sir Joseph Banks bequest.

Literature: Stuebe (1979), no. 53; Joppien and Smith (1985b), no. 2.119; David et al (1992), no. 2.194.

The British Library, London.

Greenwich only.

On 22 June 1774, Cook landed at Niue with a party including the Forsters, Hodges and Sparrman. The hostility of the local population led Cook to name this previously uncharted atoll, 'Savage Island' and prevented exploration of the island's interior, limiting observations to those that could be made from the safety of the *Resolution*. Cook recorded the principal topographical features in his journal:

It is about 11 Leagues in Circuit of a round form and good height and hath deep water close to its shores. All the Sea Coast and as far in land as we could see is wholly covered with Trees Shrubery & c amongst which were some few Cocoanut trees, but what the interior parts may produce we now not. To judge of the whole Garment by the skirts it cannot produce much, for so much as we saw of it consisted wholy of Coral rocks all overun with trees Shrubs &c, not a bit of soil was to be seen, the rocks alone supplied the trees with humidity.[1]

Hodges's drawing of the coastline complements this spare summary of the landscape, highlighting the steep coral cliffs, their narrow precipitous gullies, and the masses of rock and sandbanks, only visible at low tide, below. The beach is suggested by a pale yellow wash also used in the *Resolution*'s sails and the reflections of the choppy water. Washes of ochre and burnt sienna indicate the vegetation clinging to the rock outcrops, echoed in the colouring of Cook's ship.

[1] Cook (1955–67), vol. 2, 438.

21 [*Man of*] *NEW CALEDONIA*, September 1774

Red chalk, 54.3 × 36.8 cm

Inscribed: the title, as above, on mount (l.c.).

Provenance: drawn for the Lords Commissioners of the Admiralty; formerly in the collection of the Royal Naval Museum, Greenwich, 1873–1936; on indefinite loan from the National Maritime Museum, London.

Literature: Stuebe (1979), no. 127; Joppien and Smith (1985b), no. 2.137, pp. 99, 237; Douglas (1999), 70–3.

Engraved: by F. C. Aliamet, for Cook (1777), vol. 2, plate XXXIX.

National Library of Australia, Canberra.

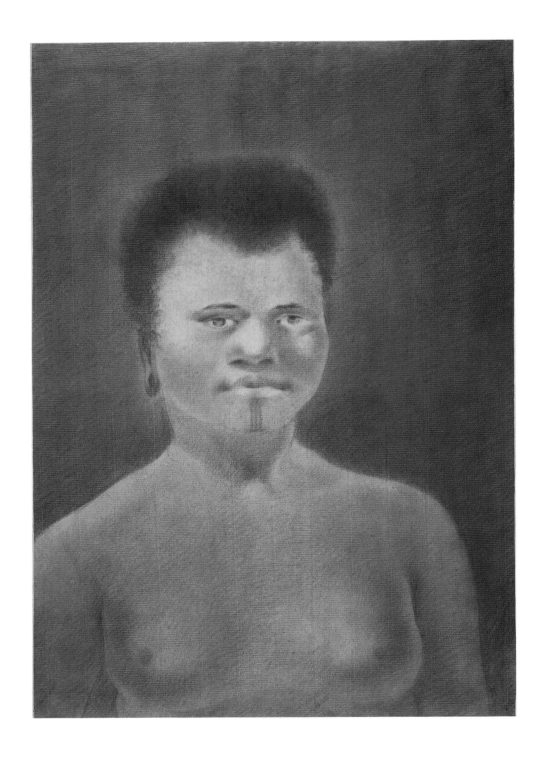

22 [*Woman of*] *NEW CALEDONIA*, September 1774

Red chalk, 54.4 × 37 cm

Inscribed: as title, on lined mount (l.c.).

Provenance: drawn for the Lords Commissioners of the Admiralty; formerly in the collection of the Royal Naval Museum, Greenwich, 1873–1936; on indefinite loan from the National Maritime Museum, London.

Literature: Stuebe (1979), no. 128; Joppien and Smith (1985b), no. 2.138, pp. 99, 238.

Engraved: by J. Hall, for Cook (1777), vol. 2, plate XLVIII.

National Library of Australia, Canberra.

Hodges must have executed these sketches during the *Resolution's* nine-day stay in September 1774 at the large island that Cook named New Caledonia. Unlike the individualized portraits of Society Islanders, these images are generic, representative types: a 'man' and 'woman', rather than named persons. Yet, this does not necessarily make them, as Joppien and Smith suggest, 'wholly impersonal'. Rather, as Margaret Jolly has noted of a related set of drawings of people of ni-Vanuatu, 'though not individuated they are extraordinarily sympathetic'.[1] Although primarily of informational value, they still record an encounter with a specific sitter, with Hodges adapting his usual schema with various subtle modifications. Nonetheless, it is interesting that he portrays the male figure in both front view and profile, anticipating methods characteristic of later ethnography. This figure is also shown wearing a woven conical hat, decorated with a slingshot, denoting a chiefly status. Such markers of social position were a significant feature of contemporary portraiture, but might be read here also as further ethnographic information. The drawing of the woman lacks comparable data about clothing, but is attentive to other 'typical' bodily adornments: her pierced, elongated earlobe, and three parallel, tattooed stripes running below the lower lip.

Engravings after these drawings appeared in Cook's official voyage narrative, and were praised by George Forster.[2] Forster's interest in Hodges's portrait studies centred on the evidence that the bodies of Polynesians provided about their state of progress. The elder Forster saw an intimate connection between physical appearance and bodily types, climate, environment and modes of subsistence:

> NEW-CALEDONIA though near the continent of New Holland, is inhabited by a set of men, who are totally different from the slender diminutive natives of that country, and in many respects distinguished from all the natives belonging to the first tribe, living in the Eastern isles of the South Seas. Many of these New-Caledonians are very tall and stout, and the rest are not below the common size; but their women, who appear here again, under the humiliating and disgracing predicament of drudges, are commonly small. They are all of a swarthy colour; their hair is crisped, but not very woolly; their chins are surrounded with respectable beards, which they now and then tie up in a knot; their features are strong and masculine, the ear-laps are cut and enlarged in the same manner as in Easter Island . . . Their limbs are strong and active, marked by fine outlines. Their females have generally coarse features, few having any thing agreeable or pleasing in their round face, with thick lips and wide mouths. Their teeth are fine, their eyes lively, the hair finely curled,

the body in such as have not borne children, is well proportioned, with a flowing outline, and fine extremities. The generality are of a mild and good natured temper, ready to please their guests in every thing in which they can be serviceable: but the ungrateful soil afford[s] them only a sparing consistence, and that too, not to be procured without much labour.[3]

Especially interesting are Forster's observations on the status of women in this culture. Drawing heavily on a model of progress developed by Scottish Enlightenment writers, such as John Millar, Forster argued that the social advancement of women provided a measure of a society's progress towards civilization. For Forster, it was virtually axiomatic that 'the more debased the situation of a nation is, and of course the more remote from civilization, the more harshly we find the women treated'.[4] Women's importance to the development of civil society rested in their role in cultivating sympathy and sensibility. Thus, the Society Islands, the Friendly Isles and the Marquesas, cultures placed by Forster at the apex of Pacific society, had all benefited from the 'tender feelings, mutual attachment, and social virtues, which naturally lead them towards the blessings of civilization'.[5] This distinction between the more advanced state of the eastern Pacific and the relative degradation found in the western isles was central to a more general division Forster conceived among Oceanic peoples. He classified them into two 'great varieties' or 'races', 'the one more fair, well limbed, athletic, of a fine size, and a kind benevolent temper; the other, blacker, the hair just beginning to become woolly and crisp, the body more slender and low, and their temper, if possible, more brisk, though somewhat mistrustful'.[6] This was not a rigid distinction, however, as he considered the islanders to be 'again divided into several varieties, which form the gradations to the other race'.[7] These divisions derived principally from observations on physical appearances, which were made most immediately available to a metropolitan audience through Hodges's drawings and their reproduction.

[1] Jolly (1992), 348.

[2] Forster [1777], vol. 2, 590.

[3] Forster [1778], 159–62.

[4] Ibid., 258. For detailed discussions of this issue, see Thomas (1996), Guest (1996) and Wilson (2002).

[5] Forster [1778], 260.

[6] Ibid., 153.

[7] Ibid.

23 [*Two head studies of South Sea Islanders*],
c.1774–75

Oil on thick canvas, possibly sailcloth, pasted on mount, 10.5 × 14.3 cm

Inscribed: 'Hodges RA' in pencil (l.l.), in unknown hand. 'C2d7
Petherick views', 'Mr Hodges was with Cook's Second Voyage
on board the Resolution. The Resolution did not go near the
Endeavour River or part of Australia. Hodges only went out in the
2nd voyage, Webber was in the Third Voyage? Australian Aborigines,
probably natives of one of the South Sea Islands (G.H.D.)', on back
of the mount, in another hand. 'Two studies from life of Australian
(South Sea Islanders deleted) Aborigines by Hodges. NB When the
Ship was stranded the whole of the Artists materials was destroyed
and the canvasses were lost so that the artist was obliged to use a
piece of Sail Cloth to paint upon. See MS Life of W. Hodges',
below, in a different hand.

Provenance: Petherick

Literature: Joppien and Smith (1985b), no. 2.146.

National Library of Australia, Canberra.

These two small, rapidly executed oil studies pose problems regarding
identification of their subjects and date of execution, but offer an
intriguing insight into Hodges's working practices on the voyage. The
contradictory nature of the inscriptions on the rear of the mount is a
salient reminder of those difficulties of attribution attending Hodges's
work. Contrary to the claims of these labels, Hodges never visited
Australia, no manuscript of the artist's life has ever come to light, and
there is no evidence corroborating the incident described in the third
inscription. There is however little doubt that the fabric is sailcloth and
the sketches by Hodges. Both the summary handling of the paint and
the treatment of facial features are consistent with Hodges's approach.
The figures bear a notable resemblance to those later incorporated in
paintings of Tahitian war canoes (cat. no. 30; fig. 51). Their directness
implies that they were taken from life, like the red-chalk portraits,
although when is unclear. Other similar thumbnail sketches are known
and reinforce the idea that Hodges's use of oil paint on the voyage
extended to studies of Pacific peoples, as well as the landscape.[1]

[1] Joppien and Smith (1985b), no. 2.145.

24 *View of the Province of Oparree [Pare], Island of Otaheite, with part of the Island of Eimeo [Moorea], 1775?*

Oil on panel, 76.2 × 123.2 cm

Provenance: painted for the Lords Commissioners of the Admiralty.

Literature: Stuebe (1979), no. 87, pp. 31–2, 147; Joppien and Smith (1985b), no. 2.53, pp. 57–8, 167; Smith (1985), 62; Smith (1992), 130.

National Maritime Museum, London, MoD Art Collection.

Greenwich only.

This has long been considered one of Hodges's most significant pictures. Joppien and Smith called it 'the most advanced painting for its time that Hodges ever painted', in acknowledgement of its impressive scale, loose handling of paint and compositional cropping, taken as evidence of an artist breaking with classical formulae and anticipating the naturalistic turn in landscape painting around the end of the century.[1] This wide panoramic view of Tahiti's northern shoreline, broad expanse of coastal waters and distant prospect of neighbouring islands, is cer-

tainly relatively free in execution. Painted on an unusually large panel, it employs a restricted palette over a thick white ground. Hodges's abbreviated brushwork and liquid impasto highlights convey a sense of luxuriant tropical heat, in the even glow of a meridian sunset. Compositionally, the placement of the islanders' canoe, cut off by the bottom of the picture plane, has few precedents, and amplifies the sense of vastness implied by the exaggerated aerial perspective, in suggesting space beyond the frame. It is of note that Hodges considered reusing this element at least, and possibly repeating the composition, since x-rays reveal almost exactly the same figures on the bottom edge of his large view of Matavai Bay (cat. no. 28).

Though much has been made of the painting's technical radicalism, its large, ambitious treatment is matched by the significance of the location. For Pare became highly prominent in both the literary and pictorial record of Cook's second voyage: on the *Resolution*'s return visit to Tahiti in late April 1774, the voyagers were intrigued to find an array of war boats assembled there, which enacted a series of spectacular rehearsals and reviews in preparation for a projected sea-borne attack upon the neighbouring island of Moorea. These activities were discussed and illustrated in detail in Cook's *Voyage* and provided the subject for the most grandiloquent of Hodges's post-voyage paintings (cat.

no. 30). Hodges's selection of Pare as the subject for a large-scale painting towards the end of the voyage is an early acknowledgement of its importance, and perhaps marks the formative stages of his plans for the pictorial commemoration of the voyage, where specific events, landscapes and peoples were frequently assigned a wider significance. *View of the Province of Oparree* was probably conceived as a pendant to the *View of the Monuments of Easter Island* (cat. no. 25); they are identical in scale and stylistically similar, using thick, liquid paint over a light ground on an improvized support, and suggesting a similar period of execution. Hodges often thought of works as complementary pairs or groups; notably in his post-voyage works, where he revisits certain motifs or ideas across several related pictures. Though it is difficult to determine any precise thematic intentions here, there is a clear contrast between the lush tropical verdure of the coastline at Pare and the bleak terrain of Easter Island, which accentuates the sense of loss suffusing Hodges's view of the latter's historic landscape.

[1] For discussion of this view of Hodges and the criticisms it is liable to, see Geoff Quilley's essay above.

25 *A View of the Monuments of Easter Island* [Rapanui], 1775

Oil on panel, 77.5 × 121.9 cm

Provenance: painted for the Lords Commissioners of the Admiralty.

Literature: Stuebe (1979), no. 6, pp. 32–5, 99–100; Joppien and Smith (1985b), no. 2.94, pp. 58, 74–6, 196–7; Smith (1985), 71–2; Smith (1992), 130–1.

National Maritime Museum, London, MoD Art Collection.

Cook moored off the western coast of the previously little-visited Easter Island on 14 March 1774, only to weigh anchor some three days later when it was found the island might furnish few of the provisions the *Resolution* required. During this brief stay, Hodges, accompanied by various colleagues, made two walking tours across the island. On the second of these excursions, along the south-eastern coastline to the far side of the island, they first encountered the colossal stone sculptures that are the subject of this painting. According to J. R. Forster, who was present, several of the party 'marched to an elevated place & stopped a little in order to refresh, or to give Mr *Hodges* an opportunity of drawing some stone-pillars at a distance'.[1] Like so much of Hodges's fieldwork from the voyage, these drawings are now lost, though their existence is indicated by the very different engraving for Cook's *Voyage* (fig. 45). This large, stately painting must also derive from them. Like its pendant, *View of the Province of Oparree*, it was probably worked up on the voyage homeward. Indeed, *A View of the Monuments of Easter Island* anticipates the work executed on return to London, not least in terms of its ambition. Beyond being a visual record of the time spent at Easter Island, it is also a variation on the well-established pictorial theme of *Et in Arcadia Ego*.[2] Alongside the topographical concern to capture the character of this barren landscape, the prominence assigned the colossal sculpture, tellingly juxtaposed with the foreground details of human remains, makes that terrain the repository of the island's past and present. On arrival, the voyagers had found the inhabitants of Easter Island in the most desperate, poverty-stricken condition. However, the stones indicated the former existence of a more advanced, civilized state. Hodges's painting might therefore be read as a melancholic reflection upon its passing. Forster was clear about the origin and function of the monuments: 'The pillars are burying places & Monuments. We found on the Pedement among the stones several human bones of the same size as ours, for I held a Thighbone against my own, & found it exactly correspond'.[3] Hodges's picture matches this description regarding the monuments' appearance and supposed purpose (not in fact correct). In the scroll-like marks inscribed on the foreground fragment, which feature on a number of the stone figures, it also includes an observation not to be found in any of the written accounts. Hodges offers therefore some characterization of what was witnessed. However, the skeletal remains at the base of the statues make an allusion to a more contemplative kind of painting.[4] This assembly of bones and ancient remnants, set against the most desolate landscape, intimates ideas of decay, vanished glory and human insignificance in the cosmic scale. This is reinforced by the dramatic contrasts of scale and tone, with the low vantage point aggrandizing the statues, the only uprights in this bleak scene, contrasted tonally against the lowering sky. In this, the composition conforms to the

Fig. 45 William Woollett after William Hodges, *Monuments in Easter Island*, engraving, from Cook (1777). National Maritime Museum, London.

ways ancient relics of Britain's own prehistory, such as Stonehenge, were represented.[5] If Hodges's depiction of the Easter Island monuments exploited conventions for the representation of his own country's ancient landscape, then he may have also intended a parallel between Pacific societies and Britain's own rude past. Such comparisons are common in the voyage literature and are a significant feature of Hodges's later pictorial reflections on the voyage.

[1] Forster (1982), vol. 3, 472.

[2] Hodges was surely familiar with his former master Wilson's 1755 painting on this theme. For a discussion of this tradition, see Panofsky (1965).

[3] Forster (1982), vol. 3, 468.

[4] It has been suggested that the oddly angled upright among the bones is Wales's quadrant, used to measure the stones – which appears in the related engraving in Cook's *Voyage* (fig. 45). However, this is unclear and might just as easily be read as part of the remains. Cf. Joppien and Smith (1985b), 76.

[5] Smiles (1994). For a contemporary description of Stonehenge similar to Hodges's vision of the Easter Island monuments, see Oppé (1946–8), 21.

Overleaf: detail of cat. no. 18 [*The* Resolution *in the Marquesas*], April 1774.

Hodges's post-voyage work

JOHN BONEHILL

On returning to England, Cook immediately repaired to London to report directly to the Admiralty, and 'lay before them a full Account of my proceedings during ye Whole Voyage . . . together with charts of Lands I have either discovered or explored and such of Mr Hodges's drawings as were not Transmited to you from the Cape of Good hope'.[1] Clearly, Cook recognized the importance of Hodges's contribution, not least in augmenting his own written record. However, Hodges's views of Pacific landscapes and peoples were also to play a crucial role in the commemoration of the second voyage. For, over the next two years or so, besides supervising the production of the engraved illustrations for the voyage's much anticipated official account, he executed a series of epic paintings offering a schematic narrative of that journey.

Hodges's contract for this work is now lost. According to the botanist Daniel Solander, he was 'to have 250 a year so long as he is engaged by the Admiralty to finish the drawings and paintings he has made during the Voyage'.[2] A letter from the Earl of Sandwich to his close friend Joseph Banks, dated 19 August 1775, further indicates what was expected of Hodges. Writing of the early plans to mark the voyage, Sandwich noted that the Admiralty had

> not quite concluded anything about the publication of Captain Cookes voyage, his own journal is in my opinion a very good one, & Mr Forster is desirous of being concerned jointly with Captain Cooke in the publication; but as I have already told you this is not yet settled among us: however that no time be lost, Mr Hodges the designer is directed to finish the drawings, particularly those that are to be selected for engraving; and I shall give directions that as fast as they are finished they shall be framed & glazed without which there will be no means of preserving them.[3]

There are already hints here of the dispute between the Admiralty and J. R. Forster over the authorship of the official voyage narrative. Excluded from its preparation and refused the right to publish his own independent account, Forster embarked on an extended war of words with Sandwich lasting some three years.[4] By way of circumventing the restrictions placed on him, George Forster produced *A Voyage round the World*, partly based on J. R. Forster's voyage journal and published in 1777 six weeks prior to Cook's official account; the following year his own remarkable, encyclopedic philosophical treatise, *Observations Made during a Voyage round the World*, was published. Central to the quarrel were the plates after Hodges's drawings and paintings. The Forsters were denied the opportunity to reproduce any of these, and so enhance the appeal of their own publications, but did clearly have access to them. Their writings frequently refer to them, and many of their descriptive passages directly echo, even rely upon, Hodges's work. Also of note in Sandwich's letter are the unusual plans for Hodges's drawings to be 'framed & glazed'.

In the months following his return to London, much of Hodges's attention was directed towards the production of five large canvases comprising a partial history of the voyage. Four are identical in size and follow a broadly similar compositional format. Though not an entirely coherent grouping, Hodges frequently conceived works as pairs or sequences with thematic correspondences, and so it is possible to infer more than an accidental relation between them.[5] They undoubtedly recognize and comment upon the historical significance of the voyage, as manifest in the expansion of geographical knowledge, the commerce and intercourse flowing from contact, and the progress induced through trade and introduction of manufactured articles. Hodges's paintings are accordingly epic in conception and demonstrate his personal aspirations for the elevated status of landscape painting, made explicit much later with his 1794–95 one-man show, to achieve 'a nobler effect'.[6]

Hodges's ambitions for these paintings were probably also informed by the speculations of his fellow voyagers, especially the Forsters. He was undoubtedly aware of contemporary debates over the history of human progress, and many of the preoccupations of his post-voyage works appear as reflections upon the European past, refracted in the encounter with the Pacific. In *An Essay on the History of Civil Society*, Adam Ferguson argued that 'descriptions given by travellers' offered direct access to the past: 'It is in their present condition, that we are to behold, as in a mirror, the features of our own progenitors; and from whence we are to draw our conclusions with respect to the influence of situations, in which, we have reason to believe, our fathers were placed'.[7] In Hodges's work for the Admiralty, such concerns were addressed through a form of contemporary history painting, that incorporated not only such philosophical speculation on the origins of civil society, but also new kinds of ethnographic and geographical knowledge within the framework of traditional classical forms. This also informed Hodges's work on the illustration of the voyage's official account.

Under the terms of his Admiralty employment, Hodges was to supervise the execution of engravings after his own works, comprising the plates for Cook's *A Voyage towards the South Pole*. Hodges led a team of artists drawn from several London workshops, including such skilled and popular engravers as Francesco Bartolozzi, James Basire, William Byrne, James Caldwell, Giovanni Battista Cipriani, John Hall, Benjamin Pouncey, John Keyes Sherwin, William Watts and William Woollett.[8] The scale and scope of the illustrational programme for the Admiralty's account – running to some thirty-five plates, encompassing maps, charts and diagrams, as well as images classifiable as still-life, genre, landscape, portraits and history – required great flexibility on the part of those commissioned, especially given the novelty of the subjects, and was a fundamentally collaborative process: Hall and Basire engraved the portraits, Pouncey and Watts specialized in landscape. Where the design required the grouping of several figures, the history painter, Cipriani, assisted Hodges: in the *Landing at Erramanga*, for example (cat. no. 35). To what extent Hodges had final say in the details of the plates, and whether or not he approved the various alterations made to his original studies, is not clear. However, the revisions were controversial. Sherwin's engraving after Hodges's *Landing at Middleburgh* was decried by George Forster for its 'Greek contours and features' (cat. no. 41).[9] Other plates were criticized along similar lines, although Forster was by no means consistent in his judgements. However, his remarks reveal the tension between the illustrative function of the plates, as authentic records of the Pacific encounter, and the endeavour to elevate their status. Whether in the designs for Cook's *Voyage* or in the heroic, grand-style Admiralty paintings, Hodges aspired to an aesthetic status commensurate with the voyage's high social and cultural value.

[1] Cook (1955–67), vol. 2, 694.

[2] Daniel Solander to Joseph Banks, 5 September 1775: Library, Royal Botanic Gardens, Kew.

[3] Captain Cook Memorial Museum, Whitby (on loan from the Mulgrave family archives).

[4] Hoare (1976), 151 and *passim*.

[5] This is the subject of an as yet unpublished paper by Geoff Quilley, '"Tahiti revisited": the historicizing visual order of the Pacific in the art of Captain Cook's voyages' (forthcoming). My thinking about these paintings is indebted to the insights of this work.

[6] Edwards (1808), 247.

[7] Ferguson [1767], 80.

[8] To this list might be added the name William Blake, who was apprenticed to Basire at this time: see Joppien and Smith (1985b), 110.

[9] Forster [1777], vol. 1, 222. Joppien and Smith (1985b), no. 2.73.

All catalogue entries in this section are by John Bonehill, except no. 39, which is by John Bonehill and Pieter van der Merwe.

26 [*Cascade Cove*] *Dusky Bay*, 1775

Oil on canvas, 135.9 × 193 cm, signed and dated 'Hodges – 75' (l.l.).

Provenance: painted for the Lords Commissioners of the Admiralty.

Literature: Stuebe (1979), no. 42, pp. 25–8, 120–1; Joppien and Smith (1985b), no. 2.25, pp. 25–6, 149; Smith (1992), 122–3; Thomas (1996), 244–9; Brunt (1997); Adams and Thomas (1999), 78–85; Lamb (2001), 243–7.

Exhibited: probably RA, 1776 (add.), or possibly RA, 1777 (168); RA, 1951–2 (47); Alexander Turnbull Library, June–September 1959 (4); Auckland, 1964 (13).

National Maritime Museum, London, MoD Art Collection.

Remarking on the principal geographical features of the lands of the southern hemisphere in *Observations Made during a Voyage round the World*, J. R. Forster recalls New Zealand's South Island:

> We observed, in the several inlets and arms forming this spacious bay, sometimes cascades rushing rapidly down, and falling from vast heights before they met with another rock. Some of these cascades with their neighbouring scenery, require the pencil and genius of a SALVATOR ROSA to do them justice: however the ingenious artist, who went with us on this expedition has great merit, in having executed some of these romantic landscapes in a masterly manner.[1]

Forster's admiration for the rugged, uncultivated topography of Dusky Bay deprives him of words to describe its sublimity: he can only evoke the pictorial drama of Rosa's depictions of the southern Italian landscape or direct the reader to Hodges's paintings. Hodges's sketches made on the spot provided the source for this monumental depiction of Cascade Cove, executed for the Admiralty on return to London. Like Forster's account, it summons Rosa's views of wild mountainous land-

Fig. 46 Daniel Lerpinière after William Hodges, *Family in Dusky Bay*, engraving, from Cook (1777). National Maritime Museum, London.

Fig. 47 *Habit of an Ancient Briton*, engraving, from Jeffreys (1772). The British Library, London.

scapes, but similarly ties these 'romantic' tendencies to a keen observation of natural phenomena.

This is, in scale, the most ambitious of the several images Hodges produced of the cascade, but also the most constricted view of the rocky outcrop.[2] The unusual composition might derive from Wilson's similarly unconventional *Lydford Waterfall Tavistock, Devon*, datable to the period immediately preceding Hodges's departure to the Pacific.[3] Here, however, even more of the picture surface is devoted to the rushing torrent of water, rendered in scumbled white paint, crashing onto a cluster of black rocks. Out of the spray emerges the rainbow recorded by George Forster and Wales.[4] Hodges's depiction of this phenomenon is extremely unusual for this period, and anticipates the observational naturalism of English landscape painting around the turn of the century. However, this conventional symbol of divine deliverance might also commemorate the relief felt by the voyagers on reaching New Zealand, following the lengthy and hazardous venture into Antarctic waters.

Hodges's view of the cataract synthesizes several occurrences in Dusky Sound. While registering the response to the beauty of the waterfall visited with Cook on 12 April 1773, it records the first encounter with an 'Indian family' five days earlier, at which Hodges was present. Silhouetted against the white mist of the falls, the solitary male figure on the rock, supported by a heavy ceremonial club (or *taiaha*), might be identified as the 'father' of the group, with his three female companions to the side (fig. 46).[5] If, as Joppien and Smith maintain, Hodges endows him with 'a kind of Polyclitan dignity', such classicizing tendencies are nevertheless clad in ethnographic detail. There might also be a comparison not only with the classical past but with British antiquity, in the figure's resemblance to 'Ancient Britons' of contemporary antiquarian illustration (fig. 47).[6] Artists, historians and social theorists all drew parallels between newly discovered cultures and earlier European societies, such as the ancient Britons, whose belligerence was taken to indicate their uncorrupted state. Adam Ferguson noted how 'the inhab-

itants of Britain, at the time of the first Roman invasions, resembled, in many things, the present natives of North America: they were ignorant of agriculture; they painted their bodies, and used for cloathing, the skins of beasts'.[7] Several participants in Cook's voyage noted similar continuities. Anders Sparrman recognized in the Maori 'many of the methods of war and murder of our Gothic Viking forefathers'.[8] The Maori encountered at Dusky Sound were seen as living instances of modern man's ancient past. Hodges's picture therefore is a *history* painting, not in the pure academic sense but in representing an encounter with that rude past.

[1] Forster [1778], 51. Cf. also Cook (1955–67), vol. 2, 119.

[2] Joppien and Smith (1985b), nos. 2.23–7.

[3] See Solkin (1982), cat. no. 135.

[4] Cook (1961), vol. 2, 782. Cf. Forster [1777], vol. 1, 90–1.

[5] For discussion of the difficulties facing the voyagers in deciding the precise relations between this 'family', see Thomas (1995).

[6] Contemporary fascination with Britain's own prehistory was such that it found expression in a diverse range of cultural activities, not least the visual arts (see Smiles (1994)). Hodges long-standing interest in the topic is testified to by two now lost works which drew on aspects of the nation's remote past: *A View of a Druid's Altar in Pembrokeshire* (Society of Artists 1768) and *Landscape and figures, the destruction of the Bards* (RA 1791).

[7] Ferguson [1767], 75.

[8] Sparrman (1944), 49.

27 *A View of Cape Stephens in Cook's Straits [New Zealand] with Waterspout*, 1776

Oil on canvas, 135.9 × 193.1 cm, signed and dated 'Hodges – 76' (l.c.).

Provenance: painted for the Lords Commissioners of the Admiralty.

Literature: Stuebe (1979), no. 49, pp. 28–9, 124–5; Joppien and Smith (1985b), no. 2.29, pp. 33–9, 151; Smith (1985), 65–8; Smith (1992), 122–3; Brunt (1997).

Exhibited: British Institution 1817 (132).

National Maritime Museum, London, MoD Art Collection.

Late in the afternoon of 17 May 1773, a few days out from Dusky Sound and en route to rendezvous with the *Adventure* in Queen Charlotte Sound, the *Resolution* encountered four waterspouts off Cape Stephens.

Few had witnessed this startling phenomenon before, and from the vivid descriptions in the voyage accounts it elicited responses ranging from the alarm and disquiet felt by the ordinary seamen, recorded by Richard Pickersgill,[1] to the inquisitive curiosity of George Forster's controlled, meticulous description:

> On a sudden a whitish spot appeared on the sea in that quarter, and a column arose out of it, looking like a glass tube; another seemed to come out of the clouds to meet this, and they made a coalition, forming what is commonly called a water-spout . . . Our situation during all this time was very dangerous and alarming; a phaenomenon which carried so much terrific majesty in it, and which connected as it were the sea with the clouds, made our oldest mariners uneasy and at a loss how to behave . . . we prepared indeed for the worst, by cluing up our topsails; but it was the general opinion that our masts and yards must have gone to wreck if we had been drawn into the vortex.[2]

Only at the end does Forster acknowledge the *Resolution*'s perilous situation, but, unlike the mariners, he is still able to appreciate the 'terrible majesty' and sublimity of the scene, in a way that accords with Hodges's pictorial record of the occasion.

Hodges probably made several sketches of the waterspouts at some point the same afternoon or very shortly after. A depiction of the phenomenon inserted in Wales and Bayly's *Astronomical Observations* (1777) is evidence of this (fig. 48). In the accompanying text the authors claimed the plate 'was engraved from a drawing of Mr. Hodges, taken at the time; in which he has exhibited the appearance of one of them in three separate states'.[3] This does not mean, however, that the engraving is a purely objective depiction of the meteorology. In attempting to illustrate this near shapeless, elemental phenomenon, it inevitably falls back on the conventions of the sublime: the intensely dramatic composition relies upon the stark contrast of the brilliant white of the coastline and spiralling water against the surrounding darkness. A series of closely engraved, broken lines describe the serrated edges of the waves, the twisting funnels of water, and the gathering storm. The only tangible shape is the barely discernible silhouette of the *Resolution*, on the verge of being completely engulfed in the waterspout's rising vortex.

This scene of human endeavour all but drowned by the uncontrollable forces of nature was developed further in the large canvas, *A View of Cape Stephens in Cook's Straits*, completed for the Admiralty the year after the voyage. Hodges's scene conforms closely to Forster's description, even including the shaft of lightning noted by Forster as one of the columns of water broke. The details of the rugged coastline, overgrown with vegetation, and inhabited by indigenous animal life, in the form of seals and exotic waterfowl, recall Hodges's other depictions of the antipodean landscape, seeming to locate the scene in a specific topography. However, several aspects of the composition indicate Hodges's deviation from a literal rendering of events. On the rocky promontory in the foreground, a 'family' group, entirely of the artist's invention, watches the hazardous passage of Cook's ship. It has been claimed that this group derives from the Maori family encountered at Dusky Bay and shown in *Cascade Cove* (cat. no. 26), but this is not entirely satisfactory. In fact, Hodges's intentions are obscure. If the woman clutching a child to her breast is a strange amalgam of Europeanized features and exotic dress, unlike Maori depicted elsewhere by Hodges, the man is a still odder conglomeration of

Fig. 49 Richard Wilson, *Ceyx and Alcyone*, 1768, oil on canvas, 101.6 x 127.1 cm. National Museums & Galleries, Wales.

sources, alternately a prophetic Moses or tragic Lear, classical orator or Druidic Bard.

This mix of elements is only one of the painting's dense web of references. Compositionally, it closely resembles Wilson's *Ceyx and Alcyone* (1768) (fig. 49), a picture Hodges undoubtedly knew very well and may have worked on when under Wilson's tutelage.[4] He directly quotes specific passages such as the arching limbs of the bare tree to the right. Hodges's explicit reference to Wilson's attempt to elevate landscape painting by invoking classical sources advertizes his own similar artistic ambitions. A scene of near shipwreck on a distant, inaccessible and stormy coast was a subject of obvious potential. Coastal scenes provided ideal artistic opportunities to treat the play of conflicting forces in nature, and were increasingly popular among painters during the later eighteenth century. Several factors suggest that Hodges strove to imbue this work with moral significance.

This human drama is played out against a sublime, elemental backdrop. Signs of the sublime – as codified most influentially by Edmund Burke – dominate the picture. Earth, air, fire and water fuse indissolubly, and in some passages indistinguishably. Obscurity, darkness and immensity were all qualities identifiable as sublime, and are summoned here by the dramatic contrasts of tone, scale and form. For Burke, sublime terror was peculiarly pleasurable: 'The passions which turn on self-preservation are delightful when we have an idea of pain and danger without actually being in such circumstances'.[5] In this analysis, such imagery appealed to the sympathetic emotions (or 'passions'). Religious references further heighten the work's emotional and moral content: the foreground group recalls the Holy Family, and the composition overall evokes the iconography of the Deluge. In addition, the composition is based not just on Wilson but also on Gaspar Dughet's *Jonah and the Whale* – known to Hodges presumably through its 1748 engraving – so referring to another instance of divine deliverance (fig. 50).[6] These allusions establish an association of maritime disaster and divine judgement

Fig. 48 After William Hodges, *Waterspouts in Cook's Straits*, engraving, from Wales and Bayly (1777). National Maritime Museum, London.

Fig. 50 After Gaspard Dughet, *Jonah and the Whale*, 1748, (engraved in reverse),
Copyright © British Museum.

that confers a moral charge to this paean to nautical achievement.

This is significant given the subject's potential reminder of another instance of near-shipwreck, from Cook's first voyage. John Hawkesworth's account of this, in his widely read 1773 compilation, *An Account of the Voyages Undertaken by the Order of his Present Majesty for*

Making Discoveries in the Southern Hemisphere, had elicited considerable critical invective, not least for the details it carried of the eroticism of Tahitian society (see also cat. no. 32).[7] However, contemporaries were still more disconcerted by his apparent dismissal of Providence in the *Endeavour*'s escape from certain shipwreck on the Great Barrier Reef, attributing the ship's salvation to chance rather than divine intervention. Hodges would certainly have been aware of the controversy on his return to London. His choice, therefore, of the *Resolution*'s deliverance from nautical disaster for such a major painting seems pointed, particularly in its multiple Biblical references. Such a treatment would certainly have appealed to the Admiralty, still reeling from the heated controversy surrounding Hawkesworth's publication. Accordingly, Hodges's painting can be seen as an admonitory reminder of the need for faith, and an acknowledgement of the claims of divine truth and order in the world.

[1] Pickersgill (1984), 72.

[2] Forster [1777], vol. 1, 110–11.

[3] Wales and Bayly (1777), 346.

[4] Joppien and Smith (1985b), 37–8.

[5] Burke [1757], 51.

[6] Rigby and van der Merwe (2002), 92.

[7] On the hostile reception of the book, see Abbott (1982), 137–86.

28 [A] view of Maitavie Bay, [in the Island of] Otaheite [Tahiti], 1776

Oil on canvas, 137.1 × 193 cm.

Inscribed: as title, on the back of the original canvas.

Provenance: painted for the Lords Commissioners of the Admiralty.

Literature: Stuebe (1979), no. 85; Joppien and Smith (1985b), no. 2.49, pp. 59–61, 164; Smith (1985), 69–71; Smith (1992), 127–8; Bindman (2002), 134–5.

National Maritime Museum, London, MoD Art Collection.

Probably executed for the Admiralty during the second half of 1776, this is the second version of the picture exhibited at the Royal Academy earlier that year as *A view of Matavie Bay in the island of Otaheite* (cat. no. 31). A larger, more grandly conceived painting, handled in a less vigorous, impasto-heavy manner, Hodges made several telling revisions to the original composition. Recent x-rays indicate that the canvas started dif-

ferently, possibly as a variant of cat. no. 24. Cook's ships anchored in the bay replace the war canoes; to the left, at Point Venus, are Wales's portable observatory and a tent set up for the *Resolution*'s sick. There are a number of additional figures, notably the foreground Madonna and Child-like group and the classically posed boatman to their left. These adjustments impart a greater structural clarity than in the earlier version, as well as placing the Navy, or the voyage's patron, firmly at the focus of the composition.

Where previously Hodges concentrated on the Tahitian fleet, this revised work focuses on the interaction between the voyagers and the community on the island's north side. It presents the encounter as one of amicable and peaceful co-operation, where modern commercial society, represented by the *Resolution* and *Adventure*, co-exists with one shown, through its manufactures and cultivation of the environment, to be taking the first steps towards the commercial state. So, Hodges's picture offers 'a Georgic vision of man as the improver and organizer of nature',[1] celebrating both the comforts and the rigours of Tahitian life. The bay bustling with fishing boats and canoes is matched by the opulent, plentiful landscape – indicating that enterprise will reap rich rewards – a view of the

island that echoes Forster's description of Tahiti's natural abundance:

> The mild and temperate climate, under the powerful, benevolent, and congenial influence of the sun, mitigated by alternate sea and land breezes, quickens the growth of the vegetable and animal creation; and therefore, in some measure also, benefits and improves the human frame, by this happy combination. Such is the great abundance of the finest fruit growing, as it were, without cultivation, that none are distressed for food. The sea is another great resource for the inhabitants of this and all the Society Isles. They catch great numbers of fine and delicious fish.[2]

Forster, in line with contemporary environmentalist theory, sees the people of Tahiti as the physical embodiment of their environment: the climate 'improves the human frame'. Hodges's apparently classicized islanders then are fitting. Their nobility, as Joppien and Smith have commented, is 'inseparable from the salubrity of the climate'.

[1] Bindman (2002).
[2] Forster [1778], 145–6.

29 *A View in the Island of New Caledonia in the South*, 1777–8

Oil on canvas, 138 × 193.5 cm.

Provenance: painted for the Lords Commissioners of the Admiralty.

Literature: Stuebe (1979), no. 30; Joppien and Smith (1985b), no. 2.140, pp. 98–9, 240; Smith (1992), 69.

Exhibited: RA 1778 (149); Alexander Turnbull Library, June–September 1959 (10); Auckland 1964 (22).

National Maritime Museum, London, MoD Art Collection.

On 4 September 1774, as the *Resolution* travelled south from Melanesia for New Zealand prior to its third and final cruise of Antarctic waters, a previously uncharted island came into view. Cook named it New Caledonia, and spent much of the following month surveying the coastline and exploring its interior. Leading one excursion into the hills, he was struck by the wild, irregular prospect below:

> At length we reached the Summit of one of the hills from whence we saw the Sea between some Advanced hills at a considerable distance on the opposite side of the Island. Between those advanced hills and the ridge we were upon is a large Vally through which ran a Serpentine river which added no little beauty to the prospect. The plains along the Coast on the side we lay appeared from the hills to great advantage, the winding Streams which ran through them which had their direction from Nature, the lesser streams coveyed by art through the different plantations, the little Stragling Villages, the Variaty in the Woods, the Shoals on the Coast so variegated that the whole might afford a Picture for Romance.[1]

Very probably Hodges was among the party, and made sketches of the same view. Stuebe has suggested that this large, ambitious landscape, worked up from now lost studies, amounts to a virtual 'illustration' of Cook's words. The same series of contrasts that 'so variegated the Scene' for Cook, between art and nature, cultivated and unimproved land, dense, forested interior and open sea, structures Hodges's panoramic prospect. Conversely, Cook's uncharacteristically lyrical description, couched in the language of the picturesque, is possibly influenced by others' interpretation of landscape: the Forsters, Wales, or indeed Hodges.

Hodges offers a seemingly objective topographic view, but one that also forms a harmonious, coherent composition. While attending to the irregularities of the terrain, in the impassable crevice and sheer rock face of the foreground, or the unexpected, shadowy shapes of the forest, each natural abutment forms a successive and sharply defined plane. Furthermore, Hodges's staffing of this landscape goes far beyond mere topographical description. Besides marking the discovery of this significant island, the painting offers a further meditation upon the nature of Pacific history. Despite the harshness of the foreground shapes, this is also a rich, fertile land. It is studded with birds in flight, possible prey for the lone, spear-carrying hunter barely discernible at far right. In the middle distance, even less distinct, several other figures huddle around a fire. Hodges's vision of a nomadic people, entrusting their survival to the natural provision of the environment, consigns them to the lowliest stage in the progress towards civil society: that of the hunter-gatherer. According to contemporary theorists, people in the rudest state 'intrust their subsistence chiefly to hunting, fishing, or the natural produce of the soil'.[2] Hodges's painting suggests the distance of this culture from the attainments of European trading nations: the *Resolution*, a potent symbol of modern commercial society, lies at anchor off the island's eastern shore, no more than a faint presence.

---

[1] Cook (1955–67), vol. 2, 533–4.

[2] Ferguson [1767], 81.

30 *The War-Boats of the island of Otaheite* [Tahiti], *and the Society Islands, with a View of part of the Harbour of Ohameneno* [Haamanino], *in the island of Ulietea* [Raiatea], *one of the Society islands*, 1777

Oil on canvas, 181.1 × 274.3 cm, signed and dated 'Hodges 77' (l.r.).

Provenance: painted for the Lords Commissioners of the Admiralty.

Literature: Stuebe (1979), no. 94, pp. 38, 151–3; Joppien and Smith (1985b), no. 2.115, pp. 82–5, 214; Smith (1985), 75; Smith (1992), 131.

Exhibited: RA 1777 (171); British Institution 1817 (49); British Institution 1851 (126); RA 1951–2 (377); Alexander Turnbull Library, June–September 1959 (5); Auckland 1964 (17).

National Maritime Museum, London, MoD Art Collection.

Returning to Matavai Bay on 22 April 1774, Cook and his party found a fleet of some 160 canoes assembled for an attack on the neighbouring island of Moorea. Although the *Resolution* left before the outbreak of hostilities, naval manoeuvres at Pare were watched and recorded with intense interest. Both Forster's and Cook's journals detail the preparations, the latter noting Hodges was 'with me and had an opportunity to collect some materials for a large drawing or Picture he intends to make of the fleet'.[1] Sketches taken on this occasion were the basis for several post-voyage works, including an oil study for the official publication (cat. no. 41) and this grandiose painting executed for the Admiralty and for display at the Royal Academy.

Exhibited in 1777 alongside several other scenes from the voyage, it is Hodges's largest known work entirely by his own hand. Given the public appetite for news of the Pacific, its subject matter and size guaranteed its prominence on the densely crowded Academy walls. However, the work's vigorous handling of paint and sharp tonal contrasts attracted adverse criticism in the daily press,[2] although not all reports were unfavourable. 'Gaudenzio', writing in the *St. James's Chronicle*, observed 'The War-Boats of the Island of Otaheite, &c., by

Fig. 51 William Hodges, *Review of the War Galleys at Tahiti*, c.1776, oil on panel, 24.1 x 47.0 cm. National Maritime Museum, London, MoD Art Collection.

Mr. Hodges, are very curious, and there is great Merit in the Views'.[3] 'Curious' is a term frequently evoked by late eighteenth-century voyages of exploration, possessing a range of connotations, usually used to register the noteworthiness of what might now be termed a society's 'material culture'.[4] Hodges's various paintings and sketches of Tahiti's war canoes likewise demonstrate a close scrutiny of their design and manufacture.

In the oil study for the plate for Cook's *Voyage towards the South Pole* Hodges builds up a wealth of informative, ethnographic detail (fig. 51), depicting the intricate decorative and anthropomorphic carved pillars of the sterns and the elaborate head-dress of the warrior on the raised fighting stage. While the large Admiralty painting similarly displays such 'curiosities', the grand spectacle of the fleet's embarkation also affords a subject that meets the demands of history, in addressing the most public of themes, war. This in turn entailed further reflection upon the history of human society. War was a subject of abiding interest to Hodges, most obviously in the central works in his one-man show of 1794–95. Aspects of those later canvases are adumbrated in the present work, as in the small 'caritas' vignette of the mother and child at bottom left, icons of domesticity and the civilizing processes and social continuity under the warrior's protection. Moreover, Hodges's painting synthesizes an eclectic range of pictorial models to demonstrate the artist's visual erudition and ambitions. If the Madonna and Child-like grouping of the shore scene recalls devotional models, then the powerful male nudes of the warriors manning the boats echo numerous classical exemplars. In addition, Hodges departs from his sketches' ethnographic fidelity by rearranging and simplifying various features of the most prominent canoe to form a stable, pyramidal composition that, as Joppien and Smith have noted, resembles a 'classical pediment'. Such quotation of revered models and compositional formats is apt for the history Hodges depicts.

The close inspection of the boats themselves, however modified by

aesthetic concerns, is indicative of Hodges's awareness of the central place of the mechanical arts and manufactures to the evaluation of societal progress. J. R. Forster noted that 'the large war-canoes cost the natives infinite labour, and afford the best specimens of their genius, industry, and mechanical arts', concluding that naval might and the capacity to wage regular war were major factors elevating Tahitian society above all others in the Pacific.[5] Contemporary social theory argued that such bellicosity was a further indication of a relatively advanced state of progress. For, if the tropical climate and abundance of nature induced a slothful society, then conflict provided an urgent redress. In *Sketches of the History of Man*, Lord Kames observed that

> Upon the whole, perpetual war is bad, because it converts men into beasts of prey: perpetual peace is worse, because it converts men into beasts of burden. To prevent such woful degeneracy on both hands, war and peace alternately are the effectual means; and these means are adopted by Providence.[6]

War, by this analysis, was a necessary, even Providential, corrective to the corrupting effects of the luxury thought to be the inevitable consequence of commercial progress and prosperity. That Hodges was open to and aware of such arguments is made explicit in his later writings, but is also suggested by his fascination with the Tahitian fleet at Pare, particularly in this, one of his most ambitious works.

Hodges's concern to heroicize the sea-borne warfare of the Pacific through classicizing quotation was entirely in keeping with the accounts of his fellow voyagers. George Forster drew an explicit comparison between the war canoes and 'the ships of the ancient Greeks', to illustrate 'that men in a similar state of civilization resemble each other more than we are aware of, even in the most opposite extremes of the world'.[7] Significantly, it is their ability to wage war, made manifest in the arts devoted to it, that signals their relative stage of progress. Hodges's epic treatment of three large war canoes, against a backdrop of a rising tropical squall, grants the scene a poetic, Homeric quality that also encourages such comparison.

[1] Cook (1961), vol. 2, 391.

[2] See John Bonehill's essay in this volume.

[3] *St. James's Chronicle, or, British Evening-Post*, 3–6 May 1777, 2.

[4] Thomas (1991), 125–51.

[5] Forster [1778].

[6] Kames (1774), vol. 1, 438.

[7] Forster [1777], vol. 2, 377–8. Cf. Forster (1982), vol 3, 502–3. See also Smith (1992).

31 *A View of Matavai Bay in the Island of Otaheite* [Tahiti], 1776

Oil on canvas, 91.5 × 137.1 cm, signed and dated 'Hodges 1776' (l.l.)

Provenance: H.T. de Vere Clifton (?); Christie's, 19 November 1948 (162), one of a pair of pictures to Spink (see cat. no. 32); Paul Mellon.

Literature: Stuebe (1979), no. 84; Joppien and Smith (1985b), no. 2.48, pp. 59–62, 163; Smith (1985), 69–71; Guest (1989), 39 *passim*; Smith (1992), 127–8.

Exhibited: RA 1776 (133); Yale University Art Gallery, New Haven, April–June 1965 (105).

Yale Center for British Art, Paul Mellon Collection.

Like cat. no. 30, the principal subject of this painting is the spectacle of Tahitian war galleys. Several types of vessel are ranged across the harbour, from small outriggers to large double sailing canoes with fighting stages and warriors in ceremonial dress. Hodges probably intended this view of Tahiti-nue, the larger of the two landmasses forming the island, to be paired with his painting of Tahiti-iti, on the southern peninsula (cat. no. 32): of identical size and exhibited together in 1776, they complement each other thematically. Both suggest the lush opulence of the landscape, given emphasis by the liquidity of the paint. Their mutuality revolves around a series of contrasts: between the coastline and the interior, male and female space, and, most obviously, war and peace. Hodges made a later version of this painting, substituting the *Resolution* and *Adventure* for the Tahitian war boats (cat. no. 28).

32 *A View taken in the Bay of Otaheite Peha* [Vaitepiha], 1776

Oil on canvas, 91.5 × 137.1 cm, signed and dated 'Hodges – 76' (l.l.).

Provenance: H.T. de Vere Clifton (?); Christie's, 19 November 1948 (162), one of a pair to Spink (see cat. no. 31); Lord Fairhaven; National Trust.

Literature: Herrmann (1973), 129; Stuebe (1979), no. 78; Joppien and Smith (1985b), no. 2.142, pp. 62–4, 160; Guest (1989), 39 *passim*.

Exhibited: RA 1776 (134); 'Pittura Inglese, 1660–1840', Palazzo Reale, Milan 1975 (86).

Anglesey Abbey, The Fairhaven Collection (The National Trust).

Exhibited at the 1776 Royal Academy exhibition alongside *A View of Matavai Bay in the Island of Otaheite*, this pendant depicts Vaitepiha Bay on the opposite (south-eastern) side of the island. Where the former indicates a society preparing for war, this painting concentrates on the benefits of peace. It offers an Arcadian vision of Tahitian life that highlights the island's rich, luxuriant landscape, and accords with its popular conception as a paradise regained. Louis-Antoine Bougainville's account of his 1768 landfall, translated by J. R. Forster the year before he departed on Cook's second voyage, promoted Tahiti as the 'New Cythera', and the parallels this suggests across space and time, between contemporary Pacific society and a distant, European past, are also summoned by Hodges's painting.[1] Its depiction of tranquil amusement in lush verdure, together with the framing of the prospect and exaggerations of aerial perspective, evoke a nostalgic vision of a remote idyll conforming to the conventions of the pastoral landscape tradition, but also located in a specific topography. Drawing on an oil sketch probably painted on the *Resolution*'s first visit to the bay in August 1773, it is rooted in the close observation of topography and the atmospheric effects of the local climate (cat. no. 10).

Various details of Hodges's composition place this apparition of secluded freedom in a distinctly primitive setting. If the young Tahitian women recall the familiar classical iconography of Diana bathing, the extensive tattooing revealed by the figure on the bank exoticizes that tradition. While it is now recognized that such markings were related to the life cycle and denoted membership of chiefly or *arioi* society, a contemporary exhibition-going public might have understood them very differently.[2] One of the most notorious features of Hawkesworth's relation of Cook's first voyage was its account of the overt eroticism of Tahitian culture, not least in the sexual encounters between islanders and voyagers. It initiated much moralizing censure, but also led to the publication of a slew of sentimental and satirical verse, usually framed in Ovidian language and imagery, which delighted in the more lascivious details of Tahitian practices, such as tattooing buttocks.[3] Hodges's painting perhaps responds to this prurient interest, yet contains a number of elements that strike a somewhat disquieting note. Presiding over this scene of carefree pleasure is an anthropomorphic carving of deified ancestors (or *tii*); while in the middle ground at far right is an elevated platform bearing a shrouded corpse (or *tupapau*). These inclusions turn the painting into a meditation on the transience of earthly pleasures as a further adaptation of the traditional theme of *Et in Arcadia Ego* (see cat. no. 25). These intimations of mortality present reminders of the fragility of this blissful state, contrasting with the warlike theme of the painting's pendant. However, it was also recognized that European intervention, no matter how supposedly beneficial in its civilizing influences, must corrupt this pristine, unspoilt landscape and its innocent peoples. It was lamented that the most tangible record of European presence in 'New Cythera' was the introduction of gonorrhea.

[1] Bougainville (1772), 242.

[2] For the significance of such marks in Tahitian culture, see Gell (1993). *Arioi* society was largely composed of younger, aristocratic islanders, and notorious amongst the voyagers for its promiscuity.

[3] See Roderick (1972); Smith (1985), 82–5; Orr (1994); Bewell (1996). On the voyagers' responses to Tahitian sexuality, see Porter (1990).

33 'Tahiti Revisited', 1776

Oil on canvas, 92.7 × 138.4 cm, signed and dated 'Hodges – 76'.

Inscribed: 'A View taken [in] yᵉ Bay of Oaite peha OTAHEITE' on the back of the original canvas.

Provenance: painted for the Lords Commissioners of the Admiralty.

Literature: Waterhouse (1953), 178–9; Stuebe (1979), no. 79; Joppien and Smith (1985b), no. 2.43, pp. 63–4, 160; Smith (1985), 64–5; Smith (1992), 132; Bindman (2002), 134–5.

Exhibited: British Institution 1817 (16); Birmingham City Art Gallery, November–January 1949 (161); RA, December–March 1969 (68).

National Maritime Museum, London, MoD Art Collection.

This prospect of the interior of Tahiti-iti is frequently assumed to be the painting exhibited at the Royal Academy in 1776 as *A View taken in the bay of Otaheite Peha*. However, various aspects suggest it is more likely a second version of that work (cat. no. 32). Hodges's handling is more controlled and the abrupt tonal contrasts characteristic of his work are moderated. There are also some slight compositional alterations that reinforce the note of melancholic reflection struck by the complex reworking of the *Et in Arcadia Ego* theme of the original version. The most significant are the addition of a *tapa* cloth beneath the *tii* which, as Stuebe suggests, might be likened to a shroud; and the introduction of a third bather, seen in a profile redolent of figures of mourning in contemporary funerary monuments. In the middle ground, two further figures – one heavily draped on the rock, left, and the other seated – contemplate the verdant landscape surrounding them. Such inclusions give added emphasis to the sense of impending loss that generally accompanies images of idyllic, Edenic plenty in this period: Ronald Paulson's consideration of melancholy in eighteenth-century British art and literature concludes that an aesthetic of the beautiful constitutes nothing less than an aesthetic of mourning. It is, he argues, a sensibility dependent upon anticipated loss.[1] 'Tahiti Revisited', the title on the frame, is of uncertain origin.

[1] Paulson (1989), 230–45.

124

34 *Landing at MALLICOLO* [Malakula], *one of the NEW HEBRIDES, c.*1776

Oil on panel, 24.1 × 45.7 cm

Provenance: H. Arthurton, London; Colnaghi, London (1957).

Literature: Stuebe (1979), no. 28; Joppien and Smith (1985b), no. 2.126, pp. 92–3, 224, Smith (1985), 73.

Engraved: by J. Basire, for Cook (1777), vol. 2, plate LX.

National Maritime Museum, London.

On the afternoon of 22 July 1774, the *Resolution* anchored just off the eastern coast of Malakula. Initial contact with the local population, Cook recorded, established a 'friendly intercourse'.[1] However, for reasons that remain unclear, relations soured, and in the confusion members of the crew discharged a flurry of gunshots. Later the same day, communication was re-established when several canoes appeared around Cook's ship. Details of this encounter were subsequently recounted by George Forster:

> We were received by a croud of no less than three hundred persons, all armed, but very friendly and inoffensive in their behaviour towards us. A middle-aged man, rather stronger than the generality of the people, gave away his bow and quiver to another, and came unarmed to shake hands with us, in signs of peace and amity; he was

perhaps a chief among them. A pig was brought at the same time, and presented to the captain, apparently as a kind of expiation for their countrymen's ill behaviour; but perhaps it was only a ratification of the peace which we had concluded. This interview is represented in a fine plate, designed by Mr. Hodges, and engraved for captain Cook's account of this voyage.[2]

Despite Forster's admiration for Hodges's picture, it is far from an exact representation of the encounter, with notable discrepancies between word and image. Though Hodges is careful to include local detail, such as the islanders' characteristic adornments and decoration, other elements are more fanciful, particularly its adaptation of several well-known classical archetypes. It is significant that the exchange of gifts Forster relates is elided here: in Hodges's painting the reciprocal gestures of the two central protagonists indicate a sanctioning of the renewed peace. Yet, while Hodges and Forster interpret this interview as a scene of peaceful accord ratified, it is possible that the offering of the animal was intended as compensation payment, and that Cook's gifts were accepted in turn as an acknowledgement of a re-establishment of social relations.[3] This and Cat. no. 36 should in theory be Admiralty pictures, but were either disposed of or never received by them.

---

[1] Cook (1961), vol. 2, 461.

[2] Forster [1777], vol. 2, 483–4.

[3] On the significance of such gift-giving in ni-Vanuatu society, see Allen (1981).

35 *Landing at ERRAMANGA [Eromanga] one of the NEW HEBRIDES, c.*1776

Oil on panel, 22.9 × 45.7 cm

Provenance: painted for the Lords Commissioners of the Admiralty.

Literature: Stuebe (1979), no. 9; Joppien and Smith (1985b), no. 2.128, pp. 93–4, 227; Smith (1985), 73–4; Smith (1992), 200–2.

Engraved: by J. K. Sherwin, for Cook (1777), vol. 2, plate LXII.

Exhibited: RA 1778 (150).

National Maritime Museum, London, MoD Art Collection.

On 4 August 1774, Cook moored the *Resolution* off the coast of the island of Eromanga. Following apparently peaceful entreaties from local inhabitants to come ashore, Cook, accompanied by a party of marines, embarked for the beach. However, his journal records that after the 'distribution of a few trinkets a Mongest them' the locals became more demanding, and an already uneasy interview became actively hostile, forcing the voyagers to retreat to the ship.[1]

Hodges was not witness to these events but Wales recorded that Cook's own account of proceedings was 'copied by Mr. Hodges, a few days after the transaction happened'.[2] Clearly, Cook and Hodges were in consultation over what might prove a significant event worthy of

visual record, and although we have no similar confirmation of other such collaborations, it must be presumed that this was common practice when the artist was not physically present. This insight into Hodges's working practices derives from the contentious nature of his representation of the aborted landing at Eromanga. For Wales's remarks were written in defence of Cook's description of this violent episode – and the accompanying engraving – in the official voyage account.

George Forster accused Cook of acting with unnecessary force at Eromanga, and 'lamented that the voyages of Europeans cannot be performed without being fatal to the nations whom they visit'. His criticisms extended to Hodges, whose pictorial version of events he dismissed as 'invented'.[3] In a lengthy, vitriolic reply, Wales defended both artist and explorer:

> No intelligent person will suppose, that in those representations Mr. Hodges meant to identify particular persons, or to give the exact position or employment of every one who were present; but it appears very possible, that he might draw a general representation of the action from a description given to him by any person of veracity, equally as well as if he had been on the spot and seen it with his own eyes.[4]

This exchange was in reference to Sherwin's engraving after Hodges's painting, rather than the painting itself (fig. 52), which was, anyway, based not only on Cook's account but also on a composition provided by Cipriani.[5] In Cipriani's hands, Cook's encounter with the Eromangans became a near epic confrontation, with the Melanesians transformed into an array of classical types. His quotation of well-

Fig. 52 John Keyes Sherwin after William Hodges, *The Landing at Erramanga, one of the New Hebrides*, engraving, from Cook (1777). National Maritime Museum, London.

known works of classical antiquity conforms to the kind of eclectic borrowing advocated by academic theory and so lends the scene the status of history. Hodges absorbed these lessons, but also introduced a number of individual elements to the figures: rendering their proportions heavier and coarsening their features. Sherwin's plate seems to be a composite of Hodges's oil study and Cipriani's drawing, leaning more towards the latter's classicizing tendencies. That such generalizing principles in art were commonly understood is demonstrated by both Wales's comments and the critical reactions to Hodges's *Landing at Erramanga* on its exhibition at the Royal Academy in 1778.

The controversy may have prompted Hodges's decision to display what is, after all, only a study in such an important public context as the Academy: both offering his original design for comparison with the engraved version, and attempting to capitalize on the attention generated by the furore. If so, he did not anticipate the picture being singled out for critical rebuke. In a mordant review the *Morning Post* condemned it for 'material faults in both its plan and execution', complaining the 'Europeans and the savages are not discriminated in their complexion'.[6] Hodges's painting failed in not meeting the demands for legibility so crucial to academic theorizing of history painting, which stipulated a visually unified account of a significant event, condensing the

narrative's temporal and spatial complexity into a single image. Such comments are revealing in that they recognize the difficulties of depicting a scene of 'confusion' or violent confrontation. For theoretically the painting of violence was problematic. Its contingent, anecdotal nature was thought incompatible with the dignity and intellectual balance expected to characterize the elevated and elevating arts. While Hodges's composition sets up a contrast between civility and savagery, played out against a backdrop of beach and ocean, for reviewers of the day, this only made for a 'disagreeable effect'.

[1] See Cook (1955–67), vol. 2, 478–9.

[2] Wales (1778), 74.

[3] Forster [1777], vol. 2, 505.

[4] Wales (1778).

[5] See Joppien and Smith (1985b).

[6] The *Morning Post, and Daily Advertiser*, 29 April 1778, 2. The same fault was identified in an otherwise complimentary review in the *General Advertiser, and Morning Intelligencer*, 2 May 1778, 4.

36 *The Landing at TANNA* [Tana] *one of the NEW HEBRIDES, c.*1775–76

Oil on panel, 24.1 × 45.7 cm

Provenance: H. Arthurton, London; Colnaghi, London (1957).

Literature: Stuebe (1979), no. 104; Joppien and Smith (1985b), no. 2.134, pp. 94–5, 233–4; Smith (1992), 214.

Engraved: by J. K. Sherwin, for Cook (1777), vol. 2, plate LIX.

National Maritime Museum, London.

Following the violence at Eromanga, Cook approached neighbouring Tana with considerable caution. On 6 August 1774, as he prepared to land on the island's northern shore, a large number of inhabitants, led by an elderly 'chief' the voyagers came to know as 'Paowang', gathered on the beach:

> every thing conspired to make us believe they meant to attack us as soon as we should be on shore; the consequence of which was easily supposed; many of them must have been killed or wounded, and we should hardly have escaped unhurt; two things I equally wished to prevent. Since, therefore, they would not give us the room we required, I thought it better to frighten them into it, than to oblige them by the deadly effect of our fire-arms. I accordingly ordered a musket to be fired over the party on our right, which was by far

the strongest body; but the alarm it gave them was momentary. In an instant they recovered themselves, and began to display their weapons. One fellow shewed us his backside, in a manner which plainly conveyed his meaning. After this I ordered three or four more musquets to be fired. This was the signal of the ship to fire a few great guns, which presently dispersed them; and then we landed, and marked out the limits, on the right and left, by a line.[1]

When published in Cook's *Voyage* this account was accompanied by Sherwin's engraving after this painting by Hodges. However, Hodges's composition is again far from literal. Rather, it breaks down the narrative's principal features into an immediate, legible image, in a manner as reminiscent of the reportage of the popular print as the language of academic painting.[2] The extensive ethnographic detail, authenticating the verbal and visual recitation of events, is subsumed within the greater pictorial drama of the scene. Hodges illuminates the encounter in a remarkably original way, utilizing the strange atmospheric effects wrought by brilliant sunlight and the smoking volcano Yasur, together with the flash of artillery fire reflected in the water. The central features of Cook's narrative are certainly present, but the finer details are omitted to produce a more striking, even theatrical general effect. Like Cat. no. 34, this should in theory be an Admiralty picture, which they either disposed of or never received.

[1] Cook (1777), vol. 2, 54–5.
[2] For example, the well-known print *The Fruits of Arbitrary Power; or the Bloody Massacre* (1770).

37 [*Tahiti, bearing South East*], *c.*1775

Oil on panel, 24.1 × 45.2 cm

Provenance: painted for the Lords Commissioners of the Admiralty.

Literature: Stuebe (1979), no. 82; Joppien and Smith (1985b),
no. 2.108, pp. 94–5, 209–10.

Engraved: by W. Watts, for Cook (1777), vol. 1, plate LIII.

Exhibited: Birmingham City Art Gallery, 1949 (162); Tate Gallery,
1949 (156).

National Maritime Museum, London, MoD Art Collection.

Hodges's inclusion of the Tahitian canoes in the foreground of this picture provides extraordinary technical detail regarding their construction, decoration and sailing methods, with the figures giving information regarding local dress. The painting's purpose was to illustrate Cook's words, following the intention to use Hodges's art 'to give a more perfect idea . . . than can be formed from written description only'. Its size and level of finish suggest that it was executed on Hodges's return, and was intended as the model for Watt's engraving for Cook's *Voyage*. It shows Point Venus and One-Tree Hill, with the volcanic peak of Mount Orofena behind, and derives from Hodges's panoramic profile in ink and wash executed on the *Resolution*'s second visit to Tahiti (cat. no. 19). That original composition has been compressed, with the viewpoint being much closer to the shore. This was not Hodges's only source, however: the rose-pink and magenta blues of the sky, conveying such a convincing sense of the tropical atmosphere, borrow from his earlier *plein-air* oils of the island (cat. nos 10–13). Hodges combines an array of data but reduces the complexity of that visual experience for the sake of coherence.

38 [*A Cascade in the Tuauru Valley, Tahiti?*], *c.*1775

Oil on panel, 49.9 × 64.1 cm

Provenance: painted for the Lords Commissioners of the Admiralty

Literature: Stuebe (1979), no. 45; Joppien and Smith (1985b), no. 2.143.

Exhibited: South London Art Gallery, 1951 (12); RA, Winter 1951–2 (65); Alexander Turnbull Library, 1959 (3); Auckland, 1964 (12).

National Maritime Museum, London, MoD Art Collection.

There is disagreement over the subject of this picture, and when and where it was painted. The title on its Admiralty frame, *A View of a Rock of Basalt in the Island of New Zealand*, has long gone unquestioned: Stuebe thought it was probably executed during the *Resolution*'s six-week stay in Dusky Sound during March–April 1773. However, Joppien and Smith observed that basalt is not commonly found in this region, suggesting the picture to be more likely a view of Tahiti, where basalt is predominant. The picture's mountainous, volcanic landscape adds weight to this idea. Further, there is written evidence of Hodges making sketches of the Tuauru Valley during the *Resolution*'s second visit to the Society Islands. Both Forsters record the artist as present in a party that explored the area on 3 May 1774, George Forster recalling: 'I recommended it to Mr. Hodges to visit the cascade which I had found in the valley; and accordingly the next day he went up with several gentlemen, and took a view of it, and of the basalt pillars under it'.[1] It seems

Fig. 53 William Hodges [*A Waterfall in Tahiti*], 1775, oil on panel, 48.9 x 61.6 cm. National Maritime Museum, London, MoD Art Collection.

likely that this painting was worked up from those *in situ* studies, probably in London.

Forster's reasons for recommending the cascade as a painterly subject are easy to understand. Both artist and naturalist responded to the artistic possibilities of such scenery but also shared an interest in the geological information provided by such phenomena, concerns readily apparent in Forster's description of the Tuauru Valley's rock formations:

> A fine cascade fell from this fringed part along the wall into the river, and made the scene more lively, which in itself was dark, wild and romantic. When we came nearer, we observed that the perpendicular rock had many projecting longitudinal angles, and on wading through the water to it, we found it to consist of real columns of black compact basaltes, such as the natives manufacture into tools . . . As it is now generally supposed that basaltes is a production of volcanoes, we have here another strong proof that Taheitee has undergone great changes by such subterraneous fires, where nature produces the most wonderful chymical operations, upon a very extensive plan.[2]

In his *Observations*, J. R. Forster also speculated on the 'great changes on the surface our globe' wrought by volcanic activity.[3] Hodges was close to such debates, subscribing to John Whitehurst's *Inquiry into the Original State and Formation of the Earth*, a text specifically concerned with establishing a 'system of Subterraneous Geography'.[4] This painting clearly shows his interest in the range of natural forces determining the shape of the landscape. The distant mountains transform into a foreground where the movement of water over strata and the resulting processes of erosion point to a landscape in the course of constant, gradual change. These elemental forces also feature in a second view of this cascade from a lower vantage point, which gives prominence to the pillars of basalt mentioned by Forster (fig. 53).[5] Both pictures have the same dimensions, are treated in the same broadly brushed manner, contrasting patches of heavy impasto with unworked areas, and compositionally similar. They were probably intended as pendant studies for either uncompleted or now lost works.

[1] Forster [1777], vol. , 369. Cf. Forster (1982), vol. 3, 504.

[2] Forster [1777], vol. 2, 369.

[3] Forster [1778], 103.

[4] Whitehurst (1778), ii. On the development of Whitehurst's theories, on which he was working during Hodges's period in Derby, see Craven (1996). More generally, see Hamblyn (1996).

[5] This was also formerly thought to show a New Zealand landscape. A third painting, again once thought to be of Dusky Bay, may also relate to the sketches done in May 1774. This includes bathing figures before the waterfall, which recall those seen in the paintings of Vaitepiha Bay (cat. nos 30–1). Cf. Joppien and Smith (1985b), nos. 2.109–10.

39 *Captain James Cook, c.1775*

Oil on canvas, 76.2 × 63.5 cm, inscribed *Captn James Cook of the Endeavour*

Provenance: probably Admiral Sir Hugh Palliser and/or his natural son, George Thomas Palliser, at The Vache, Chalfont St Giles, and sale with the house, first to Thomas Allen in 1862 and second (before 1902) to Major Harry McCalmont: family descent to Major Victor McCalmont, Mount Juliet, Co. Kilkenny, 1986: Leger Galleries, 1987.

Literature: Stuebe (1979), no. 115; Smith (1992), 225; Thomas (2003), xxvii–xxxi.

Engraved: by J. Basire, for Cook (1777), vol. 1, frontispiece: by Thornton (1), 11 September 1784, frontispiece to G.W. Anderson's *New, authentic and complete collection of voyages . . .* (pub. Alexander Hogg) and (2) 22 January 1785, frontispiece to Hogg's cheap octavo edition.

National Maritime Museum, London.

Fig. 54 Nathaniel Dance, *Captain James Cook*, 1775-76, oil on canvas, 127.0 x 101.6 cm. National Maritime Museum, London, Greenwich Hospital Collection.

This portrait is undoubtedly a study from life and was presumably aways intended to illustrate the official voyage account. It is less certain whether it was directly engraved by James Basire, rather than from (probably) a related drawing or more finished oil but, if so, neither are known. The prime evidence that such a version may have existed is the facial refinement and more finished dress in the Basire print. The inferior later prints by Thornton are basically the same as Basire's but reversed and with further changes in the dress and hair, including a ribboned queue. The 1784 folio version bears the claim, 'Accurately Drawn from an Original Painting...', and the smaller one of 1785 states that this picture was in G.W. Anderson's possession. If so, it seems more likely that Anderson's painting was itself based on Basire rather than yet another version by Hodges. A near contemporary oil now in the State Library of New South Wales does not seem to be Thornton's source but a further derivative from his print. That said, the present oil is one of Hodges's rare forays into portraiture, its naturalistic, coarse-featured rendition being quite at odds with contemporary conventions for depicting such public figures, exemplified by Nathanial Dance's elegant portrait of Cook painted for Joseph Banks at about the same time (fig. 54). Dance presents him as a man of letters or a philosopher in his study; seated at a desk, his head tilted as if in a moment of contemplation, and his right hand resting on his own chart of the southern hemisphere, substituting for the more usual papers and globe. Besides placing Cook in a well-established pictorial tradition, this formal celebration of his seafaring feats presents him as the Enlightenment man, engaged in the disinterested pursuit of knowledge. On his return from the second voyage, Cook was elected a Fellow of the Royal Society, securing his reputation as a skilled, though self-taught, scientific observer. Dance's portrait visually complemented the many literary tributes to Cook, like George Forster's, which praised him 'as a navigator, constant and indefatigable in

his pursuits, skilful in planning and executing his course'[1]. By contrast, Hodges concentrates on his sitter's countenance, without the paraphernalia of learning, though that would be unremarkable if the work were only a preliminary study.[2] While the result lacks the sophisticated sheen of a specialist portrait painter, its directness conveys something of the bluff, self-made seaman who had risen through the ranks and complements his public image as an heroic man of science.[3] Reference to his achievements is limited to the sketchy details of his uniform, the junior captain's undress of 1774-87, which dates the painting to late 1775 or early 1776. Hodges's interest is in the concentrated description of the facial structure, modelled in stark contrasts of light and dark, which bears comparison with the close observation of individual features in the contemporary portrait of Omai (cat. no. 40). The identifying inscription seems to be near-contemporary though presumably not by Hodges, who only knew him in the *Resolution*. Its addition is important, however, since – partly thanks to the much-engraved Dance portrait – the likeness alone is not self-evidently Cook. The picture's early history is unknown but the only current explanation of how it ended up in the McCalmont family is that it was at The Vache, Admiral Palliser's house, when his son sold it to the Allens in 1826, and they to the McCalmonts. Palliser (d. 1796) was Cook's early captain, patron and friend, also Comptroller of the Navy and later Governor of Greenwich Hospital,

Capt. James Cook
of the Endeavour.

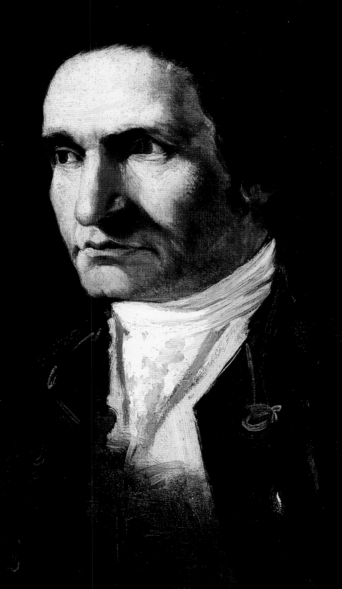

and he could have had the picture from Hodges at any point to complement the well-known monument he erected to Cook in the grounds of The Vache. Alternatively his son may have acquired it after Hodges's death, since his 1795 sale was not a full studio disposal. Joseph Farington RA. Hodges's friend and one of his children's guardians, might have been involved at that point, or even added the description, though the portrait is not mentioned in his diary.

1 Forster [1778], vol. 2, 771.
2 The fact that a narrow strip has been cut off the top of the canvas at some point and added to the bottom, to correct the original proportions, tends to support this idea.
3 On Cook's reputation, see Smith (1992), 225–40; Wilson (2002).

40 *Omai, c.*1775–76

Oil on panel, 61 × 50.8 cm

Provenance: John Hunter Collection; John Hunter's Museum (1816); Royal College of Surgeons (1820).

Literature: Stuebe (1979), no. 92; Joppien and Smith (1985), no. 2.65, pp. 64–5, 175; Smith (1985), 82; Bindman (2002), p. 136.

Engraved: by J. Caldwell, for Cook (1777), vol. 1, plate LVII.

Hunterian Museum, The Royal College of Surgeons of England.

Greenwich only.

Fig. 55 James Caldwell after William Hodges, *Omai*, engraving, from Cook (1777). National Maritime Museum, London.

Omai (more properly Mai), from Huahine, was brought to England by Lieutenant Tobias Furneaux on the *Adventure*. Adopted by Sir Joseph Banks and the Earl of Sandwich, he was introduced to fashionable London society, including the royal family, and was also painted by several artists, most notably Sir Joshua Reynolds. However, there seems little physiognomic resemblance between Hodges's portrait and Reynolds's celebrated portrayal, or even Caldwell's notably classicized engraving (fig. 55). While Caldwell and Reynolds offer a generalized treatment according with the practice advocated by the Academy president himself, Hodges submits the sitter to a more exacting visual scrutiny. Hodges often drew affinities between Pacific peoples and classical models, and the compositional format here bears resemblence to the antique portrait bust, but his typically bold handling of drapery and setting offsets such comparisons. Rather, he focuses on rendering Omai's facial features and complexion.

Little is known of the circumstances by which Hodges came to execute this painting of Omai. If commissioned by the eminent, Scots-born surgeon and anatomist, John Hunter, in whose collection the work is first listed, this would be entirely in keeping with his fascination for exotic cultures and peoples.[1] Hunter was an avid reader of travel literature, as well as a keen collector of curiosities, amassing an unparalleled specimen cabinet devoted to pathology, and comparative and evolutionary anatomy, centred on his collection of numerous rare 'national skulls', that complemented pictures of non-European people. That Hodges was aware of related debates, and moved in corresponding social and intellectual circles, seems certain.

1 Stuebe (1979), 170. See also Turnbull (1999).

JAMES COOK (1728–79)

41 *A Voyage towards the South Pole, and Round the World*

2 vols., published by W. Strahan & T. Cadell, London, 1777

National Maritime Museum, London

Cook's official, Admiralty-sanctioned account of the second voyage appeared some six weeks after the publication in March 1777 of George Forster's rival narrative, *A Voyage Round the World*. Not compelled to wait for the final proofs of the engravings after Hodges's paintings and sketches, Forster was able to issue his version of events earlier. However, illustrations were an important supplement to any such publication, and Forster's book certainly suffered for their absence. For the two volumes of Cook's *Voyage* are filled with a rich, eclectic range of visual material that supplies a wealth of data: on navigation and geography in the maps and charts, natural phenomena in the numerous views, ethnographic curiosities in the arrangements of objects and detailed sectional diagrams, as well as specif-

ic peoples, places and events in the portraits or landing scenes. These enabled the reader to trace Cook's steps, and experience vicariously the rich diversity of Polynesian peoples and landscapes.

The images offer a contrapuntal commentary on events described in the text. Interleaved at regular intervals, the narrative often directs the reader to them, as in the description of the Tahitian fleet at Pare: 'The drawings which were made of these vessels . . . not only illustrate, but . . . make the description of them unnecessary'.[1] This faith in the ability of the plates to impart information not readily reducible to language is a recurrent feature of the book, one that was continued in Cook's posthumously published account of his third voyage. Indeed, that Hodges's paintings and sketches were able to communicate in a way that even the most attentive, meticulous written testimony could not, was accepted from his initial appointment.

However, controversy surrounded the illustrations' accuracy. This plate by J. K. Sherwin after Hodges, of 'The Landing at MIDDLE-BURGH', was condemned by George Forster for its 'Greek contours and features', that were an unfaithful artistic licence.[2]

[1] Cook (1777), vol. 2, 18.
[2] Forster [1777], vol. 1, 222.

Part Two
Picturing the History of India

Hodges and India

GEOFF QUILLEY

Hodges arrived in India in January 1780. Joseph Farington suggested that he turned to India partly out of grief at the early death of his first wife,[1] but his decision also demonstrated a combination of two of the primary characteristics of his artistic career: an opportunism, based on calculated risk, to exploit the artistic and professional openings created by developing imperial expansion, together with an increasing artistic interest in the representation of history through landscape painting. The complexities involved in such an artistic project were indicated in paintings of Pacific subjects done for the Admiralty after Cook's voyage, and more particularly in his depictions of historic British buildings and locations made during 1777 and 1778 (cat. no. 73).

In a sense, India was Hodges's ideal country. The growing consolidation of British power and wealth there, with the establishment after 1765 of the East India Company as a governing body with revenue-collecting powers, offered an expanding commercial community of potential patrons, to which Hodges had privileged access through his introduction to the Governor General, Warren Hastings. Hastings became Hodges's most important patron for the rest of his life (and beyond, since Hastings also provided support to Hodges's widow and children after his death in 1797).[2] While the East India Company, founded in 1600, had been trading out of various Indian ports since that date, it was only in the 1760s, particularly through the aggressive colonial policy of Robert Clive, that a British military presence was established inland in Bengal. The assumption of the right to collect Bengal's land tax made the Company the effective ruler, on behalf of the British government, of this vast eastern province.[3] Hastings became the first Governor-General of Bengal in 1774.

In addition, India presented a land of immemorial antiquity that was the repository of its own history and civilization through the prolific richness of its monuments, and which was therefore in direct contrast to the new and in many respects little understood cultures 'without history' that Hodges had encountered in the Pacific. The arrival also of European antiquarian and scholarly interest in Indian history (of which Hastings was himself a leading instigator) continued to reveal, even during Hodges's time there, greater knowledge of Indian culture through exposure to its ancient and rich literature. In particular, the increasing understanding of Sanskrit during the 1780s, derived from Sir William Jones's translations of Sanskrit poetry and mythology, prompted speculation that it might be the *ur*-language for Greek, Latin and other Euro-Asian idioms. Such theories were presented most famously in Jones's 'Third Anniversary Discourse to the Royal Asiatic Society' (1786) and the essay 'On the Gods of Greece, Italy, and India' of the following year, in which Jones argues for a common origin to the mythologies of India, classical Greece and Rome, Egypt, China 'and even islands of America', on the premiss that

> when features of resemblance, too strong to have been accidental, are observable in different systems of polytheism, without fancy or prejudice to colour them and improve the likeness, we can scarcely help believing, that some connection has immemorially subsisted between the several nations, who have adopted them.[4]

In contrast to this antiquarian, comparative philological approach to Indian history were the received stereotypes about India as a land of Mughal despotism and oriental barbarism. The quintessential figure here was the emperor Aurungzeb, whose negative image was popularised through Dryden's 1675 verse drama *Aureng-Zebe*. Alongside this image of India was that of the Orient as the exotic and seductive realm of the *Thousand and One Nights*, the translation of which was enduringly popular through-

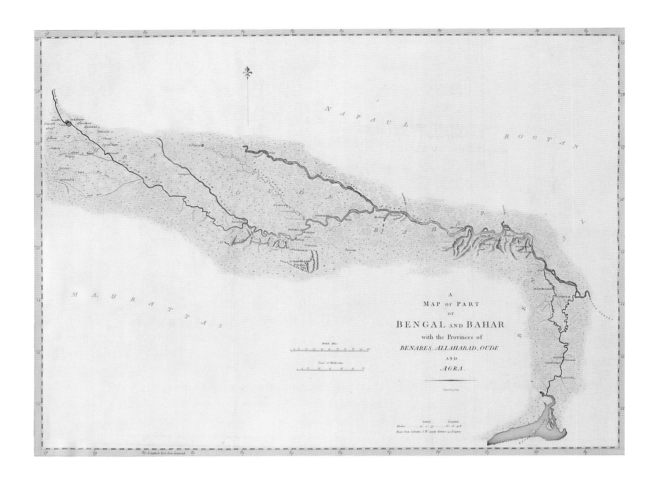

Fig. 56 *A Map of Part of Bengal and Bahar with the Provinces of Benares, Allahabad, Oude and Agra,* engraving, from Hodges (1793). National Maritime Museum, London

out the eighteenth century. These two perceptions of India in the eighteenth century sit uneasily together but can certainly be detected in Hodges's images and writings. It needs to be remembered that the British India through which Hodges travelled preceded by decades the full-scale systematic, administrative hegemony of the nineteenth-century Raj. Therefore his work, like that of Jones, cannot properly be appropriated as part of the account of Orientalism, theorized by Edward Said, as a consistent western discourse about 'the Orient' that served the political and ideological ends of western imperialism, by presenting the east as 'naturally' inferior, decadent and incapable of self-government.[5] It also needs to be remembered that the area of India visited by Hodges, though extensive, was a small part of the subcontinent (fig. 56), that reflected the still limited and uncertain territorial control of the British in India in the early 1780s.

Certainly, it was India rather than the Pacific that was the major artistic preoccupation of Hodges's career. Between 1780 and 1795, besides hundreds of drawings, paintings and prints, he produced his *Dissertation on the Prototypes of Architecture, Hindoo, Moorish, Gothic* (1787), a stage design of Calcutta, and the travel narrative *Travels in India* (1793), one of the earliest such accounts written by a professional artist. Similarly, Hodges was increasingly known during his own lifetime as a specialist in Indian scenes: the *London Chronicle*, reviewing the Royal Academy exhibition of

1787, in which Hodges showed eleven works, noted that his Indian subjects constituted 'a species of painting in which Mr. Hodges seems not to have a competitor equally industrious and able with himself'.[6]

Having spent a year in Madras, confined by ill health and the ongoing war with Hyder Ali, Hodges moved to Calcutta, arriving there in spring 1781. He had earlier been recommended to Warren Hastings as an artist desirous of recording 'the most curious appearances of nature and art in Asia'.[7] This marked the start of an extraordinarily productive two-and-a-half years in which he toured Bengal and Bihar, and produced paintings for the leading figures of British India: Sir Elijah Impey, Claude Martin and above all, Warren Hastings himself. Besides Hastings, however, the most important patron of Hodges's painting in India was Augustus Cleveland, the District Collector for Bihar, with whom he stayed for several months early in 1782, making paintings and drawings of the landscape around Bhagalpur and the Rajmahal hills. At the sale of Cleveland's effects on 4 February 1794, there were 21 oil paintings by Hodges.[8] Cleveland's reputation lay in his supposedly peaceful negotiations with the local tribes of the region, going so far as to enlist them as his army of sepoys (cat. no. 62). It is this reputation that subtends Hodges's works for him, in their frequent concern with the portrayal of the local native people, and which is the focus of Hodges's account of him in *Travels in India*. Indeed, Cleveland's noted benevolence and success in dealing with the local Indian population rendered him something of a paradigm for the image of paternalistic colonialism in India that the British were actively cultivating during the 1780s and 1790s. On his early death in 1784, he was memorialized in a monument raised at Bhagalpur by the East India Company and also in a verse tribute written on the Company's behalf, which dwells on his capacity for paternalism, centred on

> His bloodless triumphs o'er a barbarous land.
> Bright in his hand, the sword of justice gleam'd,
> But mercy from his eyes benignant beam'd,
> And mercy won the cause; the savage band
> Forsook their haunts, and bow'd to his command.
> And where the warrior's arm in vain assail'd,
> His gentler skill o'er brutal force prevail'd.[9]

This follows closely the essential threads of an ideology of paternalistic imperialism, as outlined in 1783, for example, by Hodges's friend, the poet Henry James Pye, who urged 'EUROPE's race' to 'civilize mankind' in just the same way:

> No more with arms the trembling tribes destroy,
> But soft Persuasion's gentler powers employ,
> Till, from her throne barbarian Rudeness hurl'd,
> REFINEMENT spread her Empire o'er the world.[10]

Hodges made three tours in northern and eastern India out of Calcutta. In spring 1781 he reached Monghyr [Munger] and Rajmahal, where he first met Augustus Cleveland. After returning to Calcutta in early summer, he left almost immediately in Warren Hastings's diplomatic mission to Benares [Varanasi]. With the escalation of the conflict between the British and the raja of Benares, Chait Singh, Hastings and his party were forced flee to the Company fort of Chunargarh. While here, Hodges made extensive drawings, at Hastings's instruction, of both Chunargarh and Chait Singh's forts in the surrounding region. In December, Hodges left Hastings's company and travelled to Bhagalpur at the invitation of Cleveland. He arrived back in Calcutta on 15 May 1782, and was then afflicted by illness until November, after which he left on his final tour in January 1783, reaching as far as Agra, in the company of Major Browne's delegation to Delhi. Owing to the ongoing conflict of the Anglo-Maratha war, Hodges did not himself reach Delhi, but instead made his way back to Calcutta via the fort of Gwalior, which had been taken by Company forces from the Marathas in 1780.

Hodges seems to have had specific objectives with each of these three excursions. The first was devoted solely to British territory, while the second focused on his observation of Hindu manners, art and customs centred on Benares and with Cleveland in the Jungleterry. The final, most ambitious tour was chiefly concerned with the study of Mughal sites and their related history. All these overlapping, interleaving and frequently conflicting histories were the subjects of Hodges's numerous paintings, prints and drawings of India, and more particularly of his written accounts, the letterpress to the forty-eight aquatints of *Select Views of India*, published between 1785 and 1788, and the travel narrative, *Travels in India* (1793). Hodges's overriding concern to represent the history of India through its landscape was stated explicitly in the advertisement for subscriptions for the prints in 1787, proposing them as

> faithful representations of remarkable places in that remote country, presuming they will be highly interesting on account of their novel and picturesque scenery, and more especially as they illustrate the history and antiquities of places, now so much the object of enquiry.[11]

This amounts to an abbreviated manifesto for Hodges's project as an artist-historian, and for India as the site *par excellence* for its pursuit. This was a proposal that Hodges laid out more fully at the end of *Travels in India*, in suggesting further parts of India suited to 'the enterprizing artist', whereby landscape painting might reach the zenith of its potential to be 'faithfully connected with the history of the various countries, and . . . faithfully represent the manners of mankind'.[12]

Note: catalogue entries in this section are by Geoff Quilley.

[1] Cited in Stuebe (1979), 43.

[2] On Hastings's patronage of Hodges, see Stuebe (1973) and Natasha Eaton's essay in this volume.

[3] Bayly (1989).

[4] Jones (1787), 221.

[5] Said (1978).

[6] *London Chronicle*, 28 April–1 May 1787, 413.

[7] Macpherson to Hastings 31 December 1778; Hastings Papers, British Library, Add. MS 29,142 ff. 276–7.

[8] For Augustus Cleveland's estate see the Bengal Inventory Series L/AG/34/276/ 1785. The 21 paintings by Hodges in Cleveland's collection were first advertized for sale in 1784 in the *Calcutta Gazette*. The complete collection was sold and was re-advertized in the Calcutta newspaper the *World* 1 January 1794. However, Cleveland's inventory lists further subjects, such as a representation of four hill figures and a *nautch*, as well as what is listed as '100' of Bhagulpur, probably sketches: my thanks to Natasha Eaton for this information.

[9] *Monody on the Death of Augustus Cleveland, Esq.* (1786).

[10] Pye (1783), Part 2, lines 771–82.

[11] *Morning Herald*, 18 January 1787, 1.

[12] Hodges (1793), 156.

42 *A View of Marmalong Bridge with a Sepoy and Natives in the Foreground, c.1780–81*

Oil on canvas, 68.6 × 91.4 cm

Provenance: Warren Hastings collection; removed from Daylesford by the Kingham Hill Trust to Kingham Hill School, 1936; Sotheby's, 17 November 1971 (133); private collection, London; Christie's, 21 June 1974.

Literature: Stuebe (1979), no. 325.

Yale Center for British Art, Paul Mellon Collection.

Yale only.

Marmalong Bridge, just to the south of Madras, was one of the first subjects depicted by Hodges in India, shortly after he had arrived at Madras in the summer of 1780. His time in the city was artistically unproductive, for despite his high state of anticipation at touring through the country, his plans were prevented

> by the great scourge of human nature, the great enemy of the arts, war, which, with horrors perhaps unknown to the civilized regions of Europe, descended like a torrent over the whole face of the country, driving the peaceful husbandman from his plow, and the manufacturer from his loom.[1]

He goes on to explain that though there are few opportunities for the painter in a country at war, he made however among others a drawing of Marmalong bridge, which is a very modern work, built, as I am informed, at the private expence of an Armenian merchant.[2]

The inclusion of the sepoy among the prominent figures in the foreground is no doubt a deliberate reference to the state of conflict besetting the region at the time, while the central female figure's pose is distinctly classical, and may be understood in terms of a contrast between the antiquity of the civilization of India and the modernity of Marmalong Bridge in the distance, which cuts right across the composition, dividing it horizontally. This reading is further suggested by the evocation of peace in the grouping of the figures around the sepoy, set against the brightly coloured landscape under the setting sun. The central female figure also appears elsewhere in association with sites of Indian antiquity, notably in two drawings of the holy island of Jangerah at Sultanganj (Yale Center for British Art, Paul Mellon Collection, B1978.43.1736 and B1978.43.1760, where the same figure appears to have been inserted almost as a direct quotation from the *View of Marmalong Bridge*) and, in reverse, in the drawing of the Temple of Vis Visha [Vishveshvara] at Benares [Varanasi] (Yale Center for British Art, Paul Mellon Collection, B1978.43.1810). The same figure features

again in the engraving *A View of the Tomb of the Emperor Shere Shah at Sasseram in Bahar* (published 1786).

This painting, according to Stuebe, is a pendant to *Natives drawing Water from a Pond with Warren Hastings' House at Alipur in the Distance* (cat. no. 45). Given that the principal subject here is the distant view of a bridge built 'at the private expence of an Armenian merchant', the common theme of the two views is the positive and progressive intervention of European trading nations into an ancient but essentially retrograde society, represented by the juxtaposition of traditional Indian figures and culture in the foreground with the products of foreign commercial investment in the background. In this sense, the pendants also offer a contrast between what was held to be the advanced state of commercial European society and the mostly agricultural, quasi-feudal society of contemporary India. They thus can be placed within the same broad theoretical understanding of the history of human development as a four-stage progress from hunter-gatherer to commercial civilization, that influenced Hodges's paintings of Pacific peoples and territories.

[1] Hodges (1793), 5.
[2] Ibid., 8.

43 *View of Calcutta from Garden House Road,* *c.*1781

Oil on canvas, 63.5 × 95.3 cm

Provenance: Colnaghi, 1948; Spink, 1948; gift of Sir Thomas Barlow to Manchester City Art Gallery, 1949.

Literature: Stuebe (1979), no. 234.

Manchester Art Gallery.

This is a smaller version of the large painting in the Victoria Memorial Hall, Calcutta. Both are based on a drawing in the Paul Mellon Collection (B1978.43.1779). The Manchester picture is more faithful to the drawing and appears, therefore, to be a study for the much larger Calcutta picture, which is in many ways a form of philosophical essay on the relationship of the centre of British colonial power to the indigenous Indian population, in the manner of Hodges's post-voyage works of the Pacific (cat. nos 26-33).[1]

Hodges described Calcutta effusively in *Travels in India* and produced at least five paintings of the city.[2] He arrived there from Madras in March 1781, and describes how, when sailing up the Hughli towards the city, the prospect was suddenly and impressively transformed at Garden House Reach, the vista represented here:

As the ship approaches Calcutta the river narrows; that which is called the Garden Reach, presents a view of handsome buildings, on a flat surrounded by gardens: these are villas belonging to the opulent inhabitants of Calcutta. The vessel has no sooner gained one other reach of the river than the whole city of Calcutta bursts upon the eye. The capital of the British dominions in the East is marked by a considerable fortress, on the south side of the river, which is allowed to be, in strength and correctness of design, superior to any in India.[3]

Hodges here emphasizes, therefore, the broad sweep of the river, populated with 'vessels of various classes and sizes, from the largest Indiaman to the smallest boat of the country', which presents Calcutta as a thriving commercial entrepôt, the expanding centre of East India Company trade in India. He presents his visual experience of Calcutta as a geo-temporal move towards the establishment of the British presence there, culminating with the recently completed Fort William, the subject of another major oil painting (private collection) that was engraved for *Travels in India*.

---

[1] See Natasha Eaton's essay in this volume.

[2] Stuebe (1979), cat. nos 234–8.

[3] Hodges (1793), 14.

44 *View of Calcutta, c.*1781

Oil on canvas, 91.5 × 115.5 cm

Provenance: L. Hand, London; Leggatt, October 1961; Lord
Inchcape

Exhibited: Leggatt, October 1961 (10)

Literature: Stuebe (1979), no. 237

Private collection.

Greenwich only.

The thinness of the paint surface in parts of this picture, the use of wet-
in-wet technique and the acutely observed atmospheric conditions, as
Stuebe suggests, recall Hodges's *plein-air* views done on Cook's voyage,
and suggest that this work might also have been done at least partly on
the spot. If so, the viewpoint perhaps indicates that it was done on board
a vessel anchored in the middle of the river, a method with which Hodges

was also very familiar from his experience with Cook (cat. no. 2).

Like the more carefully worked up views of Calcutta (cat. no. 43), the
composition and technique of this painting recall the Venetian views of
Canaletto or Guardi, particularly here in the delicate use of impasto
highlights and flecks of colour to delineate the distant cityscape.
Contemporary critics made the same comparison, one reviewer noting
that the *View of Calcutta, taken from Fort William* (RA 1787) 'possesses
much of Canalleti's stile'.[1] It may be that there is a deliberate evocation
of Canaletto's Venetian and London views (for example, in the way that
the boat resembles the form of a Venetian *gondola*), intending a comparison between the developing commercial, colonial centre of Calcutta
and the most celebrated past and present imperial trading metropoles of
Venice and London. Hodges suggests as much in his description of
Calcutta's liberal openness as a trading exchange, while carefully associating this with the construction of magnificent architecture, and the
progressive influence of his patron, Warren Hastings, who assumes a
Doge-like presence in Hodges's account, making his views of Calcutta
also a homage to his principal patron:

A European lands here in the midst of a great city, without passing the outer draw-bridge of a fort: here are no centinels with the keen eye of suspicion, no stoppage of baggage. The hospitality which a stranger experiences from the inhabitants, and particularly from those to whom he is recommended, corresponds exactly with the freedom of his admission into the city

[. . .]

Calcutta, from a small and inconsiderable fort, which yet remains (and in which is the famous black-hole, so fatal to many of our countrymen in 1756), and a few ware-houses, was soon raised to a great and opulent city, when the government of the kingdom of Bengal fell into the hands of the English. For its magnificence, however, it is indebted solely to the liberal spirit and excellent taste of the late Governor General; and it must be confessed, that the first house was raised by Mr. Hastings which deserves the name of a piece of architecture.[2]

One of the new large colonial houses, that Hodges likens to 'Grecian temples' 'dedicated to hospitality', is prominently shown through the trees at the left edge of Hodges's painting, promoting further this image of Calcutta as a peaceful, modern, ordered and prosperous trading mart (in contrast to the living memory of the city as the site of colonial conflict and the notorious 'Black Hole' of Calcutta).

[1] The *Morning Herald*, Tuesday 15 May 1787, 3.
[2] Hodges (1793), 14–16.

45 *Natives drawing Water from a Pond with Warren Hastings' House at Alipur in the Distance*, 1781

Oil on canvas, 69.2 × 91.5 cm, signed and dated 1781

Provenance: Warren Hastings collection, Daylesford House Inventory 1799, p.22; Daylesford House sale, 26 August 1853 (900); removed from Daylesford by Kingham Hill Trust to Kingham Hill School, 1936; Sotheby's, 17 November 1971, to Richard Green

Literature: Hastings Papers, British Library, Add. MSS. 41,609, pp.22, 38 and 41,610, p.14v; Stuebe (1979), no. 190

Private collection.

Greenwich only.

One of two views by Hodges of Hastings's house at Alipur, just south of Calcutta, that were in Hastings's collection (the other is untraced). It is the pendant to the *View of Marmalong Bridge* (cat. no. 42), which also features, for Hodges's Indian paintings, a remarkable number of figures. As Stuebe points out, this is 'an idyllic scene of Indian life'.[1] Like *A Camp of a Thousand Men formed by Augustus Cleveland* (cat. no. 62), it operates as a loose but ingenious adaptation of the conversation-piece, with the leisurely foreground activities placed in a significant dialogue with the gentle, classical forms of the house in the distance: the viewer is led to understand that the peaceful Indian idyll is somehow consequent upon the presence of the house.

The careful grouping of the figures beneath the overarching shade of the tree, and their various activities, also echoes Hodges's comments about the banyan tree in *Travels in India*, which he links directly with Hastings's government of Bengal. The banyan tree, owing to its peculiarly extensive means of propagation and its provision of shelter, was a longstanding symbol for beneficent political government in Indian culture. Although it is not a banyan tree that Hodges has depicted here, its compositional dominance, both embracing the figures beneath it and framing the view to Hastings's house in the distance, suggests that it may be understood in a similar manner:

> These trees, in many instances, cover such an extent of ground, that hundreds of people may take shelter under one of them from the scorching rays of the sun. The care that was taken in the government, and the minute attention to the happiness of the people, rendered this district, at this time, (1781) a perfect paradise. It was not uncommon to see the manufacturer at his loom, in the cool shade, attended by his friend softening his labour by the tender strains of music. There are to be met with in India many old pictures representing similar subjects, in the happy times of the Mogul government.[2]

The similarity of the right-hand pair of figures by the hut to this vignette description of Indian life 'in the happy times of the Mogul government' suggests that Hodges may have intended a veiled reference to the Mughal miniature tradition. Certainly, he, like Hastings, studied and collected such works (fig. 14). If so, it would amplify the compliment that the picture clearly intends to pay to his patron Hastings – who partly modelled his system of government on that of the great Mughal emperor, Akbar – concerning the ordered and happy state of Indian society under his regime.

[1] Stuebe (1979), 202.
[2] Hodges (1793), 27.

46 *Rocks near Sakrigali*, 1781–82

Oil on canvas, 63.5 × 83.8 cm

Provenance: Augustus Cleveland sale, 4 February 1794

Literature: Stuebe (1979), nos. 387–8

Private collection.

Greenwich only.

This is probably one of the two views of Sakrigali that were on offer at the sale of Augustus Cleveland's effects in 1794. The freedom of handling and the thinness of the paint surface in places combined with use of impasto in others suggest that it was executed on the spot, a characteristic feature of Hodges's paintings for Cleveland. This idea is further sup-

ported by the fact that it corresponds to none of the drawings at the Yale Center for British Art. It is certainly extraordinarily daring in both technique and use of colour, which again suggests an oil sketch made on the spot more than a finished work.

Hodges visited Sakrigali, in the Rajmahal hills marking the border between Bengal and Bihar, in spring 1781, and produced another painting, now lost, for Warren Hastings of the ancient pass of Sakrigali, which was engraved for *Travels in India* (fig. 18) with a description of the site's significance:

> This pass, in the time of the Hindoo and Mogul governments was the commanding entrance from Bahar into the kingdom of Bengal, and was formerly fortified with a strong wall and gate, the ruins of which yet remain. What must shew the inutility of such fortifications, and the wisdom of the British government in suffering them

to go to decay, is the ease with which they are eluded; for, in the year 1742–3, the whole Mahratta army, consisting of fifty thousand men, under Boschow Pundit, passed through the hills above Colgong, and to the south-west of this pass into Bengal. On the top of the hill is a ruined tomb of a Musselman sied, or saint. The whole scene appeared to me highly picturesque.[1]

The wildness and decay of this terrain, therefore, not only adds to its picturesque value, but may also be inferred as a sign of British strategic wisdom in abandoning the pass as a military stronghold. There is an implicit contrast between past Mughal uses of the landscape and present British ones. Contrary to the frequent assumption about Hodges's Indian paintings, that they classicize and idealize the landscape to fix it in a permanent state of 'pastness', the implication here is that the landscape is undergoing – or has the potential to undergo – profound change, as a result of the British presence in it. Hodges's improvisatory and innovatory technique in this painting is both a testament, like his paintings done on the spot on Cook's voyage, to the need to make an urgent visual record, but also in a way is appropriate to this sense of potential change.

[1] Hodges, (1793), 22–3.

47 *Tomb and distant View of the Rajmahal Hills,* probably 1781

Oil on canvas, 66.2 × 72.4 cm

Provenance: possibly Augustus Cleveland sale, 4 February 1794; G P Dudley Wallis Collection, Manchester; Christie's, 24 July 1959; Sotheby's, 20 November 1963; presented by Friends of the Tate Gallery, 1964.

Literature: Stuebe (1979), no. 368

© Tate, London 2003. Presented by the Friends of the Tate Gallery, 1964

The title of this painting derives from the correspondence of the subject to the title of a work in the Augustus Cleveland sale, 1794, though it is not possible to say precisely whether it was painted for Cleveland. It relates to a drawing in the Paul Mellon Collection (B1978.43.1765), while the figure was taken from another drawing of the Rajmahal hills (Paul Mellon Collection, B1978.43.1740). Despite the existence of prior drawings, and the painting's polished execution and seemingly carefully conceived Claudean composition, which contrast with the more experimental, *esquisse*-like quality of many of Hodges's works for Cleveland, there are certain features that support the proposition that it was executed while Hodges was visiting him on his first excursion in Bengal in spring 1781. Despite its high finish, it was clearly quickly painted, probably at one or two sittings: much of the paint surface is thin and was worked wet-in-wet, including the pillar of the arch to the right, where the paint appears to have been rubbed away before overpainting. There is a *pentimento* altering the line of the tree to change it from that in the drawing and render it more serpentine, which suggests that Hodges originally based the painting on the drawing and reworked it later. However, it is unusual to find *pentimenti* in Hodges's Indian subjects after his return from India.

While it corresponds to a description in *Travels in India* of the pass of Teliagarhi,[1] Hodges has elevated this branch of landscape painting by rendering it as an Indian version of *Et in Arcadia Ego*, a subject with which he would have been thoroughly familiar through Richard Wilson's depictions of it. Here, the identification, through the conspicuous inclusion of sheep (missing from the drawings), of the sentinel fig-

ure as a shepherd placed before the Muslim tomb, recapitulates in a colonial context the essential elements of the pastoral *Et in Arcadia Ego* iconography as developed most famously by Poussin in the seventeenth century. This offered a moralistic admonition to the effect that death is present even in Arcadia. The association here of the Mughal tomb with a sense of loss and nostalgia makes the painting comparable to Hodges's other views of Indian ruins (cat. nos 49, 53). It also recalls his similar treatments of Pacific islands as adaptations of the *Et in Arcadia Ego* subject (see cat. nos 25, 32, 33).

Hodges refers to Bengal and Bihar under British administration as 'a perfect paradise', which certainly corresponds to the idyllic vision of an Indian Arcadia here.[2] However, in this ideologically very complex picture, what Hodges presents is an unspoilt (though cultivated) paradise, from which any trace of a British presence is noticeably absent.

[1] Hodges, (1793), 24.

[2] Ibid., 27. For the ideological implications of such a statement, see Natasha Eaton's essay in this volume.

48 *View of the City of Rajmahal, c.1781*

Oil on canvas, 62.5 × 70.2 cm

Provenance: Warren Hastings sale, 11 April 1797; Christie's, 1989, as 'View of Gyah' by Thomas Daniell

Literature: Stuebe (1979), no. 363, listed as untraced.

Private collection.

Greenwich only.

The composition and use of colour in this distant view of Rajamhal in evening light are reminiscent of Hodges's Pacific paintings, particularly the *View in Pickersgill Harbour* (cat. no. 5). Hodges visited Rajmahal on his first excursion through Bengal in spring 1781, and was greatly impressed by its former architectural splendour, constructed substantially under Sultan Shuja (see cat. nos 49–51). Hodges elsewhere comments very favourably on Shuja as a patron of architecture, and throughout the *Travels* associates architectural progress with liberal and beneficent government. It may be that the view of the city framed by the ancient, glowing banyan tree, a longstanding symbol of inclusive government (see cat. no. 45), signifies the relative prosperity and liberality of Shuja's government. The elegiac mood is, however, tempered by an emphasis on the exotic, in the prominent varied trees, the city's strange spires in the distance, and above all the intense colour and heightened light-dark contrasts. If, as has been argued in relation to his Pacific paintings and some Indian views, Hodges was concerned to familiarize exotic non-European territories and cultures to a British audience, here there is no such intent: we are offered a view of India's present, encapsulated by the ruins of its past, as mysterious and strange.

49 *View of a Mosque at Rajmahal, c.*1786–87

Oil on canvas, 105.5 × 128 cm

Provenance: possibly Warren Hastings collection; possibly Daylesford House sale, 26 August 1853; Percy Moore Turner; Morton Morris & Company Ltd, London, March 1987

Exhibited: RA 1787 (79)

Engraved: *Select Views*, no. 14

Literature: Stuebe (1979), no. 356; Tillotson (2000), 122–3, 127

Government Art Collection.

It is possible that this picture, exhibited at the Royal Academy in 1787, is the view of the ruins of Rajmahal that Hodges mentions having painted for Warren Hastings.[1] Being based closely on a drawing in the Paul Mellon Collection (B1978.43.1780) and also the basis for the aquatint published in 1786, it is likely that it was completed after Hodges's return to England; it has a clear appeal to a domestic audience. As with many other depictions by Hodges of Indian monuments, this subject has a double significance, for both the history of Mughal India and also the recent military history of the British in India. He makes this explicit in the description of the aquatint version in *Select Views*:

From the taste and style of this building, it is probable it was raised by that liberal patronizer of arts, and of architecture in particular, Sultan Sujah, the third son of the Emperor Shah Jahan, and brother to the Emperor Aurangzebe, it being in the same style of magnificence with the palace built by Sultan Sujah at Rajemahel, having the same ornaments, and being on the same scale with those buildings, and bearing marks of the same antiquity.

To the English in particular this building becomes of considerable historical value; for, on the night succeeding the battle of Oodooa-Nullah, the whole of the British part of the army, after the pursuit of the enemy's forces, were lodged in this building:– This action was gained by Major Adams, in 1764, over the forces of Meer Cossim Alli, and which gave the English the complete possession of the kingdom of Bengal.[2]

Rajmahal, linked to Murshidabad, the former capital of Bengal that was eclipsed by Calcutta when Warren Hastings became Governor General, was a significant site for Hodges, of which he produced multiple depictions. Like Agra it was for him a place of ruins denoting the glories of a past era, which was historically associated with a more liberal leader,

in Agra's case Akbar, and here Shuja, who, along with his brothers Dara Shikoh and Murad, was defeated by the fourth brother Aurangzeb in the contest for the imperial succession after Shah Jahan's deposition in 1658. The ruins of Rajmahal, therefore, signalled the progressive descent of Mughal rule from a liberalism marked by cultural and architectural achievements, to the supposed despotism epitomized by Aurangzeb. In this case, the particular association with British military conquest and supremacy in Bengal could also signify for a British audience the positive colonial intervention of the commercial maritime state into what was seen as a quasi-feudal society.

Stylistically echoing earlier British views, such as that of Llanthony Abbey (cat. no. 73), this painting likewise treats architecture as a barometer of social political conditions. This view of the ruined mosque at Rajamahal, therefore, from a British perspective, offered simultaneously an emblem of past decline and of present revival.

[1] Hodges, (1793), 21, 36.
[2] Letterpress to the aquatint in *Select Views* (14), publ. 15 September 1786.

50 *Ruins of Prince Shuja's Palace at Rajmahal,* 1781

Pencil, watercolour and gouache on blue paper, 48.5 × 65.7 cm

Provenance: Christie's, the P&O Collection of Watercolours by Thomas and William Daniell, 24 September 1996, as by Thomas and William Daniell.

Private collection.

Greenwich only.

Hodges produced at least one other drawing and two paintings of the ruins of Shuja's palace at Rajmahal, which made a great impression him when he visited the site in the spring and summer of 1781. He gave a fulsome description, together with an anecdotal history about the palace, in *Travels in India.* As with many other locations, his account is fixated upon the palace's state of ruination, which precisely matches the dominant concern of this drawing, whose elegiac sense is heightened by the use of blue tinted paper:

> There yet remains a part of the palace: which was supported by vast octangular piers, raised from the edge of the river. The great hall yet remains, with some lesser apartments, aswell as the principal gate leading to the palace: these are surrounded by immense masses of ruins. This palace, in the time of Sultan Sujah, was nearly destroyed by fire: the zananah, or that part inhabited by the females of the family, was totally destroyed.
>
> A tradition prevails in this part of the country, that more than three hundred women fell a sacrifice to modesty on this occasion; none of them daring to save themselves, from the apprehension of being seen by the men.[1]

The insertion of the account of the burning of the zenanah and the self-sacrifice of the women closely echoes Hodges's fascination elsewhere in the *Travels* with the practice of *sati,* and the status of Indian women generally. Since it was commonly accepted among European theorists, including the Forsters on Cook's second voyage, that the degree of civilization of a society could be in part measured by its treatment of women, such accounts, particularly when accompanied by images of ruins, not only emphasized India's otherness but also reinforced the parallel, commonly understood among Europeans, between eighteenth-century India and medieval Europe.

[1] Hodges (1793), 21.

51 *The Gate of a Caravanserai, Rajmahal,* 1781

Sepia ink and wash, 29.5 × 46.0 cm

Inscribed: on original label 'View of the Gate of a Caravan Serai at Raje Mahal'.

Provenance: Bonhams 1982; Eyre and Hobhouse Ltd, 1983.

Engraved: *Select Views,* no. 4.

The British Library, London.

Greenwich only.

In *Travels in India* Hodges discusses serais or lodgings in the context of the variety of travellers and social types to be encountered on the road, and praises the construction of such places by the Mughals, in a rare favourable comparison of Muslim over Hindu culture. He singles out the caravanserai at Rajmahal because of its association with sultan Shuja, admired by Hodges as a patron of architecture (see also cat. nos 48–50).

In this typically economical pen and wash drawing he therefore focuses upon the building's most outstanding feature, the gate:

> The form [of the serai] is a square of equal sides; the entrance from the Bengal road is through a large and highly ornamented gate, which also possesses military strength no less than beauty. Round the four sides is a wall about twenty feet high; attached to the wall round the sides are separate apartments, covered on the top, and open to the center of the area within. In these places the traveller lodges his goods, and sleeps; the area within the square is for the beasts. Attendant on these serais are poor people, who furnish a small bedstead for the traveller to sleep on, and who are rewarded by a trifling sum, amounting to perhaps a penny English. The Mahommedan is, in general, a generous man compared with the Hindoo on these occasions.[1]

As with other representations by Hodges of Indian architecture, there is a noticeable difference between text and image here: where the description gives a full sense of the layout, plan and functions of the different part of the building, the drawing focuses upon the principle feature of the gate and in doing so follows the conventions of eighteenth-century European landscape views of buildings.[2] However, his observation that the gate 'possesses military strength no less than beauty' suggests not only the building's potential relevance to the ongoing

British military campaign in the region, but also echoes the classical architectural precept, derived from Vitruvius, of *utilitas, firmitas ac concinnitas*: the combination of function, strength and harmony of design that marks out excellence in architecture. In this sense, Hodges's choice of the gate for his subject reflects not just a European tradition of architectural representation but also a European, classically derived outlook upon architectural aesthetics.

[1] Hodges (1793), 32.

[2] Tillotson (2002), 40–1, 80–1; see also Tillotson's essay in this volume.

52 *A Tomb with Figures, c.*1782

Oil on canvas, 59.3 × 71.2 cm

Provenance: probably Daylesford House sale, 5 July 1939, as 'Figures in Foreground and Mosque in Distance' by W. Hughes; Spink & Son, London, 1950; Spink & Son, London, 1978; Eyre and Hobhouse Ltd, 1984.

Literature: Stuebe (1979), no. 421; Tillotson (2000), 144.

The Alkazi Collection, London.

Greenwich only.

Based on a drawing in the Yale Center for British Art, 'An Indian Tomb with Figures in the Foreground and a Gate in the Distance' (B1978.43.1753), which is inscribed lower left '?Lucknow', Stuebe suggests that the unidentified location might be inside the fort at Monghyr [Munger].[1] This would be more consistent with the subject matter of the painting, showing a tomb in subdued evening light with figures in the foreground. For one of the noteworthy features for Hodges when *en route* from Bhagalpur to Monghyr was the number of tombs and mausolea located at the side of the road. He states in the *Travels in India* that it was customary for the women of the family to visit them after sunset, carrying lamps, and that this created a scene that was highly picturesque and sentimental.[2] He also provided an engraved illustration of such a scene for the *Travels*, an extremely classicized and stylized composition that deliberately evokes the flat format and flowing drapery of Greek frieze sculpture.[3] While the view here differs considerably from the engraving, in that it is not a fully nocturnal scene and the figures are not exclusively female,

it still shares the same impulse towards picturesque sentiment and poetic melancholy. Hodges's curiosity about Indians' veneration of their ancestors, which surfaces frequently in the *Travels*, is linked also to his moralized accounts of ruins, which are taken as signs of imperial and moral decline. Here, the crumbling gateway and the overgrowing foliage serve to confirm this association of death and ruination, so that while the picture might offer, on the one hand, an orientalized version of the conventional pastoral subject of *Et in Arcadia Ego*, on the other hand, it also confirms a broader vision of Indian society as backward-looking and fixed in the past that was commonplace at this period.[4]

[1] Stuebe (1979), cat. no. 420.

[2] Hodges (1793), 28

[3] Illustrated in Stuebe, fig. 256.

[4] See Marshall and Williams (1982).

53 *A View of a Mosque at Mounheer* [Maner], *c.*1781?

Oil on canvas, 104.1 x 127.6cm

Provenance: possibly Augustus Cleveland sale, 4 February 1794; Maharajah Bahadur Sir Prodyot Coomar Tagore; to P. Taluqdar, 1956.

Engraved: *Select Views*, no. 18, published 1 January 1787; by Morris for the *European Magazine and London Review*, 13 (April 1788), opposite 257.

Literature: Tillotson (2000), 73–4

Standard Chartered Bank, London.

This highly accomplished view relates to a drawing in the Yale Center for British Art, 'A View of the Mosque at Mounheer from the S.E' (B1978.43.1766), which was presumably also the basis for the engraved version in *Select Views*. It also relates to another drawing (Yale Center for British Art, B1978.43.1806), subsequently also engraved for *Select Views* (17), showing the building from an alternative, more distant position. Hodges visited the site in the summer of 1781 while staying at Patna during his second excursion through Bihar in the company of Warren Hastings, and was clearly very impressed by its architectural beauty:

> This building, though not large, is certainly very beautiful: it is a square, with pavilions rising from the angles; and in the centre is a majestic dome, the top of which is finished by what the Indian architects call a cullus: the line of the curve of the dome is not broken, but is continued by an inverted curve until it finishes in a crescent. I cannot but greatly prefer this to the manner in which all great domes are finished in Europe . . . The outer surface of the dome is ornamented by plantane leaves cut in stone, covering the whole; the lines intersect each other in great lozenges, and form altogether a beautiful ornament. The great entrance to the mosque is similar to many of the doors of our large Gothic cathedrals, having columns diminishing as it were in perspective to the inner door. There is a large tank belonging to it, with several buildings rising from the water, containing pavilions. The whole, however, is much decayed.[1]

This detailed account demonstrates Hodges's sensitivity to Indian culture and his propensity, elaborated in the *Dissertation on the Prototypes of Architecture*, to make unusually detached comparative judgments between Indian, Gothic and Classical forms. However, it is noticeably at odds with the painting, which, as Giles Tillotson has pointed out, deliberately obscures the symmetry and architectural meaning of the build-

ing, in favour of presenting a view in sharp perspective that follows eighteenth-century European conventions for landscape views of buildings.[2] Rather, the painting focuses on the final observation of the building's decay, by foregrounding the gateway with its crumbling roofline enveloped by foliage. This interpretation of the site is further emphasized in the accompanying description to the mezzotint in *Select Views*, which states that the mosque was built in 1617 'in the reign of Shah Jehanguire, the son of the Emperor Akbar, by a then Soubah of the district, as a mausoleum for himself and family, as well as a mosque or religious house'. Hodges then goes on to link the ruination of the site with the unsettled history of the region:

> In the various revolutions of property, in this part of India, from one hand to another, since the erecting of this building, that which was left for the repair and support of this mosque is now lost and this building, like most in India, ruined by superstition, is rapidly falling into the dust.

This, however, is somewhat disingenuous. For, if the painting overlooks any formal significance to the architecture in terms of its cultural uses and functions, the descriptions also omit to mention that, far from being obsolete, as they suggest, the building was a continuing site of Muslim pilgrimage, centred on the tomb of the Sufi saint, Shah Daulat. Indeed, it is the tomb, not the mosque, which is the focus of the composition and of Hodges's eulogistic description. Conversely, for Hodges, it is Muslim religious 'superstition' itself, which is the cause of the building's decline, and which is key to the association of ruins with death that Hodges so frequently adduces in his Indian views (see cat. nos 47, 52).

This sublimation of the site as a living shrine of Muslim belief is emphasized in the paucity of figures and the elegiac mood that pervades the scene. As with Hodges's other views of Indian tombs and mausolea, and contrary to his known appreciation of native Indian visual traditions, it neither shows any awareness of the representational methods used by Indian artists to convey the holy significance of such sites. These adopted a planimetric view, dispaying the tomb and surrounding gardens as a form of earthly paradise (fig. 21).[3] However 'naturalistic' Hodges's perspectival view of the tomb and mosque may appear, it is important to remember that such representational means could be put to ideological ends (for instance by allowing emphatic focus on ruins), and were starkly different to Indian depictions, which tended to be regarded by the British as technically primitive and decorative.

[1] Hodges (1793), 45–6.

[2] Tillotson (2000), 73–4.

[3] See Tillotson's essay in this volume.

54 *View of the Ruins of a Palace at Gazipoor on the River Ganges, c.1785*

Oil on canvas, 61 × 71.1 cm

Provenance: possibly Daylesford House sale, 26 August 1853 (899); Sotheby's, 20 November 1963 (142)

Engraved: *Select Views* no. 7, published 4 October 1785.

Literature: Stuebe (1979), nos 287, 292; Tillotson (2000), 127–30, 137.

Inchcape Family Estates Ltd.

This is based on a drawing in the Paul Mellon Collection (B1978. 43.1722) and, with minor variations, is the basis for the aquatint in *Select Views*. Compositionally, with the banked buildings rising diagonally to the top right corner, it is very close to the view of Fatehpur Sikri (cat. no. 68), employing a strategy that simultaneously emphasizes the grandeur of the structures and draws attention to their elegiac ruination and abandonment.

Hodges visited Gazipoor [Ghazipur] in August 1781 during his second excursion up river through Bengal and Bihar in the company of Warren Hastings, and en route to Benares [Varanasi]. He clearly had magnificent ruins in mind, having recently come also from Mounheer

[Maner] where he admired the mosque and tomb (cat. no. 53), and he was no less enthusiastic in his account of the palace at Gazipoor:

At this place are the ruins of a fine palace, built in the beginning of this century. It is raised on a high bank, and on a point commanding two great reaches of the river, up and down. From the bank, which is full thirty feet from the water, is raised another basement of brick and masonry sixteen feet high, in which are some apartments: on this is the building, which is an oblong square, with great pavilions at the angles, and in the center of each side: for the whole is an open space, supported by colonades surrounding it. Within, on the floor of the building, is a channel for water about four feet wide; it encircles the floor, and, at equal spaces, there were formerly fountains. In the center of the building is a space sufficient to contain twenty people.

Nearly adjoining to this palace is a building for the purpose of raising water for the fountains, and supplying them by the means of pipes, which communicate with each other.

About two miles inland from the river are the remains of a seraii and, nearly adjoining, tombs, built at the same period as the palace. Those buildings are in a fine state of Moorish architecture, and in very good repair.[1]

As with other sites, it is surprising what Hodges contains in his written description that is omitted from his pictured representation, suggesting again that the viewpoint for the images of the palace was carefully chosen for its aesthetic values in highlighting the decay and seeming antiquity of the palace, even though he states that it was built only in the early eighteenth century. The building to the far right is presumably the water house for supplying the fountains, now defunct. It is notable, however, that he draws attention in his description to the nearby tombs and their state of 'very good repair', which offers a pointed contrast with the melancholic ruins of the pictured palace.

[1] Hodges (1793), 45–6.

55 *A View of the West Side of the Fortress of Chunargarh on the Ganges, c.*1785

Oil on canvas, 121.9 × 160.7 cm

Provenance: possibly Warren Hastings sale, Christie's, 11 April 1797 (79); presented by William Thompson to Bilston Art Gallery 1937.

Engraved: *Select Views* (3), published 20 May 1785.

Literature: Stuebe (1979), nos 242–54; Tillotson (2000), 87–8.

On loan from Wolverhampton Art Gallery.

Based, like the aquatint for *Select Views*, on a drawing in the Yale Center for British Art (Paul Mellon Collection, B1978.43.1725), this may be the view of Chunargarh that was in Warren Hastings's collection (Stuebe no. 254), though at its sale in 1797 the latter was simply entitled *A View of the Fort of Chunarghur in India*. The Hastings picture, therefore, might also be identical with the *View of the North End of the Fort of Chunar Gur in the Province of Benares in the East Indies* that was exhibited at the Royal Academy in 1786 (Stuebe (1979) no 244), which in turn might be the picture that was sold at Christie's in 1961 as *Fort Chunar with River and Boats in the Foreground*.[1] The Christie's painting was almost identical in size with the view of the west side of the fortress here, which suggests that they may have been conceived as pendants. Hodges also completed another painting of the fort from the east (private collection).

These multiple depictions and viewpoints, which are supplemented in several related drawings as well as the many associated views of the mosque at Chunargarh, indicate the level of significance of this site for Hodges and his principal patron in India, Warren Hastings. The fortress figured prominently in Hastings's campaign against Raja Chait Singh of Benares, along with several other local forts involved in the same campaign during the summer of 1781 (see cat. nos 56-59). As Giles Tillotson has commented, Hodges's depictions of them, under Hastings's instruction, 'whilst in a general way illustrating Indian locations, focus on subjects of special resonance to an English audience watching with interest the advancement there of British concerns.'[2]

Thus Hodges, in both the letterpress to the related aquatints in *Select Views* and in his lengthy account in *Travels in India*, drew attention not only to both the historical significance of the fortress but also its more immediate significance as a site of British military conquest. Despite his claim to impartiality in political matters, that 'facts alone are my object, and such alone as fell within the limited sphere of my notice', his account in *Travels in India* is inevitably and overwhelmingly biased towards Hastings.[3] He describes how he arrived at Benares, in Hastings's entourage, on 15 August, but with news of Chait Singh's successful rebellion and an impending attack on the city, they were forced to flee on the night of the 21st: some four hundred men arrived at Chunargarh, twenty miles away, at seven the following morning. With the arrival of reinforcements during August and September, an all out effort was made to suppress the insurrection by besieging the raja's other major strongholds nearby at Pateeta, Latifpur and finally Bijaigarh. Hodges portrays the raja as a stereotypical oriental despot, whose 'cruel and sanguinary disposition' was encapsulated in the torture and massacre of British soldiers, then gives a short account of the fort itself, concluding:

> This has always been considered as a post of great consequence upon the Ganges, from its insulated situation, projecting forwards to a considerable extent, and being of considerable heighth. [*sic*] It was besieged by the English in the war carried on, during the years 1764 and 1765, against the late Nabob Sujah ul Dowlah when he joined Meer Cossim, and was gallantly defended by its commandant, an Abyssinian in the service of that prince.

The first attempt of the English against Chunar was unsuccessful; but afterwards, on the fall of Allahabad, the commandant finding that the whole country had submitted to the English, and that his master's affairs were desperate, thought it needless to hold out any longer, and on the 7th of February, 1765, he surrendered the fort to Major, now General Stibbert; it was afterwards restored to the Nabob, when the peace was settled with that Prince; and in 1772, it was formerly ceded by him to the English East India Company, in exchange for the fort of Allahabad.[4]

Hodges's history is concerned not just to culminate with the details of the English acquisition of the fort, but also to stress that this was ultimately a peaceable process, after it had been restored to the nawab. The painting, in a complementary way, adopts a striking perspectival foreshortening to evoke the sublime strength and seeming impregnability of the fort, the scale of which is further stressed by the juxtaposition with the sepoy and elephant (the elephant may also be emblematic of the historical significance of the site, being both a Hindu symbol, and also a beast of war in ancient India). On the other hand, the dead stillness of the river and the picturesque, 'Gothick' appearance of the fort belie its recent history of conflict and perhaps instead confirm it as now both the peaceful site of successful colonial acquisition and the successful stronghold of the British presence, centred around Hodges's patron, Hastings.

The incongruities of scale between foreground and background and unclear definition of spatial distances, caused by the dramatic perspective, suggest that the painting was done from drawings after Hodges had returned from India, probably around 1785, when the aquatint for *Select Views* was published.

---

[1] Christie's, 8 December 1961 (195); Stuebe (1979), cat. no. 253.

[2] Tillotson (2000), 87.

[3] Hodges (1793), 48.

[4] Ibid., 55–7.

56 *View of the Fort of Pateeta, c.1781–82*

Oil on canvas, 58.5 × 68.5 cm

Provenance: Warren Hastings collection; Christie's 20 July 1956, as 'A View of Shekoabad'; Spink & Son, 1978; Christie's, 17 July 1987 (33)

Engraved: *Select Views*, no. 44, published 1 March 1788

Literature: Stuebe (1979), no. 349

Private collection.

Greenwich only.

This view of Pateeta, one of two oils completed by Hodges of this subject (see also cat. no. 57), is based directly on the drawing in the Paul Mellon Collection (B1978.43.1788) that also served as the model for the aquatint, published 1 March 1788, in *Select Views*. In the letterpress to the latter, Hodges gives a brief account of the fort:

> This fort of Peteter lies about six English miles west from the fort at Chunar Gur. It is an instance of the mud forts that are met with in Hindostan, which, in many parts of the country, may be said to cover it. I have, in many places, found them at no more than two miles distance, and in constant hostility to each other. They have been built at different times by the Zemindars, who, frequently with-holding their rents, retire to them to evade their payments to the government, under pretext of ill treatment from the Nabob or other governors.

This gives some clue to the relevance of Pateeta to the British viewer, since the fort had figured importantly in the campaign against the zamindar, Raja Chait Singh, waged by Warren Hastings in the summer and autumn of 1781 (see cat. no. 55). Noting the British government's right to dispossess the zamindar, who is 'simply a land-holder', Hodges describes the campaign and his own involvement in it at length in *Travels in India*.[1]

While Hastings's entourage, including Hodges, were in retreat and awaiting relief at the British stronghold at Chunargarh, a force under Major Popham, stationed a few miles away, successfully attacked Chait Singh's fort at Pateeta, taking it in mid-September, a victory celebrated by this painting produced for Hastings. Incongruously large figures on the rampart appear to be running up a flag by way of salute: these differ slightly from the drawing, though the other version of the subject transcribes the figures in the drawing faithfully. As in other views of Indian forts, Hodges takes a low viewpoint in order to stress the seemingly impregnable situation of the building (see also cat. no. 55). However, unlike the view of Chunargarh, there is little sense of any historical significance attached to this site other then its past and present strategic military uses.

[1] Hodges (1793), 48.

57 *View of the Fort of Pateeta, c.1781–82*

Oil on canvas, 61 × 101.7 cm

Provenance: Captain Justly Hill and by descent to Mrs Fanny Bramwell, Bideford, Devon; W. G. Archer collection, 1968; Christie's, 24 September 2003 (1)

Literature: Stuebe (1979), no. 350

Private collection.

Yale only.

Like the similar view painted for Warren Hastings (see cat. no. 56), this is based on the drawing of Pateeta in the Paul Mellon Collection (B1978.43.1788). While it retains the same grouping of figures on the rampart as in the drawing, the composition is considerably extended to the left, to include more figures and Hodges's characteristic diagonally serpentine tree.

It is the pendant to the *View of the Fort of Bidjegur* (cat. no. 58), which accounts for its changed dimensions from the view of Pateeta made for Hastings. The extra figures to the left also include in the distance a group of sepoys, distinctive in their red uniforms, again linking it to its pendant picture, which also prominently features red-coated soldiers and a cannon to the left. This emphasis on the military character of the forts, focusing on their role as British military targets and conquests in the campaign against Chait Singh during the summer and autumn of 1781, no doubt results from their being painted for one of the principal figures involved in those operations, Captain, later Major, Justly Hill (see cat. no. 58). While in the Hastings view, therefore, the figures on the fort seem to be raising some sort of flag, suggesting the successful completion of the British assault, here, as with the companion view of Bijaigarh, the siege seems to be anticipated or just being undertaken.

Hodges states in *Travels in India* that, at Hastings' request, he made several drawings of the forts at Chunargarh and Pateeta, before returning to Benares (Varanasi). He was later sent by Hastings to make drawings of the forts of Bidjegur and Latifpur, also prominent in the Chait Singh affair.[1] It is likely that this painting was executed, with its pendant, shortly after the campaign itself, perhaps in December 1781.

[1] Hodges (1793), 57, 82.

58 *View of the Fort of Bidjegur, c.*1781–82

Oil on canvas, 61.25 × 101.5 cm

Provenance: painted for Captain Justly Hill; W. G. Archer collection

Literature: Stuebe (1979), no. 226

Yale Center for British Art, Paul Mellon Collection.

Yale only.

The assault by British troops under Major Popham on the fort of Bidjegur [Bijaigarh] was the final stage in the campaign against Raja Chait Singh of Benares, who had rebelled against Warren Hastings governorship of Bengal in August 1781. By October, having lost the forts of Pateeta (see cat. no. 56) and Latifpur, Chait Singh had retreated to his stronghold at Bidjegur. Since he had also allied with the Marathas, the campaign became one of the principal episodes of the First Anglo-Maratha War. This painting, the pendant to the *View of the Fort of Pateeta* (cat. no. 57), was made for Captain Hill, one of the principal figures in the sieges of both forts. It is very similar to another view of Bidjegur (private collection) that was probably the picture exhibited at the Royal

Academy in 1786, and was the basis for the aquatint published in *Select Views* (10) on 29 May of the same year. Like these, and the pendant view of Pateeta, it contains explicit reference to the military campaign, in the inclusion of soldiers and cannon to the left. Such inclusions are unusual for Hodges's Indian views, which tend to concentrate, at least in part, on the historical significance of the sites represented, but may be explained in this instance by the fact that this painting and its pendant were produced for Captain Hill, and were no doubt intended to be souvenirs, or even testimonies, of his military successes in India as captain and later major in the Bengal Artillery, in which he served from 1763 to 1793.

In October 1781 Hodges was sent at Warren Hastings's command, in October 1781, to complete drawings of Latifpur and Bidjegur. Despite his complaints elsewhere about the deleterious effects of war upon the practice of art, Hodges welcomed this opportunity. In the letterpress to the engraving for *Select Views* even suggested that the military campaign against Chait Singh had had a positive effect in opening up previously unknown territory, since 'These places, before that time, were very little known, and that of Bidjegur only by name, no European having been in its neighbourhood'.

The view is very different from that done for Warren Hastings (cat. no. 59), being much more modest in scale and technical ambition. The dominant and virtually unmodulated green of the hillside brings to the

Fig. 57 Murshidabad artist after William Hodges, *South-east View of the Fort of Bijaigarh*, c.1790, gouache, 35.3 x 51.2 cm. The British Library, London.

fore the redness of the soldiers' uniforms, but lacks the subtle interest in atmosphere and light of Hastings's picture. The focus is very strongly upon the military significance of the site, which as Hodges states unequivocally, was in this instance also closely tied to a sense of artistic progress in opening up new Indian landscapes.

However, the degree to which Hodges's images were implicated in a colonial project that was assimilative as well as militaristic is indicated by the fact that this view was copied by Indian artists in the service of the East India Company (fig. 57). Based evidently on the widely dissemi-

nated print in *Select Views*, the artist has endeavoured to adopt a style based on European conventions, contrary to a familiar Indian tradition, even though the traditional medium of gouache has been used. Certain passages of the original, notably the cannon to the left, have been 'misread' in its production. The result is a complex hybrid that suggests at the very least that Hodges's paintings cannot be understood simply as signifiers of an oppressive colonialism; though it remains doubtful, of course, how much latitude was allowed to Indian 'Company' artists in their choice of pictorial subject.

59 *View of the Fort of Bidjegur, c.*1781–82

Oil on canvas, 99.1 × 157.5 cm

Provenance: Warren Hastings collection; Daylesford House sale, 26 August 1853 (919); presumably remained at Daylesford until removed by the Kingham Hill Trust in 1936; Hon. Esmond Rothermere, later 2nd Viscount Rothermere, Daylesford House.

Engraved: by B. T. Pouncy in Hodges, *Travels in India*, opposite p. 86.

Literature: Hastings papers, British Museum, Add. Mss. 41,609, p. 48 and 41,610, p. 23; Stuebe (1979), no. 230.

Private collection.

Greenwich only.

This large painting was made for Warren Hastings, and is closely adapted from a drawing in the Paul Mellon Collection (B1978.43.1749), with the prominent addition of the figures in the foreground. It is also the exact basis for the engraving in *Travels in India*, where Hodges states that the picture was made on the spot. At Hastings's wish, he went in October 1781 to complete views of the forts of Latifpur and Bidjegur [Bijaigarh], some fifty miles from Benares [Varanasi], during the ongoing conflict with Raja Chait Singh, whose military strongholds they were until taken by the British. Hodges accompanied the siege of Bidjegur undertaken by Colonel Popham: he describes the terrain in terms that conform closely to the view shown here. Bijaigarh's strength derived from its location at the top of a high mountain

> covered from its base to its summit with wood. This is the last of a long range of mountains, which, at this place, rudely descends to the plain. Here I enjoyed an opportunity which falls to the lot of very few professional men in my line; I mean that of observing the military operations of a siege. The camp was formed nearly four miles from the fort: there was, however, a rock about the heighth [*sic*] of the top of the mountains, and within gun shot, commanding one face of the fort, which was square. From this station the walls were battered; and after a predictable breach was made, the garrison thought fit to surrender. In the garrison were found the mother and other female relatives of Cheyt Sing, to whom every delicate attention was paid.[1]

Despite Hodges's emphasis in the text on the details of the siege, and in contrast to the other versions of this subject (cat. no. 58), there is no sign of conflict in this painting, apart perhaps from the inclusion of the rock at the left edge: this may be taken as a reference to the rock from which the siege was made, and it is noticeable that Hodges has raised its height from the drawing to render it on a level with the fort. The standing figure in the foreground is also clearly reminiscent of the Maori figure in *Cascade Cove* (cat. no. 26), and there may be a veiled comparison here between two supposedly belligerent peoples, the Maori being noted for their tendency to war. However, these are highly coded references at best, and overall Hodges has concentrated on representing with extraordinary subtlety the raking evening light across the hillside, to offer a view of the site divested of its military context and, like the view of Chunargarh (cat. no. 55), instead appropriated to an historicizing aesthetic, by which it is represented as the peaceful, naturalized site of colonial conquest. Such a gentle view of the fort corresponds with the claim about the 'delicate attention' paid to the women when the fort was taken, although this became one of the most contentious points about the campaign against Chait Singh at Hastings's trial. Hodges's pointed reference to it in *Travels* may be taken as a public statement of support for the conduct of his principal patron.

[1] Hodges (1793), 85–6.

60 *View of Benares with Aurangzeb's Mosque,* *c.*1781–82

Oil on canvas, 68.5 × 91.5 cm

Provenance: possibly Warren Hastings sale, 1797; purchased by Sir William Foster, October 1904.

Literature: Stuebe (1979), no. 199; Tillotson (2000), 1–4, 104

The British Library, London.

With minor variations, this is a smaller version of the view of Benares that Hodges produced for Warren Hastings, exhibited at the Royal Academy in 1788. One review, in response to it, surmised that Benares was comparable with Delft in its appearance and culture,[1] offering an interesting parallel to Hodges's views of Calcutta, which, being compared to Canaletto, likened Calcutta to the commercial entrepots of Venice or London.

Benares for Hodges was also the primary site of conflict between what he saw as the pure spiritual values of Hinduism and the decadent and destructive influence of Islam. This was manifest in the architectural history of the city that is the focus of this painting, with its contrast between the sacred Panchganga Ghat in the foreground and the imposing minarets of Aurangzeb's mosque. Throughout *Travels in India* Aurangzeb, the last of the six great Mughal emperors, is portrayed as the archetype of the oriental 'Grand Mogul', an eastern Muslim tyrant with seemingly unlimited arbitrary power. Hodges describes the view of the city in terms of a contrast between the beauty of the Hindu temples and Ghats, and the sublimity of the ominous intrusion of the mosque:

> from the water, its appearance is extremely beautiful; the great variety of buildings strikes the eye, and the whole view is much improved by innumerable flights of stone steps, which are either entrances into the several temples, or to the houses. Several Hindoo

temples greatly embellish the banks of the river
[. . .]

Nearly at the centre of the city is a considerable Mahomedan mosque, with two minarets: the height from the water to the top of the minarets is 232 feet. This building was raised by that most intolerant and ambitious of human beings, the Emperor Aurungzebe, who destroyed a magnificent temple of the Hindoos on this spot, and built the present mosque, of the same extent and height as the building he destroyed.[2]

Aurangzeb, a fervently devout Muslim, built his mosque on the site of the Visvanatha temple, and appears to have targeted Benares in his expansion of the Muslim Mughal empire because it was ' "the general school for Hindus" as well as a major centre for what Muslims regarded as that most abominable form of idolatry, *lingam* worship'.[3] However,

Hodges's elevation of the merits of Hindu tradition in the face of what he sees throughout the *Travels* as 'the effects of Mohamedan intolerance' might also be seen as a means of diverting attention from the morality of the British imperial presence, and as a moral justification for the British military campaign against supposedly despotic local leaders such as Chait Singh. The exhibition at the Royal Academy of Hastings's version of this subject, at the outset of his trial, could therefore be seen as an open statement of support from Hodges for his patron.[4]

[1] Stuebe (1979), 208.

[2] Hodges, (1793), 60–1.

[3] Keay, (2001), 343.

[4] See Natasha Eaton's essay in this volume.

61 *View of the Ghats at Benares*, 1787

Oil on canvas, 91.5 × 130.8 cm

Provenance: presented by the artist as his Diploma piece to the Royal Academy, 1787.

Exhibited: RA 1788; British Institution 1844 (142); Bournemouth 1957; Arts Council Touring Exhibition, 1961–2; *Treasures of the Royal Academy*, 1963

Literature: Stuebe (1979), no. 202; Tillotson (2000), 61, 122

Lent by the Royal Academy of Arts, London.

Stuebe notes that 'this highly romanticized river scene' must have been produced for the specific purpose of Hodges's diploma piece, being worked up in London from earlier drawings and paintings. Its stylistic

differences from the view of Benares [Varanasi] that Hodges exhibited at the Royal Academy in 1787, and which, though ranked as one of Hodges's 'best pictures', was criticized as being 'a little too hard', suggest that he was concerned to produce a highly polished work in full accordance with academic demands for the presentation of landscape painting.[1] Here, the composition and technique are very precisely finished, though not in the interests of topographical recording, for this is not a topographically accurate view, but rather a freely adapted composite of the principal buildings and monuments of Benares. In this sense, Hodges appears to be openly suiting his subject matter to the academic recommendations for landscape espoused by Sir Joshua Reynolds in his *Discourses*: these stated that the highest branch of landscape painting was general and idealized, in the manner of the seventeenth-century artist Claude Lorrain, as opposed to its lower form, the simple record of a given location.

Nor should it be surprising that Hodges opted for a view of India, and especially Benares, as the suitable subject for his Diploma piece. He was by this date best known for his Indian works. In addition, Benares held special significance for the British in India, because of its antiquity and central importance to Indian history. In *Travels in India* Hodges praised Benares as the ancient seat of Brahman learning – perhaps the oldest city in the world – and saw it as a 'pure' repository of living Indian history, that had been least influenced by Islamic culture. On his arrival there in August 1781 in the company of Warren Hastings, he confessed 'real pleasure' in the prospect of 'being able to contemplate the pure Hindoo manners, arts, buildings, and customs, undepraved by any intermixture with the Mahomedans', the more so 'since the same manners and customs prevail amongst these people at this day, as at the remotest period that can be traced in history'.[2]

Benares, therefore, had a direct analogy with the apprehension by Cook's voyages of certain Pacific cultures as being modern incarnations of classical civilization. For the self-styled artist-historian, Benares was an ideal subject in comprising a history that was visible to the cultivated eye. However, it was also, according to the seventeenth-century traveller François Bernier, 'the Athens of India'.[3] So, Hodges's observation of what seemed to be classical Greek forms on a column in a Hindu temple in Benares provoked his cross-cultural architectural study, the *Dissertation on the Prototypes of Architecture, Hindoo, Moorish, Gothic* (cat. no. 69). On these counts, his choice of Benares as the subject for his Diploma piece is highly appropriate, offering perhaps a veiled form of flattery to the Academy, itself styled as a modern counterpart to classical seats of learning. To offer an idealized vision, following Claudean principles of landscape painting, of the Indian equivalent to classical Athens would be Hodges's personalized compliment to the institution that had embraced him.

---

[1] *Morning Herald*, Tuesday 15 May 1787, 3.

[2] Hodges (1793), 47, 59.

[3] Bernier (1914), 334.

62 *A Camp of a thousand Men formed by Augustus Cleveland three miles from Bhagalpur, with his Mansion in the distance,* 1782

Oil on canvas, 122.0 × 160.0 cm, inscribed as title in the artist's hand on a label on the reverse

Provenance: painted for Augustus Cleveland, then by descent.

Literature: Tillotson (2000), 95–6.

Pym's Gallery, London.

During his time in India, Hodges made several visits to his friend and patron, Augustus Cleveland, at his house at Bhagalpur, staying for an extended period between January and May 1782. In *Travels in India* he writes in adulatory terms of Cleveland, who was the district collector for the region. Together they made an excursion into the local country of the Jungleterry and Hodges describes their encounters with the local people, who he speculates may be the first aboriginal settlers of the region, possibly outcast from ancient Hindu communities.[1] He elaborates on the theme of their otherness, representing them as bandits and outlaws making night raids on local farmers, preying on travellers, and impervious to any military force used against them. According to Hodges, Cleveland single-handedly pacified these people by going alone and unarmed to negotiate with the chiefs, until by 'a variety of attentions, by little presents, and acts of personal kindness, he . . . subdued their ferocious spirits'.[2] The hyperbole of Hodges's heroicization of Cleveland is indicated by the challenge to his account made by Cleveland's predecessor as head of the district, who presented himself as the initiator such measures.[3] Hodges, however, in what might be seen as a classic account of colonial assimilation, tells how Cleveland had uniforms made for the tribesmen, armed and drilled them, and turned them into a local group of sepoys, so that in less than two years

> he had a fine corps of these people embodied, for the express purpose of preserving from injury the very country that had for centuries before been the scene of their depredations. A camp was formed for a corps of a thousand men, three miles from Bauglepoor, where their families resided with them, and where strict military discipline was observed. Thus the ingenuity, address, and humanity of one man effected, in the space of little more than two years, more than could even have been hoped for from the utmost exertions of military severity.[4]

This painting, therefore, celebrates Cleveland's supposedly benign authority as a civilizing influence in this region, presenting five men proudly upright in their new uniforms against a backdrop of an extensive local landscape, across which is ranged the camp in the distance. Anchoring the scene, brightly highlighted against the cloudscape, is the classical structure of Cleveland's house. The painting is a remarkable adaptation of the domestic conversation-piece, and perhaps recalls Johann Zoffany's inventive appropriation of this genre to a colonial Indian context. It inverts the usual semantics of the conversation-piece by showing the house and grounds not as the cultivated product of the owners, who would be conventionally shown standing in the foreground to one side, as the sepoys are here, but by representing these foreground figures instead as the result of the civilizing work of the house. The presence of the owner, Augustus Cleveland, is rendered implicit in this highly favourable portrayal of the ordering effects of his colonial administration. Hodges employed a similar strategy on behalf of his other principal patron in India, Warren Hastings, when representing his house at Alipur (see cat. no. 45).

The painting, despite its large size, like many other works for Cleveland, appears to have been painted on the spot: this is suggested by the vibrant handling, directness of the portraits (which recall Hodges's portrayals of Pacific Islanders), and the lack of any discernible underdrawing or other preparatory studies. This would also explain the idiosyncracies of the figure drawing, which in places is very awkward.

[1] Hodges (1793), 87–8.
[2] Ibid., 89.
[3] Browne (1788), Introduction.
[4] Hodges (1793), 90.

63 *A Group of Temples at Deogarh, Santal Parganas, Bihar, c.1782*

Oil on canvas, 68.5 × 91.5 cm

Provenance: presented by James C. Lyell, 1917.

Literature: Stuebe (1979), no. 265; Tillotson (2000), 52–3

The British Library, London.

This is one of two painted views of Deogarh by Hodges. The other (fig. 6), which was engraved for *Select Views* (no. 22), is in a private collection; a drawing relating to it has recently been discovered in the Victoria Memorial Hall, Calcutta. Either of these paintings could be the picture

made for Augustus Cleveland and sold in the Cleveland sale, Calcutta, 1794. However, the tight handling and poetic, reflective treatment of the subject in the second view, as well as it being the basis for the later print in *Select Views*, all suggest that it was completed after Hodges's return to England. This would suggest that the painting in the Oriental and India Office Collection might be Cleveland's picture: its more experimental composition and concern with contemporary, ordinary Indian life and custom also accord with other Cleveland pictures (cat. no. 62).

Deogarh is located at Santal Parganas in the district of Bihar, near Bhagalpur. Hodges visited the site in the company of Augustus Cleveland in February 1782. In *Travels in India* he described it as

a small village, famous for the resort of Hindoo pilgrims, this being a sacred spot. There are five curious pagodas here, of perhaps the very oldest construction to be found in India. They are simply pyr-

amids, formed by putting stone on stone, the apex is cut off at about one seventh of the whole height of the complete pyramid, and four of them have small ornamental buildings on top, evidently of more modern work, which are finished by an ornament made of copper, and gilt, perfectly resembling the trident of the Greek Neptune. These Pagodas have each a small chamber in the center of twelve feet square, with a lamp, hanging over the Lingham . . . At Deogur

multitudes of pilgrims are seen, who carry the water of the Ganges to the western side of the peninsula of India.[1]

Unlike fig. 6, which takes a viewpoint from outside the complex and evokes a mysterious, exotic and seemingly desolate scene comparable to Hodges's views of Easter Island (cat. no. 25), the painting here, conforming much more closely with the description in the *Travels*, is set within the grounds of the temples and focuses upon them as objects of pilgrimage, showing, for Hodges, an unusually high number of figures distributed across the scene. While the former attempts to represent the immemorial antiquity of the buildings, the latter is concerned to show them as functioning structures serving the pilgrimage cult centred on the *lingam*, the phallic icon of Siva. The inclusion of a building under construction at the bottom right of this picture further heightens this contrast: while Hodges states that the site contained 'five curious pagodas', the painting shows the actuality, whereby several more temples were dedicated and under construction from around 1780. However, both views feature the distinctive architectural motif that captures Hodges's attention, the apex of the temples that, 'perfectly resembling the trident of the Greek Neptune', makes a cross-reference between Indian and classical western architectural forms (see also cat. nos 53, 69). It is striking, however, that this representation of a Hindu site as flourishing and expanding is in marked contrast to an equivalent Muslim shrine, such as the *Mosque at Mounheer* (cat. no. 53), and further emphasizes the relative value of Hindu and Muslim culture for the British in India in the eighteenth century.

[1] Hodges, (1793), 94.

64 *View in the Jungle Ferry,* [Jungleterry] *Bengal, c.*1786

Oil on canvas, 65 × 52.7 cm

Provenance: C. A. Woollett, 1914; Christie's, 15 July 1988 (58)

Exhibited: probably RA 1786 (90)

Engraved: *Select Views*, no. 47 (published 27 April 1788)

Literature: Stuebe (1979), nos 375, 377

Private collection.

Greenwich only.

The very tight execution and classically conceived composition of this picture, which differs markedly from the fluidity and freedom of handling of works produced in India and which clearly recalls Richard Wilson and Claude, suggests that it was done after Hodges's return from India, specifically for exhibition and inclusion in *Select Views*. In this regard, the overtly classicized composition would have helped familiarize the exotic landscape to an English audience, although one reviewer

found fault with the consequent lack of realism. Citing the *View of the North End of the Fort of Chunar Gur* (in the same 1786 exhibition) as the only work of India by Hodges that 'conveys any idea of the hot atmosphere in that climate', he goes on to complain, 'All his other productions appear, in point of aerial effect, more like views near the North Pole.'[1]

However, Hodges is still evidently concerned to emphasize the peculiarities of the landscape, particularly the fantastic and other-worldly mountain in the centre distance with its outcrops of trees. He states that the view is taken near the village of Barkope in the Jungleterry region, near Bhagalpur in the district of Bihar.[2] Hodges visited the area in the spring of 1782, in the company of his friend and patron Augustus Cleveland. He was struck by the landscape, of which he gave a detailed description in *Travels in India.*

> This interior part of the country consists of much wood, intermixed with cultivated ground, and many villages, chiefly inhabited by husbandmen. Among others, I could not but notice the village of Barkope, adjacent to which are many hills, rising almost to the consequence of mountains, and every one of them is insulated by the plain country. The appearance of this part of the country is very singular, having immense masses of stone piled one on another; from the interstices of which are very large timber trees growing out, in some places overshadowing the whole of the rocks: the trees are of various kinds. In many of these rocks I found the teek, a timber remarkable for its hardness and size; and this accompanied with the mango, no less remarkable for its softness, and which produces the fine fruit of that name. The tamarind and other trees are also produced here. On some of the highest of these hills I observed durgaws, or burial places, with little chapels annexed, belonging to the Musselmans.[3]

The careful description of the terrain and trees recalls Hodges's association with the Forsters' methods of geographical and botanical classification on Cook's second voyage. However, topographical precision is clearly not Hodges's primary concern in this elegiac view of an exotic landscape, which, with its framing trees opening onto a clearly defined middle ground and far distance, its evocation of fugitive evening light and a solitary figure by the lake, appears to be closer to eighteenth-century lines of poetic reflection than empirical accounts of non-European territories. In this sense, it may be taken as an Indian equivalent of Hodges's reflective, 'philosophical' paintings of Pacific subjects done for the Admiralty after his return from Cook's voyage (see cat. nos 26, 33).

[1] *General Advertiser*, 23 May 1786.

[2] Hodges (1785–8), no. 47.

[3] Hodges (1793), 87.

65 *View of the Jungle Ferry [Jungleterry] in Bengal; the animals painted by Mr Gilpin, c.*1785

Oil on canvas, 129.5 x 180.3 cm

Provenance: acquired by the 3rd Earl of Egremont c.1830, then by descent

Exhibited: probably RA 1785 (257)

Literature: Stuebe (1979), no. 376

Lord Egremont.

Only recently identified in the collection at Petworth, this substantial painting was listed in the 1920 catalogue of the collection by Collins-Baker as simply 'Camels in a Wood' by Hodges. It has now been cleaned and restored (fig. 58), which reveals it, though still dark, to be an important example of Hodges's views of the Jungleterry region in Bihar, with the distinctive profile of the mountain of Tewer in the background. Given its size and ambitious, complex composition, centred on the play of evening light through a wooded landscape, which was a favourite subject of Hodges, treated in *A View in Pickersgill Harbour* as well as in another view in the Jungleterry (cat. nos 5, 64), it is likely that this was an exhibited work. Its dimensions also appear to approximate those of the *View of the Falls of Mootegerna*, exhibited at the Royal Academy in 1787, visible in Ramberg's engraving of the Great Room (fig. 16) and the dimensions of which at its sale in 1936 were given as 53 × 77 inches. Of Hodges's exhibited works depicting the Jungleterry, the only one that fits the painting here is the work exhibited in 1785 and jointly completed with the animal painter Sawrey Gilpin (with whom Hodges also collaborated on another painting in the same exhibition, *View on the Hills that divide the kingdom of Bengal from the province of Bahen; the animals painted by Mr. Gilpin* (1)).

Examination of the painting during restoration indicated that the animals had been added once the landscape had been substantially completed; *pentimenti* to the water around the group in the bottom-right corner also suggest revisions to the landscape after the animals had been added. It is a remarkably integrated and involved composition for such collaboration.

It shows a wooded landscape around a lake, at dusk, with several groups of Indian figures encamped on the banks of the water with their camels and packs. In the distance a pair of women are collecting water. Hodges painted at least five other views of the Jungleterry, mostly for Augustus Cleveland, with whom he visited the region in February 1782 (see cat. no. 62). No related drawing is known.

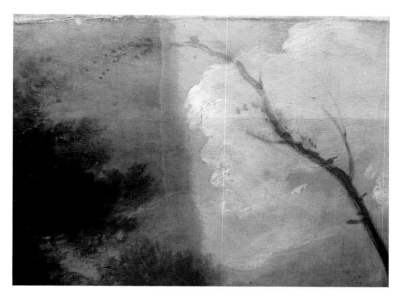

Fig. 58 William Hodges, *View of the Jungle Ferry [Jungleterry] in Bengal; the Animals Painted by Mr. Gilpin*, detail during restoration.

66 *Hill and Lake of Ture,* 1782

Oil on canvas, 35 × 48.4 cm

Provenance: Augustus Cleveland sale, Calcutta, 4 February 1794 (1)

Literature: Stuebe (1979), nos. 374, 440

Private collection.

While Stuebe only tentatively suggests that this might be the painting of this title that was in the sale of Augustus Cleveland's effects, the location of the picture has recently been securely identified as the hill and lake of Ture in the Jungleterry region of Bihar.[1] This means that it was almost certainly painted for Cleveland, which discounts Stuebe's suggestion that it is a late work. It has the same dimensions and a very sim-

ilar compositional format to the *View of Part of the South Side of the Fort of Gwalior* (fig. 4), which was painted in India, and possibly on the spot. Likewise, if done for Cleveland, this work must also have been completed while Hodges was in India, and most probably while he was enjoying an extended stay with Cleveland at his house near Bhagalpur between January and May 1782 (see also cat. nos 62, 64).

It shows a lakeside scene with riders and other figures and pays great attention to the high colouration created across the landscape by the setting tropical sun. In its directness of vision and freedom of handling, it is comparable to other works executed for Cleveland, such as the remarkable *Rocks at Sakrigali* (cat. no. 46), and also bears similarity to works done on the spot on Cook's voyage.

[1] My thanks to Charles Greig for this information.

67 *Funchal, Madeira, c.1784*

Oil on canvas, 69.8 × 91.5 cm

Provenance: Sotheby-Parke Bernet, London, 30 May 1979; Spink & Son, 1979

Literature: Stuebe (1979), no. 553; Joppien and Smith (1985b), no. 2.M2

Engraved: 'A View of the Town of Fonchial, the Capital of the ISLAND of MADEIRA', William Hodges and Isaac Wells, published by A McKenzie, 27 November 1787

© The Kelton Foundation, 2003.

Yale only.

Hodges's homeward passage from India on board the *Worcester* was broken by a short stop at Funchal, Madeira, to take supplies. Hodges probably made several drawings of the coastline during this time, and worked up this painting from those studies on his return to London. He had painted this harbour before, during or shortly after Cook's visit to the island in July 1772 (cat. no. 1). In comparison with the smooth gradations of that earlier painting, the present picture is characterized by a heavy tonality that presents a much more dramatic view of this coastline.

68 'A View of the Ruins of Part of the Palace and Mosque at Futtypoor Sicri'; plate 11 of *Select Views in India, Drawn on the Spot, in the Years 1780, 1781, 1782, and 1783, and executed in Aqua Tinta by William Hodges, R.A.* (London, printed for the author; and sold by J, Edwards, 1785–88)

Hand-coloured aquatint

Literature: Stuebe (1979), 45–6, 192, 231–2; Tillotson (2000), 119–21, 124–5.

The British Library, London.

Hodges visited Futtypoor Sicri [Fatehpur Sikri] on his third and final tour through north India, which was also his most ambitious, taking him as far as Agra and Gwalior, in the company of an ambassadorial mission to Agra led by Major Brown. They were encamped there from 23–6 March 1783, when Hodges made drawings of Akbar's ruined palace, including that, now in the Paul Mellon Collection (B1978.43.1723, fig. 59), upon which this aquatint for *Select Views* is based. In the accompanying letterpress Hodges gave a fulsome, anecdotal history of the site, calculated to maximize the appeal of the print to his British audience.

The town of Futtypoor was formerly known by the name of Sicri, and received its present appellation from the Mogul Emperor Akbar, who entitled it Futtypoor, i.e. Place of Victory, from a decisive defeat which he gave near it to the Patans at the beginning of his reign. – He adorned the spot of engagement with a beautiful mosque, a convent for Dervishes, and a fortified palace, and, on the banks of an extensive lake near the town, he erected pleasure houses, and a spacious inclosure for playing at the Chougaun, an amusement similar to the Scotch exercise of Goff, only with this difference, that the players at Chougaun are mounted on horses, and use long maces

Fig. 59 William Hodges, *A View of the Ruins of Part of the Palace and Mosque at Futty Poor Sicri [Fatehpur Sikri]*, 1783, pencil and wash, 49.5 x 66.8cm. Yale Center for British Art, Paul Mellon Collection

Fig. 60 Calcutta artist after William Hodges, *Distant View of the Jami Masjid and Buland Darwaza, Fatehpur Sikri*, c.1800, water-colour, 24.1 x 34.3 cm. The British Library, London.

headed with iron. The artificial bank, which formed the lake, has been since broken down, and that part which was covered with water thrown into cultivation – which, however more useful, is certainly less beautiful; but Futtypoor was still more delightful to the Emperor, from the circumstance of its being the residence of a holy Dervish, Shekh Selum Chishtee, whose memory is still highly venerated throughout Hindostan. Akbar had lost several sons in their infancy, and was fearful he should leave no male issue. In order to prevent so great an affliction, he besought the prayers of the holy Shekh, and sent two of his pregnant wives to lye-in at his hermitage, hoping that their issue would receive benefit from the Shekh's prayers. Two sons were born, and the eldest was named Selum, in compliment to the Shekh, and succeeded his father by the title of Jehanguir. – Futtypoor has ever since been a celebrated resort for pregnant ladies, who come to pray at the tomb of the saint, and whose descendants, living near it, reap great benefit from the oblations of such pilgrims.

Hodges's account of Fatehpur Sikri in *Travels in India* is much more matter-of-fact, making no mention of the curious circumstances surrounding the birth of Akbar's heir nor of the site still being active as 'a celebrated resort for pregnant ladies'.[1] Instead, he focuses on the layout of the palace and the poor soil and water of the region. While observing that the palace building is 'in a high style of Moorish architecture', he states baldly that it is 'in total ruin, not a single apartment remaining; and the only part which gives any idea of its former beauty is the principal gate', which, accordingly, is the principal feature of his print.

The disparity of these two accounts perhaps offers some insight into the purpose and intended audience for *Select Views*. Published individually from 1785 to 1788, the prints for the final bound volume total forty-eight works, covering the entire range of Hodges's experience in India. Often hand-coloured (by Hodges himself), they constitute a high quality, prestigious commercial venture designed to appeal to the increasing

sensibilities towards, and taste for, Indian culture among the domestic British public. Whereas Hodges's later publication of *Travels in India* followed the tradition of informative and dispassionate travel accounts and presented its author as both artist-historian and gentleman-connoisseur,[2] the subjects depicted in *Select Views* and the accompanying historical notes are clearly aimed at a broader, more popular domestic market. They frequently show sites that refer to the recent history of the British in India, particularly its military successes, or present more sensationalist historical anecdotes in the descriptions, 'human interest' narratives attracting the reader's capacity for sympathy and patriotic sentiment. It was certainly highly influential, forming the principal reference for subsequent views of India, both by the Daniells and also by Indian artists: the India Office Library has a watercolour by an anonymous Indian artist copied directly from Hodges's aquatint, demonstrating the volume's wide circulation, not just among a domestic British audience, but also in India itself (fig. 60). However, the fickleness of the Indian market was witnessed by Thomas Daniell in a letter of 1788 to Ozias Humphry: noting that the bazaar in Calcutta had abundant prints for sale, he wrote, 'Hodges's Indian Views . . . although framed & glazed are bought for less money than the glass alone could be purchased in the bazaar *times are changed*'.[3] Despite its importance in presenting new and documented views of Indian architecture, *Select Views* was evidently not a commercial success.[4]

Dedicated to the East India Company, *Select Views* presents a very favourable view of British settlement in India, under the auspices of the Company, that frames Company activity as part of a wider progressive expansion of a paternalistic, commercial empire. However, its open affiliation to the East India Company at this time may have been counterproductive to Hodges's commercial aspirations for the volume. Though clearly very costly to the artist in terms of financial and professional investment (it was his major project for these years), its lack of commercial reward no doubt had to do with the timing of the publication at the most controversial moment of Warren Hastings's resignation and

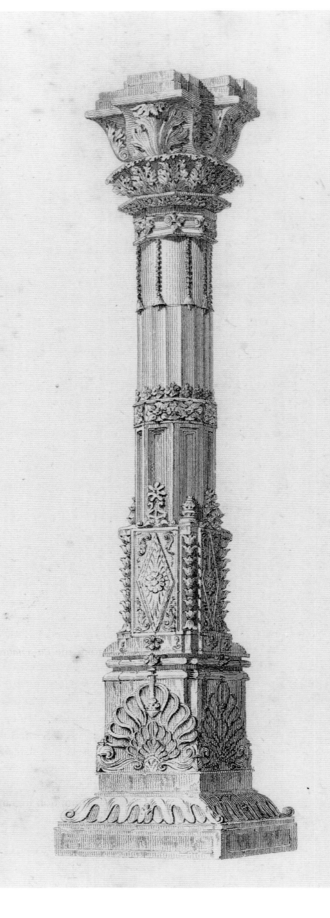

impeachment. Whatever Hodges may have hoped, views of India presented in a public commercial context, particularly when dedicated to the East India Company, by an artist known to enjoy Hastings's extensive patronage, could not in the late 1780s be divested of their overwhelming political associations, which undoubtedly affected *Select Views'* commercial viability.

1 Hodges, (1793), 131.
2 See Beth Fowkes Tobin's essay in this volume.
3 Thomas Daniell to Ozias Humphry, 1 March 1788, Royal Academy Library, MS no. HU/4/13/25–5.
4 See John Bonehill's essay in this volume; also Tillotson (2000), 119–22.

69 T. Medland after Hodges, 'Column taken from the Temple of Vis Visha at Benares', from *Travels in India* (London, 1793)

Medium: engraving

Literature: Tillotson (2000), 135–40.

National Maritime Museum, London

Hodges's interest in Indian architecture was not simply illustrative. Nor was it annexed either to the larger concern with the history of India or to the ideological ends of the growing British imperial presence there. However, his concern with architecture was ultimately historicist and culturally relative. Through analysis of style, he was at pains to demonstrate the correspondences and points of contact between India and ancient Greece and Rome. Such an understanding of history was something with which Hodges was very familiar. Johann Reinhold Forster on Cook's voyage had theorized, through the analysis of the diffusion of language, on the historical relations and relative degrees of human progress between different island societies in the Pacific; and numerous commentators from Joseph Banks on had postulated an equivalence between the newly 'discovered' cultures of the Pacific and classical civilization.[1] Similarly, in the 1780s Sir William Jones and others, under the auspices of Warren Hastings, were making philological investigations into Indian history though its languages and literature, and noticing strong similarities between Sanskrit and ancient Greek as well as between Indian and classical mythologies. In this sense, therefore, Hodges's thinking on Indian architecture may be seen as a parallel to contemporary philological studies, in asserting such correspondences through the study of architectural language.

This centred on the column from a Hindu temple in Benares [Varanasi], the so-called 'Athens' of India, that is the subject of this 'very careful engraving'. In *Travels in India* Hodges describes his surprise at finding what he identified as a Grecian scroll on an Indian column, and that it was this that led him to write his *Dissertation on the Prototypes of Architecture, Hindoo, Moorish, and Gothic*.[2] Originally published in 1787 as a separate folio, the *Dissertation* was accompanied by two large engraved plates showing *A View of the Tomb of the Emperor Shere Shah at Sasseram in Bahar* and *A View of the Gate of the Tomb of the Emperor Akbar at Secundrii* (fig. 23). The entire text, minus the engravings of the emperors' tombs, but accompanied instead by this engraving of the temple column, was later reprinted as part of *Travels in India* (1793), on the basis that it was 'perfectly calculated for a work professedly dedicated . . . to the history and progress of the arts in India'.[3]

The *Dissertation* was substantially a defence of Indian architecture against the assumption ingrained in western architectural theory of the pre-eminence of classical Greek style. Instead, Hodges proposes a radical cultural relativism in his account of the history of architectural style, rooted, as he states, in his own travel experience. His theory also shows the extent of the influence of Johann Reinhold and George Forster and other similar writers upon his thinking, since it is essentially proto-anthropological. Broadly put, Hodges proposes that all architecture derives from two fundamental forms, that of the cave and the hut, that were the two basic forms of shelter available to primitive humanity. The hut is the prototype for the Greek temple form, while the cave is the prototype for Indian, Egyptian and Gothic forms. Drawing on his experience of Pacific cultures, he argues that the degree to which these forms are adapted to architectural purposes depends on local environment:

> Architecture undoubtedly should, and must be adapted, to all the climates and countries which mankind inhabit, and is variously, more than any other, influenced and modified by the nature of the climate and materials, as well as by the habits and pursuits of the inhabitants.[4]

Each style, therefore, can have beauty according in some measure to the way it responds to the environment from which it derives. On this basis, Hodges questions the acceptance of Greek aesthetic principles as the standard of architectural excellence, and asks why

> blind to the majesty, boldness, and magnificence of the Egyptian, Hindoo, Moorish, and Gothic, as admirable wonders of architecture, [we] unmercifully blame and despise them, because they are more various in their forms, and not reducible to the precise rules of the Greek hut, prototype and column.[5]

If this seems to anticipate the championship of Gothic architecture in the nineteenth century by Pugin or Ruskin, terms such as 'majesty' and 'boldness' root Hodges's text much more firmly within the established eighteenth-century discourse on the sublime, as elaborated by Edmund Burke in his *Philosophical Enquiry into the Origin of our Ideas of the Sublime and the Beautiful* (1757). Hodges's theory of the prototypes of architecture, contrasting the hut with the cave, corresponds in broad terms to Burke's opposition of the beautiful to the sublime: the hut, prototype for Greek ideal perfection, is aligned with the beautiful, while the cave is

associated with mountains, which by this date had an almost clichéd connotation of the sublime. Where Burke cites characteristics of the sublime as darkness and grandeur, Hodges, in establishing a connection between the Egyptian temple and the Indian pagoda, states:

> Gloom and darkness are common and desirable to both; for Fancy works best when involved in the veil of obscurity.[6]

However, Hodges's discourse is also rooted in an awareness of contemporary colonial expansion. In noting the column at Benares as an exceptional combination of the hut and cave prototypes, having Greek ornamentation in a Hindu temple, he explains the historical progress and development of architecture and such admixture of styles as a positive result of colonialism:

> When emigrations to foreign countries take place, their prototype will follow the colonist, and genius will at last stretch and improve it to the last degree of perfection of which it is capable.[7]

Given Hodges's earlier comments on the beneficial architectural impact on Calcutta of European settlement in India, particularly influenced by his patron Warren Hastings (see cat. no. 44), such a statement might be taken to refer to contemporary developments as well as past ones.

---

[1] See Bindman (2000) and the author's essay in this volume.

[2] Hodges, (1793), 63.

[3] Ibid., 63.

[4] Ibid., 64.

[5] Ibid., 64.

[6] Ibid., 76.

[7] Ibid., 68.

70 *Mrs Hastings near the Rocks of Colgong, 1790*

Oil on canvas, 127.0 × 182.9 cm

Provenance: painted for Warren Hastings, Warren Hastings Collection, Daylesford House Inventory 1799, p. 5; Daylesford House sale, 26 August 1853 (918); Winter Collection sale, 24–6 June 1919 (656); Appleby Bros., London, 1965; Christie's, 10 December 1971, to S. Sabin; Paul Mellon Collection, 1972

Exhibited: *The British View of India: Selected English Paintings from the Paul Mellon Collection*, Yale Center for British Art, 10 March–12 April 1978

Engraved: Thomas Medland in Thomas Pennant, *The View of Hindoostan* (London, 1798), vol. 2, 291, plate 10

Literature: Stuebe (1973); Stuebe (1979), no. 263

Yale Center for British Art, Paul Mellon Collection.

This highly dramatic and innovative painting was painted for Warren Hastings in the spring of 1790 and commemorates the extreme devotion between Hastings and his wife Marian. Though painted well after Hodges returned from India, it depicts an incident of 1782, when Hastings fell severely ill. His wife then made an urgent and dangerous three-day journey down the Ganges in order to be with him, narrowly escaping being wrecked at the rapids of Colgong. The painting subsequently became the centrepiece of Hastings's collection at his newly built house at Daylesford, hanging above the chimney-piece in the picture room there.[1]

Hodges draws on several traditions in order to dramatize the subject and to render its moral and virtuous significance, but in a way that takes account of the very private character of the commission. In the first instance, it encapsulates a contrast between the sublimity of the storm and perilous position of the boat, and the beauty of the surrounding landscape. This is not overtly shown here, but both artist and patron would have known of it, and Hodges described it in *Travels in India* in precisely the same contrasting terms, making direct reference to the incident depicted:

At Colgong there is a considerable stream, that falls into the Ganges, which by its continued force, and particularly in the time of the periodical rains, has detached two large rocks, and formed them into islands, covered with woods, full seventy yards from the shore. There is a passage between the islands and the shore filled with sunken rocks, which form violent eddies. The passage is sometimes only to be effected by small boats; and in the time of the rains is esteemed exceedingly dangerous. I knew an instance in which it had nearly proved fatal.

The country about Colgong is, I think, the most beautiful I have seen in India. The waving appearance of the land, its fine turf and detached woods, backed by the extensive forests on the hills, brought to my mind many of the fine parks in England; and its over-looking the Ganges, which has more the appearance of an ocean at this place than of a river, gives the prospect inexpressible grandeur.[2]

It is notable that the contrast between the sublime and the beautiful is conceived as a contrast also between the uncontainable violence of the Ganges and the serenity of English parkland. Yet this is evidently one of those 'valuable subjects for the painter' that India has to offer,[3] and which may expand the range of meaning of the landscape genre in proportion to the expansion of empire. Hodges achieves this expanded significance not only through recourse to the established eighteenth-century discourses of the beautiful and the sublime, but also by invoking a set of biblical and classical references, which transform this arcane, private and sentimental subject into a full-scale exercise in historical landscape. The double rainbow on the right, towards which the labouring helmsman seems to be struggling to steer the vessel, is undoubtedly intended as a sign of divine deliverance, by reference to the Deluge. It also recapitulates the inclusion of the rainbow in *Cascade Cove, Dusky Bay* (cat. no. 26). The contrast of the swirling eddies and the monstrous rocks also recalls the classical myth of Scylla and Charybdis. All these elevated references serve to impress the viewer with the degree of private, domestic virtue of Mrs Hastings, whose reaction to the storm is, of course, hidden from view. This evocation of ideal femininity, however, is also implicated in colonial discourse, in the contrast between the straining figure of the helmsman, whose loyal efforts on behalf of his European mistress are illuminated by a heavenly shaft of sunlight, and the rest of the crew, who have shipped oars, seemingly in resignation to their fate: one clings to the prow helplessly. In this sense, the picture's moral message is similar to that of much shipwreck imagery of this period. However, in being a scene of dramatic nautical near-calamity in a colonial setting, which transforms an essentially private episode into a didactic account of general moral virtue, via reference to the image of the faithful colonial servant, it also shares much in common with the signally important instance of modern history painting, John Singleton Copley's *Brook Watson and the Shark* (RA 1778).

Hodges's painting, therefore, is a significant example of his move at this time (see also cat. no. 76) towards a form of 'historical' landscape represen-

Fig. 61 *Mrs Hastings near the Rocks of Colgong*, c. 1790, oil on silk (?) laid on glass, 23 × 33cm. Private collection.

tation that could impart morally instructive lessons to the viewer, and which would reach its apogee in the exhibition of *War* and *Peace* in 1794–95.

He also produced an exact miniature copy of this large painting. This small version (fig. 61, private collection), seemingly painted on silk laid on glass, is known to have hung in Marian Hasting's study during her lifetime, suggesting that it was painted specifically for her, perhaps as a gift from her devoted husband. Given the precision and exactness of execution, as well as its unusual materials, it is surely a copy after the painting, produced as a presentation piece. It demonstrates Hodges's propensity for technical experimentation: on his return from Cook's voyage, he had worked with Matthew Boulton, the Birmingham industrialist, on a new printing technique of 'mechanical painting', that attempted a cross between aquatinting and oil painting.[4] The use here of a precious material such as silk as the painting support and the added use of glass seem designed to emulate the prestige and translucency of enamel, or other forms of miniature painting, that Hodges would have known through his acquaintance with the leading miniaturists Richard Cosway and Ozias Humphry.[5] It is likely also that he was aware, through his Midlands contacts, of George Stubbs's experimental use of enamel painting with Boulton.

[1] Stuebe (1973).

[2] Hodges (1793), 25–6.

[3] Ibid., 31–2.

[4] Robinson and Thompson (1970).

[5] Humphry had trained with Hodges at Shipley's drawing school; they were both close to Farington, another pupil of Wilson; Humphry also later went to India. Hodges had collaborated with Cosway in 1787 on a painting exhibited at the Royal Academy, *View from the breakfast room in a gentleman's house in Pall-Mall, with the portrait of a lady by Mr. Cosway* (53). See Stuebe (1979), 3–8, 57.

Part Three

Representing Britishness

Hodges's British subjects

GEOFF QUILLEY

Throughout his career, in between his long periods abroad, Hodges travelled through and painted the British landscape. Prior to the voyage with Cook, these works consisted predominantly of architectural views, either of London (cat. no. 71) or of country seats associated with his friend and colleague at the Society of Artists, the architect James Paine (cat. no. 72, fig. 2). Farington states that, during the late 1760s, Hodges spent some time as a theatrical scene painter in Derby, where it is likely that he got to know Joseph Wright of Derby.[1] Wright subsequently painted a portrait of a 'Mrs Hodges', thought to be Hodges's first wife, Martha Nesbit.[2]

A further important contact in Derby was the eminent natural historian John Whitehurst, to whom Hodges may have been related on his mother's side, and who was one of the eminent philosophical circle in Derby during the 1760s and 70s that included the Lunar Society. He later married Whitehurst's niece, and it is likely that during his time at Derby he stayed in Whitehurst's house.[3] He later also subscribed to Whitehurst's *An Inquiry into the Original State and Formation of the Earth* (1778), an important investigation into geology and physical geography. It is therefore quite plausible that Hodges's socio-historic, climatological understanding of landscape, which clearly informs his post-voyage paintings of the Pacific, was derived in some measure from Whitehurst's influence.

After his return from Cook's voyage, Hodges evidently revisited the Midlands and undertook a short tour of Wales: several resulting paintings were exhibited at the Royal Academy in 1778. These works engage overtly with the representation of history through the depiction of architecture and landscape, an interest that would characterize his views in India. They also form part of an ongoing concern with the representation of Britain and Britishness, through its culture, historical sites, contemporary architecture and topographies, that preoccupied Hodges throughout his career.

After his return from India, this was most noticeable in his increasing treatment of literary subjects. The articulation of British national identity at this date increasingly invoked the depth of its cultural traditions and history in terms of an uninterrupted connection with the past, and in particular with its literary heritage. After 1789 such identity was couched especially in terms of an opposition to the ideologies of revolutionary France, which were centred on a severance of the present from the past. The 'invention' of British tradition was represented most obviously through a canonical set of British 'worthies', historical figures of significance to the formation of what was held to be the British (or English) character, such as Milton, Newton or Inigo Jones. Core to this was Shakespeare, who, along with his home town of Stratford, was the subject of a growing cult, led by Garrick in the mid-century, and flourishing in the 1780s and 1789os, with the scandal surrounding Ireland's forged play *Vortigern*, and the honestly patriotic but no less spectacular Shakespeare Gallery set up by the entrepreneurial publisher, John Boydell.[4] Hodges produced three works for the Shakespeare Gallery, following on from his first treatment of a Shakespearian subject in the 1788 exhibition at the Royal Academy of *Landscape with the Story of Imogen and Pisanio taken from Shakespeare's Play of Cymbeline, Act III Scene 4* (untraced). Such subjects offered opportunities for further development of the genre of historic landscape, through the treatment of literary subjects of nationalistic significance and moral association. Hodges also at this time produced landscapes on biblical subjects, all of which are now lost,[5] as well as complex historicizing capriccios such as *Landscape, Ruins and Figures* (cat. no. 76). This was at the same time that he was preparing and publishing *Select Views in India* and *Travels in*

India, works which, through their intertextuality, are directly concerned with the elaboration of the idea of the 'moralized' landscape. In this sense, Hodges's depictions of Britain were formulated against his experience of the wider reaches of empire, and thus may be understood as representations of an imperial nation through its landscape and historical monuments.

The culmination of his representation of landscape as a moral subject came with the exhibition at Orme's Gallery in Old Bond Street in 1794–95 of the pendant paintings *The Effects of Peace* and *The Consequences of War*, explicitly intended as allegorical representations of the political state of contemporary Britain.[6] Once again, Hodges's picture of Britishness was framed within a wider imperial discourse. The view of Peace, 'exemplifying the happy state of England in the Year 1795', was contrasted with the same landscape overrun by war and 'shewing the misery of internal commotion'. While Farington and others worried at Hodges's inclusion in the latter of what were taken to be Turkish soldiers, it is possible that this comprised instead a comparative reflection upon Indian history and the Mughal empire, to offer a moral parallel with contemporary British imperial ambition: throughout *Travels in India* Hodges repeatedly laments 'the effects of Mahomedan intolerance' in the extensive ruins, which offer 'a melancholy proof of the consequences of a bad government, of wild ambition, and the horrors attending civil dissentions'.[7] Certainly, the idea of 'the horrors of civil dissentions' was one associated by Hodges with the Mughal empire, so that the introduction of Muslim soldiers into a scene allegorizing Britain might be taken to refer to Britain in its wider imperial frame of reference.

All that remains of these important and pioneering works is the account given in Edward Edwards's *Anecdotes of Painting*, consisting of a partial transcription of Hodges's own catalogue description of the exhibition. Complementing the final passage of *Travels in India*, this offers his fullest theorization of the genre of historical landscape. His aspiration that the introduction of moral subjects into landscape painting might result in 'juster habits of Thought, and Conduct consequently improved' stems directly from Sir Joshua Reynolds's theorization in his Discourses of the public function of painting, to induce virtuous thoughts and actions in the spectator. However, his wider premiss, that landscape may be visually interpreted according to moral and political criteria expands upon another observation in the *Travels*:

> From the apparent state of a country, a just estimate may generally be formed of the happiness or the misery of a people. Where there is a neatness in the cultivation of the land, and that tilled to the utmost of its boundaries, it may reasonably be supposed that the government is the protector and not the oppressor of the people.[8]

This statement prefaces an open approval of British rule in Bengal, but is also implicitly an approbation of the English agrarian economy. In its far-reaching implications, however, it could almost serve as an apology for Hodges's life work.

Hodges's text as transcribed by Edwards is given in full in the Appendix.

[1] Farington.

[2] Nicolson (1968).

[3] Farington; Maxwell Craven, pers. comm.

[4] On Boydell and the Shakespeare Gallery, see Friedman (1976) and Bruntjen (1985).

[5] These included *Landscape with the Story of Hagar and Ishmael* (Royal Academy, 1790), *A Warm Evening Scene & Figures – and the Israelites crossing the Red Sea* and *Holy Family*, Stuebe (1979), nos 612–13.

[6] See Harriet Guest's essay in this volume. The paintings have been untraced since their exhibition at the European Museum in 1813, and though Edward Edwards claimed that prints existed after them and that they were at one time in the collection of Sir John Soane, there is no evidence for either assertion: see Stuebe (1979), nos 641, 643.

[7] Hodges (1793), 62, 123.

[8] Hodges (1793), 17.

Note: catalogue entries in this section are supplied by Geoff Quilley.

71 *The Adelphi under Construction, c.*1771

Oil on canvas, 46.4 × 60.3 cm

Provenance: Sidney Sabin, 1975, attributed to William Marlow

Literature: Stuebe (1979), 14 n.35

Yale Center for British Art, Paul Mellon Collection

Though formerly attributed to William Marlow, there is no documentary evidence for such an attribution other than the fact that Marlow produced other views of the Thames at this date, including two views of the Adelphi (Museum of London and Government Art Collection).

On stylistic grounds, however, the painting here differs considerably from Marlow's works. Even if considered a sketch or study for the finished Adelphi views, the brightly varied palette, use of impasto and of liquid paint for the deftly painted highlights and details, the fluidity of handling, and treatment of water and sky, particularly with regard to the attention paid to transient light and cloud effects, are still very inconsistent with Marlow's style. These are, however, all features typical of Hodges's. The interest in atmospheric effects is very similar to the view of Table Mountain completed in 1772 on Cook's voyage (cat. no. 2), while the use of delicate flecks of impasto to articulate the details of the buildings is typical of Hodges's architectural landscapes, such as the view of Worksop Manor (cat. no. 72). In addition, the composition, centred on the low horizon, with the curving sweep of the water's edge forming the foreground and leading to a distant skyline, is one that Hodges used recurrently throughout his career, and particularly in his views of

Calcutta (cat. no. 43). This is also precisely the sort of subject that Hodges would be expected to treat at this period, just prior to his departure with Cook. The state of completion of the Adelphi, built by John and Robert Adam between 1768 and 1772, and showing here nine of the projected fifteen arched vaults finished, indicates that this painting was made in about 1771. At this time Hodges was specializing in architectural views, particularly of buildings associated with the architect James Paine, and also London sites: his earliest exhibited painting was *A View of London Bridge from Botolph Wharf*, shown at the Society of Artists exhibition in 1766, while his striking contribution to the 1772 exhibition was the large-scale collaboration, with William Pars, *A View in the Pantheon in Oxford Street* (fig. 5). A large proportion of his exhibited works over the previous three years consisted of views of country houses.

This painting exemplifies the problems of attribution associated with Hodges, which are compounded by a lack of documentary evidence, particularly relating to his pre-voyage works. However, on the above grounds it is proposed that, following the suggestion of Stuebe and others, this picture should more properly be attributed to Hodges than Marlow.

72 *A View of Worksop Manor in Nottinghamshire, the Seat of His Grace the Duke of Norfolk*, 1777

Oil on canvas, 85.0 x 134.0 cm, signed and dated 1777.

Provenance: probably painted for Edward, 9th Duke of Norfolk; by descent.

Exhibited: Society of Artists 1778 (82) (possibly also previously Society of Artists 1772 (131)); Sotheby's, December 1995 (80).

Literature: Stuebe (1979), no. 531; Harris (1979), 251, plate 302; Christie (2000), 43–4.

By kind permission of His Grace the Duke of Norfolk, Arundel Castle.

Greenwich only.

Hodges exhibited a view of Worksop Manor twice at the Society of Artists, in 1772 and again in 1778. It is possible that the same painting was shown on both occasions and is the work now at Arundel Castle; but the fact that this is signed and dated suggests that, if not a separate work from that shown in 1772, then it was perhaps reworked after Hodges returned from the voyage with Cook. On the other hand, at the same time that this picture was showing at the Society of Artists in 1778, Hodges also exhibited four other architectural views at the Royal Academy, three of which relate to a tour of the West Midlands and Wales,[1] so it is to be wondered why he exhibited *Worksop Manor* separately. This may have to do with the designer of the building: the architectural views shown at the Society of Artists prior to the voyage were predominantly of buildings by the architect, James Paine, who was a director of the Society until 1772. In 1778 Paine exhibited three views at the Society of Artists of 'a villa as intended to be built at Berks'.[2] Thus Hodges's exhibition there of *Worksop Manor* might have been a supportive gesture for the architect, who had evidently been of considerable help in opening up routes of patronage to Hodges in the late 1760s and early 1770s, to show Paine's most celebrated past design alongside his plans for a future one.

Paine's design for Worksop Manor was developed in the wake of the destruction by fire of Robert Smithson's late-Elizabethan building. Originally conceived on a courtyard plan, it was 'the largest country house commission since Blenheim',[3] though only one wing was completed, building work ceasing in 1767. However, this was sufficiently impressive to merit its description as 'a fine piece of architecture, and one of the noblest mansion houses in England'.[4] Much of the house's design, particularly its ornament, was prompted by the Duchess of Norfolk, who was the scheme's prime mover.

Hodges's portrayal of the house emphasizes its size and grandeur through the use of an oblique, dramatically foreshortened perspective, a device that he employed frequently for his architectural views. He also focuses on the sociability of the house, showing the bustling activity of figures, horses and visiting coaches in the great courtyard before the north front. This may be intended to complement the family's reputation for hospitality, which is also emblematically represented in the flanking sculptures over the pediment of the central portico, personifying 'Peace and Plenty as Emblems of Hospitality'.[5] It is a bravura piece, full of Hodges's characteristic light brushstrokes alongside the use of impasto, which stylistically links it to the subsequent views of Indian architecture, for example cat. no. 53, and to the works produced from his contemporary tour of Wales and the Midlands (see cat. no. 73).

It can be grouped more specifically with Hodges's views of other buildings by Paine, and the 1771–2 paintings of Robert Adam's Adelphi (cat. no. 71) and James Wyatt's Pantheon (*The Pantheon, Oxford Street, London*, Temple Newsam House, fig. 5), both also depictions of prestigious buildings by leading British architects. *Worksop Manor*, therefore, demonstrates Hodges's early interest in contemporary architecture, which, as Paine himself wrote, could be taken as the indicator of the progress of the nation and the 'good sense, taste, and opulence of its people'.[6] In this sense, particularly for an artist such as Hodges, for whom architecture was closely tied to the character and condition of society, a view such as *Worksop Manor* may be taken as emblematic of the prosperity and health of the nation as a whole.

[1] These were *View of Brampton Bryan Castle in Herefordshire* (146), *View of Part of Ludlow Castle in Shropshire* (147), *View of Richmond Bridge* (148) and *View of Dudley Castle and Priory, in Staffordshire* (151). The views of Midlands and Welsh castles were clearly executed as part of the same series as the *View of Llanthony Abbey* (cat. no. 73).

[2] Graves (1907), 187.

[3] Pevsner (2001), 392.

[4] *A New Display of the Beauties of England; or, a Description of the most elegant or magnificent Public Edifices, Royal Palaces, Noblemen's and Gentlemen's Seats, and other Curiosities, natural or artificial, in the different Parts of the Kingdom*, 2 vols (2nd edn, London, 1787), 160.

[5] Paine (1783), vol. 2, plate 101.

[6] Ibid., vol. 1, v.

73 *Ruins of Llanthony Abbey*, 1777–78

Oil on canvas, 96.5 × 73.7 cm

Provenance: Leo Schuster Collection; Sabin Galleries 1975

Literature: Stuebe (1979), no. 503

National Museums & Galleries, Wales

As Stuebe states, on grounds of style and geographical location, this painting can be dated to Hodges's tour of the West Midlands and Wales of 1777–78, owing to its striking similarity in composition and execution to the *View of Ludlow Castle* (V&A, fig. 62), dated 1778. Hodges clearly produced several similar views from the same tour that are now untraced, for besides the Ludlow picture, he exhibited two other depictions of Midlands castles at the Royal Academy that year: *View of*

Brampton Bryan Castle in Herefordshire and *View of Dudley Castle and Priory, in Staffordshire*. This group of subjects is evidence of Hodges's awareness of the increasing cultural and antiquarian interest in British historical monuments, particularly as they related to the growing cult of Picturesque touring. Indeed, Shropshire and Wales, particularly the area around Hereford and the Wye Valley, were becoming an increasing focus for the Picturesque gaze at this date.

While Llanthony Abbey was not a renowned tourist site, it had been engraved by the Bucks in 1732 and by 1777 was given greater publicity through the publication of Wyndham's tours through Monmouthshire and Wales undertaken in 1774 and 1777. In his account of the Abbey, Wyndham draws on Giraldus Cambrensis' twelfth-century description of it as 'encircled with an amphitheatre of immense mountains' and 'solitary and remote from all worldly noise'.[1] Hodges has taken similar poetic licence in monumentalizing the scale of the building by placing diminutive figures beside it.

Ruined abbeys could hold multiple meanings with regard to British national history. While partaking of the general significance of ruins as melancholic signs of the transience of human endeavour and as past reminders about the fragility of the present, they also held a particular value around the mid-century as the embodiment of the triumph of Protestantism over the 'superstition' of the Roman Catholic church.[2] As a poetic motif the ruined abbey offered a spur to historical reflection, to 'Teach the free Thoughts on Wings of Air to range, O'erlook the present, and recall the past!'[3]

The past they recalled, however, was the medieval era when England was under the ecclesiastical rule of Rome. The abbey signified in this sense as the former abode of 'monks libidinous', characterized as slothful, greedy and a luxurious drain on the surrounding region and people.[4] Giraldus describes Llanthony as

> a happy and delightful spot . . . had not the extravagance of English luxury, the pride of a sumptuous table, the increasing growth of intemperance and ingratitude, added to the negligence of its patrons and prelates, reduced it from freedom to servility.[5]

Llanthony, therefore, could be seen as a particularly apt sign of medieval religious superstition and the feudal luxury and tyranny associated with it; and Hodges's painting, in part by virtue of its conspicuous representation of the Abbey as a Picturesque aesthetic object, serves as a vehicle for historical reflection on the stages of national social progress, themes that he would elaborate in greater detail in his Indian paintings and the commentary of *Select Views in India* and *Travels in India*.

Hodges returned to similar subjects at the end of his career, exhibiting views of Kirkstall and Fountains Abbeys at the Royal Academy in 1794 along with a painting entitled *The Abbey, taken from the Romance of the Forest*, clearly referring to Ann Radcliffe's highly popular, recently published novel, which in the same year was adapted for the stage by

Fig. 62 William Hodges, *View of Part of Ludlow Castle in Shropshire,* 1778, oil on canvas, 119.4 x 88.9 cm. V&A Picture Library.

James Boaden. Produced around the same time as his works for Boydell's Shakespeare Gallery and his other historical landscapes, and following on from his brief tenure as scene painter at the Pantheon in Oxford Street, such a title indicates the degree to which the subject of the ruined abbey for Hodges continued to carry overtly moralized novelistic and historical associations.

[1] [Wyndham] (1775), 206–11.

[2] Charlesworth (1994), 72.

[3] Keate (1769), 24.

[4] 'The Ruin'd Abby; or, The Effects of Superstition', in Shenstone (1777), 304.

[5] Cited in Bradley (1906), 248.

74 W. Byrne and J. Schuman after Hodges, *South View of Windsor, taken from the Great Park*, 1787

Inscribed 'Painted by W. Hodges RA Engraved by W. Byrne & J. Schuman'

Etching and engraving, 33.1 × 45.6 cm

Engraved: also engraved by Schuman for Boydell

Literature: Stuebe (1979), no. 526

Copyright © British Museum, London.

This fine engraving was made after a now-untraced painting exhibited at the Royal Academy in 1787 (128). It was widely regarded as one of Hodges's finest works, being described in one review as

> A very good portrait of the Royal residence; – and we add, we are sorry to see an asterisk marked against it in the Catalogue, – importing that it is for sale: – it ought to have found a *purchaser* near the castle.[1]

According to Stuebe, this was also another example of Hodges's successful collaboration with the animal painter, Sawrey Gilpin, who supposedly painted the stags in the foreground. The picture gives an extensive, panoramic view across the park and countryside with the focal point of the castle in the centre distance, in an evocation of an ordered, harmonious landscape that is to be understood as at once natural and political. It shows more than mere topography, since Windsor was

> a highly significant site in eighteenth-century eyes, and had been celebrated in verse by numerous English writers, most notably by

Alexander Pope (*On Windsor Forest*, 1713). Poetic descriptions of the Windsor landscape invariably endowed it with classical features, usually by invoking a comparison with Mount Olympus.[2]

Here, the castle, as the symbolic apogee of the monarchical system, as well as material evidence of its longevity, is also, by implication, at the centre of an ordered, harmonious constitution.[3] The composition evokes the Roman seventeenth-century landscapes of Claude Lorrain and also those of Hodges's teacher, Richard Wilson: indeed, the subject may be intended as a direct comparison with Wilson's own celebrated *View in Windsor Great Park* (National Museums and Galleries, Wales), which had been exhibited at the Royal Academy in 1778 to very positive reviews.

Certainly, Hodges intended the print to be a prestigious production following the same format he was simultaneously adopting for the striking prints of *A View of the Tomb of the Emperor Shere Shah at Sasseram in Bahar* and *A View of the Gate of the Tomb of the Emperor Akbar at Secundrii* (fig. 23), that is, associating the image with an extensive text outlining the site's historical significance, which was published both in English and French. This was also the format used for the ongoing series of prints for *Select Views in India*. In this sense, Hodges implicitly offers Windsor as the centre of Britain's empire as well as the nation, through such comparison with Mughal dynastic sites.

---

[1] The *Morning Herald*, 15 May 1787, 3.

[2] Solkin (1982), no. 94.

[3] On the ideological significance of the panoramic landscape at this period, see especially Barrell (1992).

75 *A Cottage; a Study from Nature*, 1787

Oil on canvas, 43.3 × 58.0 cm

Provenance: Spink and Sons; Sotheby's, 14 July 1999 (26)

Exhibited: possibly RA 1787 (404)

Literature: Stuebe (1979), no. 578

Private collection

Identified as being by Hodges from an eighteenth-century label formerly on the back of the frame, it seems reasonable to suppose that this is the painting that was exhibited at the Royal Academy in 1787, since there appears to be no other title among Hodges's exhibited or auctioned works matching the specific content of this piece. If so, it was one of eleven pictures exhibited by Hodges at the Academy that year, when

he was also elected as a full Academician. Most of the other ten were, like his Diploma piece for the Academy, of Indian subjects, for which he was evidently becoming critically well known. He was also respected for his representation of history through such subjects, and when such references were lacking, as here, he was criticized for it. One reviewer called this painting 'So so! . . . [a] little effort of Mr. Hodge's [*sic*] pencil' and referred the reader to his criticism of no. 198, *A Desart Coast*:

> Confine yourself to interesting scenes, and you will please, Mr. Hodges; – give us Asiatick palaces, mosques, &c. and they will be charming history; but your powers of the pencil require support from the subject, – both in regard to its novelty and interest. – It is a great painter, only, who can give importance to trifles.[1]

This shows the degree to which Hodges was projecting himself – and was increasingly regarded – at this date as a painter of Indian scenery and history.

Despite the reviewer's acerbic judgment of this painting, it is by no means an unsatisfactory exercise in landscape painting, showing an

influence perhaps of Gainsborough's cottage-door landscapes or even George Robertson's contemporary views of the landscape around Coalbrookdale. The epithet 'A Study from Nature' probably indicates that, like much of Hodges's work in the Pacific and India, this painting was done, at least partly, on the spot, an idea that is supported by the vibrant handling and the closely observed treatment of light. If so, it is significant that this was part of Hodges's habitual painterly practice, and not a method specific to the unusual demands of producing works in the environment of colonial travel.

1 *Morning Herald*, 15 May 1787, 3.

76 *Landscape, Ruins and Figures*, 1790

Oil on panel, 95.0 × 132.5 cm

Exhibited: probably RA 1790 (124)

James Mackinnon.

Greenwich only.

Owing to its size, classical subject matter, and the fact that it is painted on an expensive single wood panel, it is very likely that this painting was executed for exhibition at the Royal Academy. The only title from among Hodges exhibited works, or from his works sold at auction in 1795, that matches this picture is the *Landscape, Ruins and Figures* at the Academy exhibition of 1790. The reviewer in the *St. James's Chronicle* called it 'A pleasing picture, in the stile of his master WILSON:

The colouring rich, and the figures well introduced.'[1] The reference to Wilson is unmistakable, the ruins directly recalling his *The Temple of Minerva Medica, Rome* (c.1753–4), a monument also widely known through Piranesi's *Vedute di Roma*.

The mistaken eighteenth-century understanding of the ruins as a temple of ancient religion perhaps casts some light on the otherwise mysterious activities in the foreground: a group of quasi-classical nymphs appear to be in the process of making a votive offering to a herm figure on the right. On the bank in the foreground appears to be a classical tripod. Perhaps what is most striking is the way figure of the seated nude is taken straight from Hodges's views of Vaitepiha Bay, Tahiti (cat. nos 32, 33). It may be, therefore, that this capriccio on a classical subject is intended to be an essay in comparative religion, making connections between the culture of Polynesia and the Society Islands and that of classical Rome or Greece, in a manner similar to such propositions by Banks, the Forsters and others. On the other hand, the association with Tahiti might suggest an erotic theme, an idea supported by the fact that the herm figure that is the object of devotion is adapted from the antique sculpture *Venus with a Herm* that Hodges also used in his representation of *The Merchant of Venice* for Boydell's *Shakespeare Gallery*, also in 1790 (cat. no. 78).[2] The association of Venus with Tahiti was, of course, a well established one.

The painting certainly demonstrates Hodges's concerted efforts to develop the genre of historical landscape painting at this date. Clearly also, the expensive use of a single panel of this size suggests that he intended the subject to be an elevated and prestigious one. Recent conservation revealed several *pentimenti* in the figure grouping and the lower right side, suggesting that Hodges worked on the painting over a long period. Given the material of the support, which is similar to that of other panels used for Pacific subjects, and the central use of the Tahitian figure, it is not inconceivable that he first embarked on the work in the years immediately following his return from Cook's voyage.

[1] *St. James's Chronicle*, 30 April–1 May 1790, 4.
[2] Stuebe (1979), 343.

198

77 William Hodges, George Romney and Sawrey Gilpin, *Jaques and the Wounded Stag in the Forest of Arden*, 1789

Oil on canvas, 92.1 × 123.2 cm

Provenance: Boydell's *Shakespeare Gallery*; Christie's, 17 May 1805 (41); Sir Charles Burrell; E. Parsons; Folger Shakespeare Library, 1926; Lincoln Kirstein, 1962; The American Shakespeare Theatre, Stratford, Connecticut

Exhibited: Boydell's *Shakespeare Gallery*, 1789; British Institution, 1817 (96); British Institution, 1844 (116); *Shakespeare in Western Art*, Tokyo, Isetan Museum of Art, 1992; *Shakespeare in Art*, Ferrara, Palazzo dei Diamanti and London, Dulwich Picture Gallery, 2003

Engraved: Samuel Middiman, 1791

Literature: Winifred H. Friedman, *Boydell's Shakespeare Gallery* (London and New York, 1976); Stuebe (1979), no. 625

Yale Center for British Art, Paul Mellon Fund

One of three paintings that Hodges completed for Boydell's *Shakespeare Gallery*, this was submitted at the same time as his *Antigonus and the Bear from The Winter's Tale, Act III, Scene III*, to which it was supposed by Humphry Repton to be the pendant.[1] Reviews, however, contrasted the latter unfavourably with *Jaques and the Wounded Stag*, which in critical terms was one of Hodges's most successful works. It was praised not only for its appropriate interpretation of the text but, like the *View of Windsor* exhibited in 1787, as the successful outcome of an artistic collaboration. The *Public Advertiser* devoted an unusually lengthy and detailed review to it, commenting

> The depth you see in the forest evinces great skill in the painter, and has a most picturesque effect; and a sedate, solemn hue, is given to the whole. The scene is calculated for meditation.[2]

This final remark suggests both Hodges's contemporary concern to pursue the moral and didactic potential of the landscape genre, and that there was also critical acceptance for such development when presented, as here, within a clear context of patriotic and literary heritage.

The scene depicted is from Act 2, Scene 1, lines 29–43, in which the plight and pain of a stag wounded by hunters is 'Much marked of the melancholy Jaques'. The text, given such closely faithful treatment, is clearly carefully chosen: it appeals not just to a nationalistic cultural sentiment focused on Shakespeare but also, in its portrayal of Jaques' sympathy for the stag, to the contemporary discourse of sensibility. This was epitomized by novels such as Henry MacKenzie's highly popular *The Man of Feeling* (1771), who displays a capacity for pity and sensibility to

excessive lengths. It is perhaps not coincidental, therefore, that the pose of Jaques echoes that of the contemporary 'man of feeling', Sir Brooke Boothby, as portrayed by Hodges's colleague Joseph Wright of Derby in his 1781 portrait (Tate), where Boothby, the friend and champion of the philosopher of sensibility Jean-Jacques Rousseau, is also shown reclining by a stream in a pose of melancholic contemplation, with one of Rousseau's texts in his hand. Here, the model for Jaques was the poet and publisher William Hayley, perhaps best known as the biographer of his friend Romney and as the patron of William Blake. He was a central figure in the radical circle of artists in the 1790s, who would have been familiar with Rousseau-esque ideas on nature and civilization, and was reputedly something of a 'man of feeling' himself.

[1] Stuebe (1979), 344.
[2] *Public Advertiser*, April–May 1789, 3.

78 J. Browne after William Hodges, *Shakespeare, Merchant of Venice, Act V Scene I. A Grove & Lawn before Portia's House. Jessica, Lorenzo, and Stephano,* published by J. and J. Boydell, 1 December 1795

Etching and engraving, 44.0 × 58.9 cm

Literature: Stuebe (1979), no. 628

Copyright © British Museum, London.

The painting (now untraced) after which this large, high-quality engraving was made, was the third and last of the works Hodges executed for John Boydell's *Shakespeare Gallery,* exhibited there in 1790. Once again, his visual interpretation of Shakespeare was highly regarded, one review describing it as 'eminently brilliant'.[1] Others noted Hodges's capability for moonlight scenes. The *Public Advertiser* enthused that 'The Moonlight, by Mr. Hodges, is a perfect deception, and the most pleasing landscape of the sort which we ever saw';[2] and another reviewer concluded that 'Moon-light and dark subjects seem to suit the pencil of this Artist better than gayer scenes'.[3]

Hodges's treatment of nocturnal effects recalls not only the celebrated moonlights of Joseph Wright of Derby but also Hodges's own similar Indian scenes, such as the dramatic *View of the Jungle Ferry, Bengal, Moonlight* (private collection, exhibited RA 1786), or *A Mahometan Woman attending the Tomb of her Husband, a Moon-light Scene* (untraced, RA 1787).

His clear success in such elevated adaptations of theatrical and literary subjects may well have influenced his appointment early in 1791 as 'Inventor and Painter of the Decorations', by Robert Bray O'Reilly, manager of the Pantheon Opera House in Oxford Street.[4] While Hodges's tenure was short-lived and unsuccesful, he was clearly increasingly interested in the representation of theatrical and literary subjects at this period, producing subjects not just from Shakespeare but also from contemporary literature and the Bible.[5] His wider association with the theatre is also indicated in his large scale *Design for a Proposed New Opera House in Leicester Square*, *c.*1790 (Museum of London), a view of a building also planned by O'Reilly, before he took the lease on the Pantheon, but never realized.[6]

[1] Stuebe (1979), 342.

[2] *Public Advertiser*, 17 March 1790, 3.

[3] *St. James's Chronicle*, 23–5 March 1790, 2.

[4] Price (1987), 2–4

[5] Stuebe (1979), 338–49.

[6] See Galinou and Hayes (1996), no. 37.

Appendix

Hodges's descriptive catalogue to the exhibition of *The Effects of Peace* and *The Consequences of War*, as transcribed by Edward Edwards and published in his *Anecdotes of Painters who have resided or been born in England; with critical remarks on their productions* (London: Leigh and Sotherby, 1808).

To the Public

It is usual for every exhibitor of works of art to state, with different degrees of modesty, the nature of those objects to which he presumes to solicit the public attention and encouragement.

I have the less scruple to avail myself of the custom, as my peculiar plan demands some little explanation, that my design may be fully known, and my labours fairly appreciated.

The branch of painting, towards which my studies have been principally directed, is landscape. These studies were begun under the greatest modern master of that art, Wilson. I must be permitted to value myself upon such an advantage, which I hope very extensive travels through various countries must have improved.

Upon maturely reflecting on the nature of my profession, I have been led to lament a defect, and humbly to endeavour at a remedy. I found in the ancient and many of the modern masters of landscape, the greatest combinations of nature, and the most exact similitude, the happiest composition, and pencilling governed by the hand of Truth. But I confess there seemed very rarely to me any moral purpose in the mind of the artist. The storm has been collected over the peaceful trader, or the brilliant skies of Italy have illumined merely the forms of inanimate nature. We have seen foliage frowning on one side, and the blasted trunk exhibiting its dreary desolation on the other; but the whole has evinced only the ordinary progress of life, and the effects of elemental war.

It could not escape me, that the other branches of the art had achieved a nobler effect – History exhibited the actions of our heroes and our patriots, and the glory of past ages – and even Portrait, though more confined in its influence, strengthened the ties of social existence. To give dignity to landscape painting is my object. Whatever may be the value of my execution, the design to amend the heart while the eye is gratified, will yield me the purest pleasure by its success. I flatter myself even with an influence that shall never be acknowledged; and the impression of these slight productions may be felt in *juster* habits of Thought, and Conduct consequently *improved*. From slight causes, the Author of our minds has ordained that we should derive most important convictions. Perhaps the enthusiasm of the artist carries me too far; but I hope and trust that my progress in this design may be serviceable to my country, and to humanity.

The first fruits of this purpose I now present to the Public. Making it, as every good man should do, a matter of conscience, I shall not desist from the prosecution of my object. My pictures will constantly be lessons, sometimes of what results from the impolicy of nations, or sometimes from the vices and follies of particular classes of men. These illustrations will be wide and various – from Europe and Asia, wherever the moralist can draw the substance of his animadversion, I shall select the subject of my pictures. The task is arduous and new, but I resolve to pursue it with vigour and fidelity.

Requesting attention to the descriptive character of the pictures now exhibited, I leave my cause with confidence to the judgment, and, I should hope, the feelings of the people.

W.H.

The Effects of Peace, and the Consequences of War

In the first are intended to be shown the blessings enjoyed by the happiest constitution, and supported by a vigorous executive government.

The scene represents a sea-port thronged with shipping, expressive of Commerce; the great public buildings denote its Riches; a large bay opening to the ocean, merchant ships going out, others returning, shew the extension of its trade to the most distant corners of the globe.

From the interior of the country a river empties itself into the bay, across which is a bridge, for the convenience and communication of commerce: the loaded wagon evincing the labours of the manufacturer.

A rich corn field marks the industry of the peasant, and the high state of agriculture in the country.

On the foreground of the picture is displayed the happy state of the peasantry.

Shrouded in a rich wood is a cottage, covered with the vine and the fig-tree, and the family enjoying the breeze in a mild, soft evening. The group of figures exhibits three generations – from venerable age to infancy – with the sympathy of maternal affection, and surrounded by domestic animals, while the father and brothers are at work in the field.

The two dogs in the front of the picture point out the beneficence of the landlord, by the care his tenant has taken of them in the recess of the hunting season.

The Consequences of War

The same scene as the above picture, under the most melancholy difference – the city on fire – ships burning and sinking in the harbour – the once happy cottagers destroyed or dispersed – the building dismantled, and the last remnant of the wood is the scathed tree. Batteries of cannon now occupy the rich fields of husbandry – soldiers of a distant region now usurp the happy retreat of the peasant – and vultures perch where domestic pigeons brooded over their young.

Bibliography

A Catalogue of Pictures, painted by J. Wright of Derby, and exhibited at Robins' rooms under the Great Piazza, Covent Garden (1785), London

Abbott, John Lawrence (1982), *John Hawksworth: Eighteenth-Century Man of Letters*, Madison

Adams, Mark and Thomas, Nicholas (1999), *Cook's Sites: Revisiting History*, Dunedin

Adams, Ron (1984), *In the Land of Strangers: A Century of European Contact with Tanna, 1774–1787*, Canberra

Alexander, John T. (1989), *Catherine the Great: Life and Legend*, Oxford

Allen, Brian (1995), 'The East India Company's settlement pictures: George Lambert and Samuel Scott', in Pauline Rohatji and Pheroza Godrej (eds.), *Under the Indian Sun: British Landscape Artists*, Bombay, 1–16

Allen, D.G.C. (1992), 'Artists and the Society in the eighteenth century', in D.G.C. Allen, and John L. Abbott, (eds.), *'The Virtuoso Tribe of Arts and Sciences': Studies in the Eighteenth-Century Work and Membership of the Society of Arts*, Athens, GA, 91–119

Allen, Michael (ed.) (1981), *Vanuatu: Politics, Economics, and Ritual in Island Melanesia*, Sydney

Andrews, Malcolm (1989), *The Search for the Picturesque: Landscape Aesthetics and Tourism in Britain, 1760–1880*, London

Archer, Mildred (1965), 'The East India Company and British art', *Apollo* 92

Archer, Mildred (1972), *Company Drawings in the India Office Library*, London

Archer, Mildred (1992), *Company Paintings: Indian Paintings of the British Period*, London

Asher, Catherine (1992), *Architecture of Mughal India*, Cambridge

[Barbauld, A. L.] (1793), *Sins of Government, Sins of the Nation; or, A Discourse for the Fast, Appointed on April 19, 1793. By a Volunteer*, 4th edn, London

Barrell, John (1986), *The Political Theory of Painting from Reynolds to Hazlitt: 'the Body of the Public'*, New Haven and London

Barrell, John (1992), 'The Public Prospect and the Private View: The Politics of Taste in Eighteenth-Century Britain', in *The Birth of Pandora and the Division of Knowledge*, London, 41–61

Barrell, John (2000), *Imagining the King's Death: Figurative Treason, Fantasies of Regicide, 1793–1796*, Oxford

Bayly, C.A. (1989), *Indian Society and the Making of the British Empire*, Cambridge

Beaglehole, J.C. (1974), *The Life of Captain James Cook*, London

Benedict, Barbara (1990), 'The "curious attitude" in eighteenth-century Britain: observing and owning', *Eighteenth-Century Life* 14, 59–98

Bernier, François (1914), trans., A. Constable, *Travels in the Mogol Empire AD 1656–68*, London

Bewell, Alan (1996), ' "On the Banks of the South Sea": botany and sexual controversy in the late eighteenth century', in David Philip Miller and Peter Hanns Reill, (eds.), *Visions of Empire: Voyages, Botany, and Representations of Nature*, Cambridge 173–93

Bhabha, Homi (1994), *The Location of Culture*, New York

Bindman, David (2002), *Ape to Apollo: Aesthetics and the Idea of Race in the Eighteenth Century*, London

Bougainville, Louis Antoine de (1772), *A Voyage Round the World*, trans., J. R. Forster, London

Bourdieu, Pierre (1984), *Distinction: A Social Critique of the Judgement of Taste*, ed. Richard Nice, Cambridge, Mass.

Bradley, Sir Joseph Alfred (1906), *A History of Monmouthshire: from the Coming of the Normans into Wales down to the present Time*, vol. 1, part 2a: *The Hundred of Abergavenny (Part 1)*, London

Brewer, John (1995), 'Cultural production, consumption, and the place of the artist in eighteenth-century England', in Brian Allen (ed.), *Towards a Modern Art World*, New Haven and London, 7–26

Brewer, John (1997), *The Pleasures of the Imagination: English Culture in the Eighteenth Century*, London

Browne, Major J. (1788), *India Tracts: containing a Description of the Jungle Terry Districts, their Revenues, Trade and Government*, London

Brunt, Peter (1997), 'Savagery and the sublime: two paintings by William Hodges on an encounter with Maori in Dusky Bay, New Zealand', *The Eighteenth Century: Theory and Interpretation*, 38/3, 266–86

Bruntjen, Sven H.A. (1985), *John Boydell (1719–1804): A Study in Art Patronage and Publishing in Georgian London*, New York

Burke, Edmund (1757; 1958), *A Philosophical Enquiry into the Origin of our Ideas of the Sublime and the Beautiful*, J.T. Bolton, (ed.), London

Calder, Alex, Lamb, Jonathan and Orr, Bridget (eds.) (1999), *Voyages and Beaches: Pacific Encounters, 1769–1840*, Honolulu

Chard, Chloe (1999), *Pleasure and Guilt on the Grand Tour: Travel Writing and Imaginative Geography*, Manchester

Charlesworth, Michael (1994), 'The ruined abbey: Picturesque and Gothic values', in Stephen Copley and Peter Garside (eds.), *The Politics of the Picturesque: Literature, Landscape and Aesthetics since 1770*, Cambridge

Christie, Christopher (2000), *The British Country House in the Eighteenth Century*, Manchester

Christie, Ian R. (1982), *Wars and Revolutions: Britain, 1760–1815*, Cambridge, Mass.

Christie's (November, 1968), *Hastings Sale*, London

Clayton, Timothy (1997), *The English Print 1688–1802*, New Haven and London

Cohn, Bernard S. (1996), *Colonialism and its Forms of Knowledge: The British in India*, Princeton

Coleridge, (1969), *Coleridge: Poetical Works*, Ernest Hartley, (ed.), Oxford

Connell, Brian, (ed.) (1958), *Portrait of a Golden Age: Intimate Papers of the Second Viscount Palmerston, Courtier under George III*, London

Cook, James (1777), *A Voyage towards the South Pole, and Round the World*, London

Cook, James (1955–67), *The Journals of Captain James Cook on his Voyages of Discovery*, 3 vols., J. C. Beaglehole, (ed.), Cambridge

Daniell, Thomas and William (1810), *A Picturesque Voyage to India*, London

David, Andrew with Joppien, Rüdiger and Smith, Bernard (eds.) (1988), *The Charts and Coastal Views of Captain Cook's Voyages*, vol. 1: *The Voyage of the* Endeavour *1768–1771*, London

David, Andrew with Joppien, Rüdiger and Smith, Bernard (eds.) (1992), *The Charts and Coastal Views of Captain Cook's Voyages*, vol. 2: *The Voyage of the* Resolution *and the* Adventure *1772–1775*, London

Donald, Diana (1996), *The Age of Caricature: Satirical Prints in the Reign of George III*, New Haven and London

Douglas, Bronwen (1999), 'Art as ethno-historical text: science, representation and indigenous presence in eighteenth and nineteenth-century voyage literature', in Nicholas Thomas and Diane Losche (eds.), *Double Vision: Art Histories and Colonial Histories in the Pacific*, Cambridge, 65–99

Edwards, Edward (1808), *Anecdotes of Painters who have Resided or been born in England; with Critical remarks on their Productions*, London

Elliott, John and Pickersgill, Richard (1984), *Captain Cook's Second Voyage: The Journals of Lieutenants Elliott and Pickersgill*, ed. Christine Holmes, London

Evans, Dorinda (1982), *Mather Brown: early American Artist in England*, Middletown, Conn.

Farington, Joseph (1978–98), *The Diary of Joseph Farington*, 17 vols., ed. Kenneth Garlick and Angus Macintyre, New Haven and London

Fawcet, Joseph (1795), *The Art of War: A Poem*, London

Ferguson, Adam (1767; 1966), *An Essay on the History of Civil Society*, Duncan Forbes (ed.), Edinburgh

Forster, George (1777; 2000), *A Voyage Round the World*, Nicholas Thomas and Oliver Berghof (eds.), Honolulu

Forster, Johann Reinhold (1778; 1996), *Observations Made During a Voyage round the World*, ed. Nicholas Thomas, Harriet Guest and Michael Dettelbach, Honolulu

Forster, Johann Reinhold (1982), ed. *The* Resolution *Journal of Johann Reinhold Forster 1772–1775*, 4 vols., Michael E. Hoare, Cambridge

Foucault, Michel (1991), 'Governmentality', in N. Rose, G. Burchell (eds.) *The Foucault Effect: Essays on Governmentality*, London

Friedman, W. H. (1976), *Boydell's Shakespeare Gallery*, New York

Galinou, Mireille and Hayes, John (1996), *London in Paint: Oil Paintings in the Collection at the Museum of London*, London

Gascoigne, John (1994), *Joseph Banks and the English Enlightenment: Useful Knowledge and Polite Culture*, Cambridge

Gell, Alfred (1993), *Wrapping in Images: Tattooing in Polynesia*, Oxford

Gerard, Alexander (1774), *An Essay on Genius*, London

Ghulam Hussein Khan (1789), *Seir Mutaqherin: History of Modern Times*, Calcutta

Graves, Algernon (1907), *The Society of Artists of Great Britain, 1761–1783, The Free Society of Artists, 1763–1783: A Complete Dictionary of Contributors and Their Work from the Foundation of the Societies to 1791*, London

Grewal, J.S. (1970), *Muslim Rule in India: Assessment of British Historians*, Calcutta

Guest, Harriet (1989), 'The Great distinction: figures of the exotic in the work of William Hodges', *Oxford Art Journal*, 12/2, 36–58

Guest, Harriet (1992), 'Curiously marked: tattooing, masculinity, and nationality in eighteenth-century British perceptions of the South Pacific', in John Barrell (ed.), *Painting and the Politics of Culture: New Essays in British Art 1700–1850*, Oxford, 101–34

Guest, Harriet (1996), 'Looking at women: Forster's observations in the South Pacific', in Forster, Johann Reinhold, *Observations Made During a Voyage round the World*, ed. Nicholas Thomas, Harriet Guest and Michael Dettelbach, Honolulu, xli–liv

Hallett, Mark (2001), ' "The business of criticism": the press and the Royal Academy exhibition in eighteenth-century London', in David H. Solkin, (ed.), *Art on the Line: The Royal Academy Exhibitions at Somerset House 1780–1836*, New Haven and London, 65–71

Hamblyn, Richard (1996), 'Private cabinets and popular geology: the British audiences for volcanoes in the eighteenth century', in Chloe Chard and Helen Langdon (eds.), *Transports: Travel, Pleasure, and Imaginative Geography, 1600–1830*, New Haven and London, 151–78

Harlow, V. T. (1952–64), *The Founding of the Second British Empire, 1763–1793*, London and New York

Harris, John (1979), *The Artist and the Country House*, London

Hayley, William (1809), *The Life of George Romney, Esq.*, London

Head, Raymond (1991), *Catalogue of Paintings Drawings, Engravings and Busts in the Collection of the Royal Asiatic Society*, London

Hill, Draper (1965), *Mr. Gillray The Caricaturist: A Biography*, London

Hoare, Michael (1976), *The Tactless Philosopher: Johann Reinhold Forster (1729–1798)*, Melbourne

Hodges, William (1785–8), *Select Views in India drawn on the Spot in the*

Years 1780, 1781, 1782, and 1783, London

Hodges, William (1787), *Dissertation on the Prototypes of Architecture, Hindoo, Moorish, and Gothic*, London

[Hodges, William] (1790), 'An Account of Richard Wilson Esq. Landscape Painter, F. R.A.', *The European Magazine and London Review* 17

Hodges, William (1793; 2nd edn 1794), *Travels in India during the years 1780, 1781, 1782 and 1783*, London

Hoock, Holger (2000), 'The King's Artists: The Royal Academy as a National Institution, *c*.1768–1820', unpublished D. Phil, Oxford University

Hulme, Peter (1986), *Colonial Encounters: Europe and the Native Caribbean, 1492–1797*, London and New York

Janowitz, Anne (1990), *England's Ruins: Poetic Purpose and the National Landscape*, London

Jeffreys, Thomas (1772), *A Collection of the Dresses of Different Nations*, 4 vols., London

Johnson, John, (ed.), (1823), *Memoirs of the Life and Writings of William Hayley, Esq.*, 2 vols., London

Jolly, Margaret (1992), ' "Ill-natured comparisons": racism and relativism in European representations of ni-Vanuatu from Cook's second voyage', *History and Anthropology*, 331–63

Jones, Sir William (1787), 'On the Gods of Greece, Italy, and India, written in 1784, and since revised, by the President', *Asiatick Researches* 1, Calcutta

Joppien, Rüdiger (1976), 'Three drawings by William Hodges (1744–1797)', *La Trobe Library Journal* 18, 25–33

Joppien, Rüdiger (1979), 'Philippe-Jacques de Loutherbourg's pantomime *Omai, or a Trip round the World* and the artists of Captain Cook's Voyages', in T. C. Mitchell (ed.), *Captain Cook and the South Pacific*, British Museum Yearbook 3, London, 81–136

Joppien, Rüdiger and Smith, Bernard (1985a), *The Art of Captain Cook's Voyages: Volume One: The Voyage of the Endeavour 1768–1771*, New Haven and London

Joppien, Rüdiger and Smith, Bernard (1985b), *The Art of Captain Cook's Voyages: Volume Two: The Voyage of the Resolution and Adventure 1772–1775*, New Haven and London

Joppien, Rüdiger and Smith, Bernard (1988), *The Art of Captain Cook's Voyages: Volume Three: The Voyage of the Resolution and Discovery 1776–1780*, New Haven and London

Kames, Lord [Home, Henry] (1774), *Sketches of the History of Man*, 2 vols., Edinburgh

Keate, George (1769), *Netley Abbey: An Elegy*, 2nd edn, London

Keay, John (2001), *India: A History*, London

Klonk, Charlotte (1996), *Science and the Perception of Nature: British Landscape Art in the Late Eighteenth and Early Nineteenth Centuries*, New Haven and London

Kriz, K. Dian (1997), *The Idea of the English Landscape Painter: Genius as Alibi in the early Nineteenth Century*, New Haven and London

Lamb, Jonathan (2001), *Preserving the Self in the South Seas 1680–1840*, Chicago and London

Lippincott, Louise (1995), 'Expanding on portraiture: the market, the public, and the hierarchy of the genres in eighteenth-century Britain', in Ann Bermingham and John Brewer (eds.), *The Consumption of Culture 1600–1800: Image, Object, Text*, New York and London, 75–88

[Marra, John] (1775), *Journal of the Resolution's Voyage, In 1772, 1773, 1774, and 1775*, London

Marshall, P. J. (1973), 'Warren Hastings as a Scholar Patron', *Essays in Honour of Dame Lucy Sutherland*, Aldershot

Marshall, P. J. (1981; 2000), *The Writings and Speeches of Edmund Burke*, vols. 7–8, Oxford

Marshall, P. J. (1999), 'Warren Hastings: the making of an imperial icon', *Journal of Imperial and Commonwealth History* 27/3

Marshall, P. J. and Williams, G. (1982), *The Great Map of Mankind: British Perceptions of the World in the Age of Enlightenment*, London

Meek, Ronald (1976), *Social Science and the Ignoble Savage*, Cambridge

Millar, John (1773), *Observations Concerning the Distinction of Ranks in Society*, 2nd edn, London

Mitchell, W. J. T. (2002), 'Imperial landscape', in Mitchell (ed.), *Landscape and Power*, 2nd edn, Chicago and London, pp. 5–34

Mortimer, John Hamilton and Jones, Thomas (1772), *Candid Observations on the Principal Performances now Exhibiting at the New Room of the Society of Artists*, London

[Mortimer, Thomas] (1763), *A Concise Account of the Rise, Progress, and Present State of the Society for the Encouragement of the Arts, Manufactures, and Commerce*, 4 vols., London

Nicolson, Benedict (1968), *Joseph Wright of Derby: Painter of Light*, London

Oppé, Paul (ed.) (1946–8), 'Memoirs of Thomas Jones, Penkerrig, Radnorshire, 1803', *The Walpole Society*, 32, pp. 1–142

Orme, Robert (1782), *Historical Fragments of the Mogul Empire*, London

Orr, Bridget (1994), ' "Southern passions mix with northern art": miscegenation and the *Endeavour* voyage', *Eighteenth-Century Life*, 18/3, pp. 212–31

Paine, James (1783), *Plans, Elevations, and Sections of Noblemen and Gentlemen's Houses, and also of Bridges, Public and Private, Temples, and other Garden Buildings*, 2 vols., London

Panofsky, Erwin (1955), '*Et in Arcadia Ego*: Poussin and the elegiac tradition', in *Meaning in the Visual Arts*, Harmondsworth, 340–67

Paulson, Ronald (1989), *Breaking and Remaking: Aesthetic Practice in England, 1700–1820*, New Brunswick and London

Pearson, Anthony (1976), 'John Hunter and two Cherokee Indians', *Annals of the Royal College of Surgeons of England*, 58, 374–81

Pevsner, Nikolaus (2001), rev., Elizabeth Williamson, *The Buildings of England: Nottinghamshire*, London

Pilkington, Matthew (1824), *A General Dictionary of Painters*, 2 vols., London

Pocock, J. G. A. (1999a), *Barbarism and Religion: Narratives of Civil Government*, Oxford

Pocock, J. G. A. (1999b), 'Nature and history, self and other: European perceptions of world history in the age of encounter', in Alex Calder, Jonathan Lamb and Bridget Orr (eds.), *Voyages and Beaches: Pacific Encounters 1769–1840*, Honolulu, 25–44

Pope, Stephen (1999), *The Cassell Dictionary of the Napoleonic Wars*, London

Porter, Roy (1990), 'The exotic as erotic: Captain Cook at Tahiti', in Roy Porter and G. S. Rousseau, (eds.), *Exoticism and the Enlightenment*, Manchester, 117–44

Price, Curtis (1987), 'Turner at the Pantheon Opera House, 1791–92',

Turner Studies, 7/2, pp. 2–8

Prown, Jules (1966), *John Singleton Copley*, 2 vols., Cambridge, MA

Pye, Henry James (1783), *The Progress of Refinement: A Poem in Three Parts*, Oxford

Rennell, James (1788), *Memoir of a Map of Hindoostan; or the Mogul Empire*, London

Reynolds, Sir Joshua (1975), *Discourses on Art*, R. Wark (ed.), New Haven and London

Rigby, Nigel, and van der Merwe, Pieter (2002) *Captain Cook in the Pacific*, London

Robinson, E. and Thompson, K. R. (1970), 'Matthew Boulton's mechanical paintings', *Burlington Magazine* 112, 497–507

Roderick, Colin (1972), 'Sir Joseph Banks, Queen Oberea and the satirists', in Walter Veit (ed.), *Captain James Cook: Image and Impact*, Melbourne

Rohatgi, Pauline (1995), 'The Lost Art of Captain Francis Swain Ward', in Pauline Rohatgi and Pheroza Godrej (eds.) *Under the India Sun*, Mumbai

Rosaldo, Renato (1989), 'Imperialist Nostalgia', *Representations 26*

Russell, R. and Islam, K. (1969), *Three Mughal Poets*, Delhi

Sachdev, Vibhuti and Tillotson, Giles (2002), *Building Jaipur: The Making of an Indian City*, London

Said, Edward W. (1978), *Orientalism*, New York

Said, Edward W. (1993), *Culture and Imperialism*, New York

Salmond, Anne (1997), *Between Worlds: Early Exchanges Between Maori and Europeans, 1773–1815*, Honolulu

Salmond, Anne (2003), *The Trial of the Cannibal Dog*, London

Sands, John O. (1990), 'The sailor's perspective: British naval topographic artists', in Derek Howse, (ed.), *Background to Discovery: Pacific Exploration from Dampier to Cook*, Berkeley, pp. 185–200

Sekora, John (1977), *Luxury: the Concept in Western Thought, Eden to Smollett*, Baltimore and London

Sharar, A.H. (1975), *Lucknow: The Last Phase of an Oriental Culture*

Shenstone, William (1777), *The Works, in Verse and Prose, of William Shenstone, Esq.*, 3 vols., 5th edn, London

Smiles, Sam (1994), *The Image of Antiquity: Ancient Britain and the Romantic Imagination*, New Haven and London

Smiles, Sam (2000), *Eye Witness: Artists and Visual Documentation in Britain 1770–1830*, Aldershot

Smith, Bernard (1985), *European Vision and the South Pacific*, 2nd edn, New Haven and London

Smith, Bernard (1992), *Imagining the Pacific: In the Wake of the Cook Voyages*, New Haven and London

Solkin, David H. (1982), *Richard Wilson: the Landscape of Reaction*, London

Solkin, David H., (ed.) (2001), *Art on the Line*, New Haven and London

Stewart, Susan (1993), *On Longing: Narratives of the Miniature, the Gigantic, the Souvenir, the Collection*, Durham, NJ

Stott, Anne (2003), *Hannah More: The First Victorian*, Oxford

Stuebe, Isabel (1973), 'Hodges and Hastings: a study in eighteenth-century patronage', *Burlington Magazine*, 657–66

Stuebe, Isabel Combs (1979), *The Life and Works of William Hodges*, New York

Suleri, Sara (1992), *The Rhetoric of English India*, Chicago

Sumner, Ann and Smith, Greg (eds.) (2003), *Thomas Jones (1742–1803): An Artist Rediscovered*, exhibition catalogue, National Museums and Galleries, Wales

Sweetman, John (1988), *The Oriental Obsession*, Cambridge

Thomas, Nicholas (1991), *Entangled Objects: Exchange, Material Culture, and Colonialism in the Pacific*, Cambridge, Mass.

Thomas, Nicholas (1994), 'Licensed curiosity: Cook's Pacific voyages', in John Elsner and Roger Cardinal, (eds.), *The Cultures of Collecting*, Cambridge, Mass., 116–36

Thomas, Nicholas (1996), 'Liberty and licence: the Forsters' accounts of New Zealand sociality', in Chloe Chard, and Helen Langdon, (eds.), *Transports: Travel, Pleasure, and Imaginative Geography, 1600–1830*, New Haven and London, 243–62

Thomas, Nicholas (2003), *Discoveries: the Voyages of Captain Cook*, London

Tillotson, Giles (2000), *The Artificial Empire: The Indian Landscapes of William Hodges*, Richmond

Tillotson, Giles, (ed.), (1998), *Paradigms of Indian Architecture*, London

Travers, Robert (2001), 'Contested Notions of Sovereignty in Bengal under the British, 1765–85', unpublished D. Phil, Cambridge University

Turnbull, Paul (1999), 'Enlightenment anthropology and the ancestral remains of Aboriginal people', in Alex Calder, Jonathan Lamb and Bridget Orr (eds.), *Voyages and Beaches: Pacific Encounters, 1769–1840*, Honolulu, 202–25

van der Merwe, Pieter (2001) 'The Glorious First of June: a Battle of Art and Theatre', in Michael Duffy and Roger Morriss (eds.) *The Glorious First of June: a Naval Battle and its Aftermath*, Exeter

Victoria and Albert Museum (1982), *The Indian Heritage*, London

Wales, William and Bayly, William (1777), *The original Astronomical Observations, made in the course of A Voyage towards the South Pole, and Round the World*, London

Wales, William [1778], *Remarks on Mr. Forster's Account of Captain Cook's Last voyage round the World*, in George Forster, *A Voyage Round the World*, 2 vols., Nicholas Thomas and Oliver Berghof, (eds.), Honolulu, II, 699–754

Waterhouse, Ellis (1953), *Painting in Britain 1530–1790*, London

Watts, W. (1779), *The Seats of the Nobility and Gentry, in a Collection of the most interesting & picturesque Views*, London

Welch, Stuart Cary (1978), *Room for Wonder*, New York

Wheeler, Roxann (2000), *The Complexion of Race: Categories of Difference in Eighteenth-Century British Culture*, Philadelphia

Whitehurst, John (1778), *Inquiry into the Original State and Formation of the Earth*, London

Wilson, Jon E. (2000), 'Governing Property, Making Law: Land, Local Society and Colonial Discourse in Agrarian Bengal, c.1785–1835', unpublished D. Phil, Oxford University

Wilson, Kathleen (2003), *The Island Race: Englishness, Empire and Gender in the Eighteenth Century*, London and New York

[Wyndham, P. J.] (1775), *A Gentleman's Tour through Monmouthshire and Wales, in the Months of June and July, 1774*, London

Index